# Secured Finance Transactions

## Key Assets and Emerging Markets

Consulting Editor **Paul U Ali**

**Consulting editor**
Paul U Ali

**Publisher**
Sian O'Neill

**Editor**
Carolyn Boyle

**Marketing manager**
Alan Mowat

**Production**
John Meikle, Russell Anderson

**Publishing directors**
Guy Davis, Tony Harriss, Mark Lamb

***Secured Finance Transactions: Key Assets and Emerging Markets***
**is published by**
Globe Law and Business
Globe Business Publishing Ltd
New Hibernia House
Winchester Walk
London Bridge
London SE1 9AG
United Kingdom
**Tel** +44 20 7234 0606
**Fax** +44 20 7234 0808
**Web** www.gbplawbooks.com

Printed by Antony Rowe Ltd

ISBN 978-1-905783-10-6/1-905783-10-8

# Table of contents

# Introduction

**Paul U Ali**
University of Melbourne

---

This book provides a practitioner-oriented perspective on secured finance transactions, focusing mainly on security interests over key asset classes and the legal framework for security interests in important emerging markets. The contributors to this book are expert legal practitioners from the broad field of banking and finance law, as well as leading academic commentators on the law of secured finance.

Security interests – basically, rights in property taken to support the performance of financial and other obligations – are an integral feature of contemporary financing transactions. They operate as a hedge against credit risk by coupling an obligee's personal claim against an obligor with rights to the latter's assets, permitting the obligee – should the obligor fail or be unable to perform – to satisfy its claim in full out of those assets ahead of competing claims against the obligor. Banks and other financiers routinely take comprehensive security interests, such as enterprise-wide floating charges and 'security packages' including mortgages and charges over individual asset classes, when making loans to corporate borrowers (particularly, small to medium-sized corporate borrowers), in order to protect themselves against the borrower's default or insolvency.

Security interests also perform a vital role in more complex financing transactions, including project finance, securitisation and structured finance. These transactions often involve the establishment of special purpose vehicles (SPVs) to raise funds from investors in the capital markets through the issue to investors of tranched debt securities, with the payment obligations represented by those securities supported by the 'horizontal partitioning' of the issuing vehicle's assets: the assets are the subject of a security interest in favour of the investors and the benefit of that security interest is shared by the investors in accordance with their differently ranked claims for principal and interest.

**Sharing of security interest**

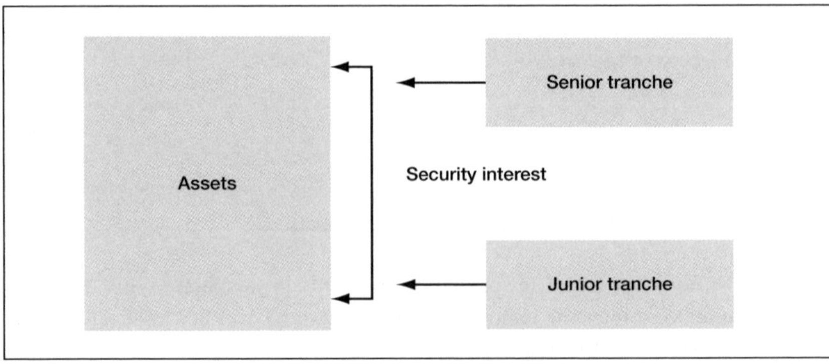


The rights in property that arise when a security interest is created also make possible the 'vertical partitioning' of assets: the assets that support an issuing vehicle's obligations to one group of investors can be ring-fenced or segregated from the assets that support the same vehicle's obligations to a second group of investors by granting the different groups of investors separate security interests over the different pools of assets. Moreover, this enables the same SPV to be re-used for different financing transactions.[1]

**Ring-fencing of assets**

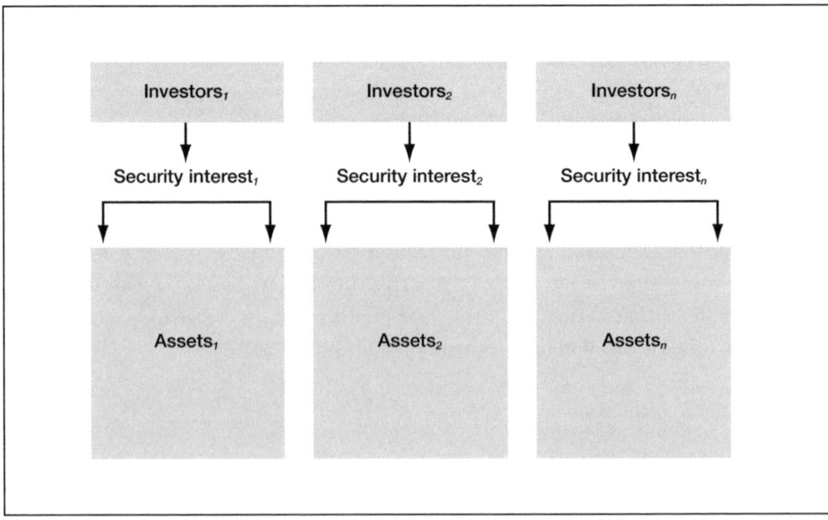


1 This concept has been taken a step further with the introduction of special legislation providing for the incorporation of 'protected cell companies' (where the segregation of assets is effected by statute) in many offshore jurisdictions: see M Lombardi and M Leese, "Guernsey Protected Cell Companies in Securitisation" in J Borrows (ed), *Current Issues in Securitisation* (Sweet & Maxwell, London, 2002), pp 71-73.

The role of security interests in mitigating credit risk, coupled with this ability to carve up assets for the benefit of investors and other creditors, has meant that the importance of security interests has remained undiminished even though, in recent times, conventional secured lending has come under considerable competitive pressure from alternative forms of fundraising, in particular securitisation.[2] Indeed, where fundraising is the predominant objective, borrowers should, in principle, be able to 'securitise' their assets without the need for an intermediated issuing entity (by using security interests to ring-fence the assets backing the issue of debt securities from the borrower's other assets).[3]

Before outlining the contents of this book, brief mention should also be made of two innovative financing structures in which security interests play a central role. The first, whole business securitisation, makes full use of the advantages of the common law floating charge – namely:

- the ease with which a single floating charge can be taken over the entire business assets of a borrower; and
- the ability of the holder of a floating charge, following the borrower's default or insolvency, to take control of the borrower's business and block the appointment of an administrator (in this context, in the United Kingdom, by making use of the so-called 'capital market exception').[4]

Whole business securitisations are essentially back-to-back loans. An SPV issues securities to investors and lends the proceeds from the issue of the securities to a corporate borrower; the payments made by the borrower on the loan are used to service the securities. This fundraising mechanism has been able to deliver greater leverage and longer terms to maturity than conventional secured lending, due to the greater tolerance for higher gearing ratios on the part of investors in the capital markets compared to banks. However, on the other hand, as the loan to the borrower has effectively made by the investors, this funding mechanism has, in practice, largely been limited to borrowers with stable cash flows and which enjoy a strong market position and operate in markets with high barriers to entry.[5]

---

2 See E J Janger, "The Death of Secured Lending" (2005) 25 *Cardozo Law Review* 1759, at 1760-1762 and 1777-1778.

3 See Moody's Investors Service, "Non-Bankruptcy-Remote Issuers in Asset Securitization" (March 12 2001). This is analogous to covered bonds (except that segregation of the assets backing covered bonds is achieved by statute, rather than by a security interest): see S Nasarre-Aznar and O Stocker, "Covered Bonds in Europe" in JJ de Vries Robbe and P U Ali (eds), *Securitisation of Derivatives and Alternative Asset Classes* (Kluwer Law International, The Hague, 2005), pp 190-191.

4 See P U Ali, "Whole Business Securitization" in SL Schwarcz, *Structured Finance: A Guide to the Principles of Asset Securitization* (Practising Law Institute, New York, 2005), §9:4.4. In the United Kingdom and Australia, this floating charge is typically supplemented by fixed charges to ensure that the secured party has a first-ranking claim against the borrower's assets. In contrast, this result can be achieved by the use of a single security interest in the United States, Canada and New Zealand due to the personal property security regimes that apply in those countries: see Ali, ibid, §9:4.5. As regards whole business securitisation in civil law jurisdictions, see P Doat and P Nugue, "Whole Business Securitisations in Civil Law Jurisdictions: The French Example" in de Vries Robbe and Ali, *ibid.*

5 See Ali, *ibid*, §9:3.

**Whole business securitisation**

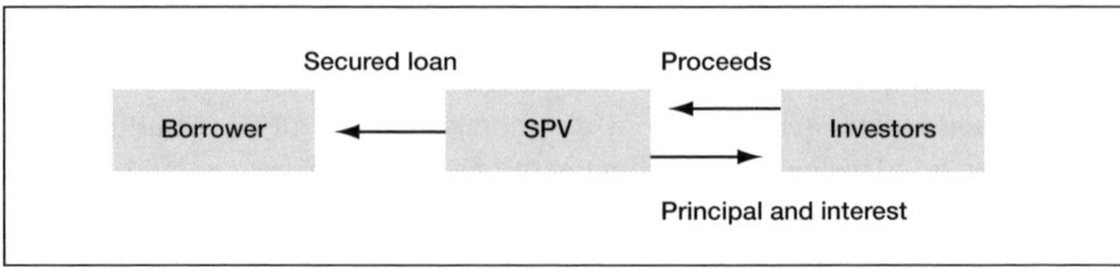


The second of these innovations, inventory securitisation, enables borrowers to use their inventory to raise funds while overcoming the legal and practical difficulties encountered in conventional secured lending by attempting to create a fixed charge over inventory.[6] Funds are raised through the issue by an SPV of debt securities. The SPV lends the proceeds from the issue of the securities to the borrower. That loan is secured by a pledge of the borrower's inventory and the borrower's payments on the loan, which are funded by the sale of the inventory, are used to service the securities (this is similar to the whole business securitisation structure discussed above).[7] Alternatively, the proceeds from the issue of the securities are used by the SPV to acquire inventory from the borrower and the securities are serviced by the on-sale of the inventory (this is similar to a conventional securitisation, save that the assets being securitised are goods rather than receivables).[8]

This book is divided into four parts. Part 1 examines three key legal issues. The first chapter addresses recharacterisation risk and the implications of the House of Lords' decision in *National Westminster Bank plc v Spectrum Plus Limited* for certain major asset classes, including insurance proceeds, equipment rents, securities and other investment assets, custodian accounts and goods, as well as securitisation. The second discusses the role of the security trustee in structured finance transactions. The third considers the – increasingly distant – prospects for reform of the English personal property security regime. This chapter contains important lessons for other common law jurisdictions, including Australia, which is now in the midst of a similar reform exercise, as regards the adoption of a North American 'Article 9'-style personal property security regime.[9]

Part 2 addresses the taking of security interests over key asset classes. The first chapter discusses credit support for derivative transactions and examines the different types of suitable collateral, including cash and government securities. The

6 See R M Goode, *Legal Problems of Credit and Security* (Sweet & Maxwell, London, 3rd ed, 2003), pp 127-128.
7 See Moody's Investors Service, "Debut of Inventory Securitisation in Europe: Moody's Rating Approach" (May 21 2002).
8 *Ibid.*
9 See Australian Attorney-General's Department, "Review of the Law on Personal Property Securities: Registration and Search Issues" (Discussion Paper 1, November 2006); Australian Attorney-General's Department, "Review of the Law on Personal Property Securities: Extinguishment, Priorities, Conflict of Laws, Enforcement, Insolvency " (Discussion Paper 2, March 2007); Australian Attorney-General's Department, "Review of the Law on Personal Property Securities: Possessory Security Interests" (Discussion Paper 3, April 2007).

second discusses the efficacy of security interests over intellectual property as a fundraising mechanism with reference to Australian IP legislation. The third examines the United Nations Convention on the Assignment of Receivables in International Trade and its application to the financing of receivables and security interests over receivables. The fourth discusses security interests over the credit balances of bank accounts in the context of the legislative guide to secured finance prepared by the United Nations Commission on International Trade Law. The fifth provides a detailed overview of the various debt financing mechanisms employed in private equity transactions, including 'second lien' finance. The sixth looks at the different secured financing arrangements encountered in aircraft finance, including aircraft mortgages. The seventh provides an overview of the financing arrangements customarily employed in the mortgage-based financing of ships.

Part 3 discusses the legal infrastructure for security interests in key emerging markets. The first chapter in Part 3 provides an overview of the creation and enforcement of security interests in Eastern Europe, accompanied by more detailed commentary on secured finance in the Czech Republic, Poland and Russia. The second discusses the different types of security interest encountered in financing transactions and the alternatives to security interests in Mexico. The third discusses the security interests available in China and also the implications for secured finance of the recently enacted Property Law. The fourth discusses security interests and their alternatives in Brazil in the context of project finance.

Finally, Part 4 examines credit derivatives as an alternative to security interests in relation to managing credit risk.

*Paul U Ali is an associate professor in the Faculty of Law, University of Melbourne and a member of the faculty's Centre for Corporate Law and Securities Regulation. Prior to becoming an academic, Dr Ali was, for several years, a lawyer in Sydney. Dr Ali has published widely on banking and finance law, securitisation and structured finance, including two books on secured finance, Marshalling of Securities (Clarendon Press, Oxford, 1999) and The Law of Secured Finance (Oxford University Press, Oxford, 2002). In 2006, Dr Ali was appointed by the Australian federal attorney general as a member of the Personal Property Securities Review Consultative Group.*

# Fixed charges

**Robin Parsons**
Sidley Austin LLP

## 1. Introduction

Victorian England burgeoned with industry and creativity and the judges in England's Chancery courts struggled to keep pace. Joint stock companies needed to raise working capital and their financiers increasingly looked to their current assets as a form of security. These assets – raw materials, work in progress, stock-in-trade and, above all, book debts – were different in nature from land or other assets that had traditionally been offered by way of security, in that they were transitory in nature and circulated in the course of carrying on the business. The new security had to cover future assets as well as present assets and accordingly could only be identified generically by reference to a class, and because they were dealt with in the course of the company's business it was not practicable for the financier to be involved in these dealings; critically, it was not practicable for the financier to execute a release on each occasion that goods were sold or a book debt was collected. It is against this background that the judges invented the concept of a floating charge.[1]

As a judicial invention, the concept of a floating charge took some time to develop and there is no recognised definition of the term even after 150 years. This is one of the difficulties. The nearest that the courts have come to defining a floating charge is the classic explanation given by Lord Justice Romer in *Yorkshire Woolcombers*:[2]

> *I certainly think that if a charge has the three characteristics that I am about to mention it is a floating charge.*
>
> *(1) If it is a charge on a class of assets of a company present and future; (2) if that class is one which, in the ordinary course of the business of the company, would be changing from time to time; and (3) if you find by the charge it is contemplated that, until some further step is taken by or on behalf of those interested in the charge, the company may carry on its business in the ordinary way as far as concerns the particular class of assets I am dealing with.*

This is not a definition because the judge made it clear that a floating charge might be created which does not possess all three of these characteristics. Each of the three is no more than a characteristic or hallmark.

1 For a fuller description of the juridical history of floating charges, see the speech of Lord Scott in *Spectrum* beginning at paragraph 95 and *Gough on Company Charges*, 2nd edition, pages 102-108.
2 [1903] 2 Ch 284, 295.

However, the Privy Council in *Agnew v Commissioner of Inland Revenue*[3] *('Brumark')* and the House of Lords in *National Westminster Bank plc v Spectrum Plus Limited*[4] have made it clear that the third characteristic is the critical one, Lord Scott even going so far as to say that he was inclined to think that if the charge bore this characteristic it would qualify as a floating charge, whatever might be its other characteristics. Indeed, it is the emphasis given to the third characteristic in *Brumark* that has given rise to widespread concern among lawyers that charges which have hitherto always been regarded as effective fixed security may be susceptible to the risk of recharacterisation as floating security.

In this chapter, I will attempt to explain why I think that this concern is largely misconceived, but before doing so I would like to explain why secured creditors should be concerned about the risk of recharacterisation and to deal further with the existing case law.

## 2. Why does it matter if a security which purports to be fixed is recharacterised as a floating security?

Floating security (including security which purports to be fixed, but which is recharacterised as floating) is less advantageous to the secured creditor in three respects.

First, floating security by its nature tends to give the secured creditor less control of the asset. Thus, the company can subsequently sell the asset to a third party and the third party will acquire good title to the asset, provided that the floating charge has not crystallised at the time of the sale and the third party has no notice of any restriction in the floating charge prohibiting the sale. Similarly, the company can subsequently create a fixed mortgage or a fixed charge on the asset in favour of a third party and the third party will take priority over the floating charge, provided that the floating charge has not crystallised at the time that the subsequent security interest is created and the third party has no notice of any restriction in the floating charge prohibiting the creation of subsequent security interests.[5] This is why well-advised purchasers or mortgagees or chargees will wish to examine the floating charge and may ask for a certificate of non-crystallisation. Third parties taking security from the company will almost invariably require the consent of the holder of the floating charge, as it has become standard practice for floating charges to contain negative pledges.

Also, an administrator may dispose of or take action relating to property which is subject to a floating charge as if it were not subject to the floating charge, something that may only be done in relation to property subject to a fixed charge with an order of court.[6]

The second respect in which floating security is less advantageous to the secured

---

3 [2001] 2 BCLC 188.

4 [2005] UKHL 41.

5 Registration of the floating charge at the Companies Registry is effective to give constructive notice of the charge, but not of the restriction: *Wilson v Kelland* [1910] 2 Ch 306. If the subsequent mortgagee or chargee makes a search, he may have actual notice.

6 Paragraphs 70 and 71 of Schedule B1 to the Insolvency Act 1986.

creditor than fixed security concerns priorities. I have already mentioned the risk that a floating security may lose priority to a subsequent fixed security. In addition, the claims of the holder of floating security in certain cases rank after the claims of certain unsecured creditors (including preferential claims and the claims of unsecured creditors up to the prescribed part) and the expenses of certain insolvency proceedings.

Claims which are preferential in a winding-up[7] or receivership,[8] or where the holder of the floating security takes possession,[9] have been cut back by the abolition of Crown preference and are now limited to claims for occupational pension scheme contributions, the remuneration of employees within certain statutory limits and levies on coal and steel production.[10]

Further, where the company becomes subject to insolvency proceedings, a "prescribed part" of a company's net property becomes available for the satisfaction of unsecured debts.[11] This prescribed part is fixed by secondary legislation[12] and is on a sliding scale depending upon the value of the net property, subject at present to a maximum of £600,000.

In many cases, the holder of floating security will not be overly concerned with preferential creditors (because the claims that rank preferentially are now much more limited) or unsecured creditors (because the amount of their priority is capped); of much greater concern (because their amount cannot be accurately assessed and therefore the effect on cash flow if the security is enforced is unpredictable) will be the expenses of administration[13] and (once Section 1282 of the Companies Act 2006 has come into force)[14] the expenses of a winding-up.

The third respect in which floating security is less advantageous to the secured creditor than fixed security concerns potential invalidation or avoidance. Section 245 of the Insolvency Act 1986 provides that a floating charge created at a relevant time is invalid except to the extent of (among other things) the value of the consideration for the creation of the charge as consists of money paid, or goods or services supplied, to the company at the same time as, or after, the creation of the charge. "Relevant time" in a case where the charge is created in favour of an unconnected person is a period of 12 months ending with the onset of insolvency. This will not apply where the asset in question is financial collateral subject to a security financial collateral arrangement,[15] but this extends to a floating charge only where the financial collateral is "delivered, transferred, held, registered or otherwise designated so as to be in the possession or under the control of the collateral taker"[16] (which may well not be the case). A floating charge created by a company registered

7 Section 175 of the Insolvency Act 1986.
8 Section 40(2) of the Insolvency Act 1986.
9 Section 196 of the Companies Act 1985.
10 Section 386 of, and Schedule 6 to, the Insolvency Act 1986.
11 Section 176A of the Insolvency Act 1986.
12 The Insolvency Act 1986 (Prescribed Part) Order 2003.
13 Paragraph 99(3) of Schedule B1 to the Insolvency Act 1986.
14 Section 1282 of the Companies Act 2006 has the effect of reversing the decision in *Buchler v Talbot (Re Leyland Daf Limited)* [2004] BCC 214.
15 The Financial Collateral Arrangements (No 2) Regulations 2003, Regulation 10(5).
16 *Ibid*, definition of 'security financial collateral arrangement'.

in Great Britain must be registered at the Companies Registry within 21 days of its creation, failing which it will be void against a liquidator or administrator or any creditor of the company.[17] This is not the case in relation to a charge which is fixed, unless it is a charge required to be registered for any other reason.[18] A security financial collateral arrangement is exempted from the registration requirement. [19]

## 3. The tension between the financier and the company

It can therefore be seen that the financier's clear preference will always be to attempt to take security which is fixed. However, in many cases the creation of a fixed charge on the borrower's circulating assets could have the effect of paralysing the company's business because it would mean that the consent of the financier would be required for every dealing with the charged assets. The theory is that if the effect of a fixed charge is to create an immediate proprietary interest in an asset in favour of the chargee, any dealing with the asset in a manner which is inconsistent with that interest would require the chargee's consent.

Very little can be done with regard to circulating assets other than book debts. It is simply not practicable, for example, to place restrictions on dealings with stock in trade in a manner that would give the chargee sufficient control to demonstrate that he had an immediate proprietary interest. Other devices could be used, such as the sales agency arrangement in Exfinco,[20] with a view to achieving the same commercial result.

For many years, clearing banks took debentures from companies incorporating what purported to be a fixed charge upon present and future book debts, placing their reliance upon the decision in *Siebe Gorman & Co Limited v Barclays Bank Limited*.[21] In that case, Barclays Bank had taken such a debenture. The debenture contained a covenant to pay into the company's account with the bank all moneys which it might receive in respect of the book and other debts subject to the purported fixed charge and not without the consent of the bank to sell, factor, charge or assign them in favour of any other person. There was also an undertaking to execute a legal assignment of the book or other debts if the bank so required.

Justice Slade (as he then was) decided that the charge was fixed, commenting: "This conclusion that the charge is a specific charge involves the further conclusion that, during the continuance of the security, the bank would have the right, if it chose, to assert its lien under the charge on the proceeds of the book debts, even at a time when the particular account into which they were paid was temporarily in credit."[22]

He also said that he was inclined to the opinion that if he had found that the chargor of book debts, having collected them, had the unrestricted right to deal with the proceeds of them so long as the account remained in credit, the charge could

---

17 Section 395 of the Companies Act 1985.

18 See Section 396 of the Companies Act 1985 and *Arthur D Little Limited (in administration) v Ableco Finance LLC*, referred to below.

19 The Financial Collateral Arrangements (No 2) Regulations, Regulation 4(4).

20 *Welsh Development Agency v Export Finance Co* [1992] BCC 270; [1992] BCLC 148.

21 [1979] 2 Lloyd's Rep 142.

22 *Ibid* at page 159.

have been no more than a floating charge. For the charge to work, the bank therefore had to have some sort of notional control of the proceeds paid into the account.[23]

This was taken a step further in *Re New Bullas Trading Limited*[24] The draftsman of the debenture in this case wanted a fixed charge on present and future book debts. He knew that it would be impossible to argue that the chargee in that case (which was not a clearing bank and therefore did not operate the current account into which the proceeds of the book debts were to be paid) would have any control of the proceeds in the current account, however notional. He therefore conceived the clever idea of dividing the book debt from its proceeds. The chargee would obtain a fixed charge on the book debt, but would only attempt to obtain a floating charge on the proceeds of the debt when paid into the account.

The Court of Appeal held that the charge was fixed, Lord Justice Nourse commenting that there was no reason in law to prevent the parties from agreeing to divide its security in this way. He seems to have thought that it should be allowed as the parties were free to contract for whatever form of security they chose.[25]

Both of these approaches have now been rejected.

## 4. The rejection of *Siebe Gorman* and the disavowal of the *New Bullas heresy*

*Siebe Gorman* was not followed by Justice Hoffmann in *Re Brightlife*,[26] who pointed out that in that case the judge had found as a matter of construction that the bank would not have been obliged to allow drawings from the account. He was able to distinguish *Siebe Gorman* from the case before him, where the chargee did not operate an account into which the proceeds of the debts could be paid.

The High Court of New Zealand declined to follow *Siebe Gorman* in *Supercool Refrigeration and Air Conditioning v Hoverd Industries Limited*[27] on almost identical facts. Justice Tompkins held that as the company was not placed under any restriction on how the company used the proceeds in the account, the bank did not have effective possession of those proceeds.

In the *Brumark* decision, Lord Millett, sitting as a member of the Privy Council, said that whether a charge falls into the category of a fixed or a floating charge cannot depend solely upon the manner in which the parties choose to describe it in the instrument creating it. He said:[28]

> *The question is not merely one of construction. In deciding whether a charge is a fixed charge or a floating charge, the court is engaged in a two-stage process. At the first stage it must construe the instrument of charge and seek to gather the intentions of the parties from the language they have used. But the object at this stage of the process is not to discover whether the parties intended to create a fixed or floating charge. It is to ascertain the nature of the rights and obligations which the parties intended to grant*

23 *Ibid* at page 158.
24 [1994] 1 BCLC 485.
25 *Ibid* at page 492.
26 [1987] Ch 200.
27 [1994] 3 NZLR 300.
28 [2001] 2 BCLC 188, 200.

*each other in respect of the charged assets. Once these have been ascertained, the court can then embark on the second stage of the process, which is one of categorisation. This is a matter of law. It does not depend on the intention of the parties. If their intention, properly gathered from the language of the instrument, is to grant the company rights in respect of the charged assets which are inconsistent with the nature of a fixed charge, then the charge cannot be a fixed charge however they may have chosen to describe it.*

The two-stage process has been followed in subsequent cases, in particular in *Smith (Administrator of Cosslett (Contractors) Ltd) v Bridgend County Borough Council.*[29] It was also cited with approval in *Spectrum*.

Nevertheless, the court in *Spectrum* seemed to impose an additional requirement. The traditional view is that the exercise of construing the charge document and categorising the nature of the rights and obligations of the parties does not take into account subsequent conduct, unless that conduct gives rise to waiver, variation or estoppel. However, *Brumark*[30] and *Spectrum*[31] would seem to indicate that the restrictions on the chargor dealing with the charged asset must not only be set out in the charge document, but also be operated in practice.[32]

In *Spectrum*, the House of Lords had to consider a charge which was expressed to be a fixed charge over present and future book debts, where the chargor was prohibited from disposing of, or creating security over, the uncollected book debts and where the chargor was obliged to place the payments made to it by its debtors in a designated account with the chargee bank. The charge did not prevent the chargor from drawing on the account for its business purposes, provided that its overdraft limit was not exceeded. In reaching its decision that the charge should be characterised as a floating charge, the House of Lords expressed the view that the essential characteristic of a floating charge that distinguished it from a fixed charge was that the asset subject to the charge was not permanently appropriated to the payment of the debt; instead, it floated over the assets subject to the security until the occurrence of some future event which had the effect of crystallising it. Until crystallisation, the chargor was left free to use the charged asset and to remove it from the security.

The House of Lords was faced with conflicting authorities on whether, in categorising a charge on book debts as a fixed or floating security, a court could ignore the rights of the chargor to the proceeds of the book debts. The House of Lords held that since the essential value of a book debt as security lay in the money that could be obtained from the debtor in payment[33] (I will refer to this as the 'essential

---

29 [2002] 1 AC 336.

30 [2001] 2 BCLC 188, 204, per Lord Millett.

31 [2005] UKHL 41, paragraph 160, per Lord Walker.

32 In *Fanshaw v Amav Industries Limited* (*'Re Beam Tube'*) [2006] EWHC 486, Justice Blackburne held that the moneys standing to the credit of the so-called 'BLL suspense account' were only subject to a floating charge even though they were never at the free disposition of the chargor. This is because (see paragraph [48] of the judgment) the terms of the debenture allowed the proceeds of the collections account to be used by the company until default and only purported to create a floating charge on the balance on the account. The judge found as a fact that the moneys standing to the credit of the BLL suspense account remained the property of the chargor and were not the property of the chargee. He further found that the payments into the account were intended to give effect to the terms of the debenture.

33 *Ibid*, Lord Scott at paragraph 110.

value test'), it was not sufficient, in order for the security to be classified as fixed, that control was exercised by the chargee over the book debts for as long as they remained uncollected: such control also needed to be exercised after collection over the use of the proceeds of the book debts by the chargor.

The House of Lords considered a number of factors in reaching its decision in *Spectrum*:

- the intentions of the parties as expressed in the documentation, including the label given to the transaction and the restrictions contained in it;
- the rights retained by or granted to the chargor to deal with its debtors and collect in money;
- the chargor's rights to draw on the account into which the collected debts had been paid; and
- the reality of control which the chargee was entitled to, and actually did, exercise over the proceeds of book debts.

However, the House of Lords gave most weight to actual controls which were exercised over the operation of the bank account in question. Lord Walker said that it made no difference whether the account was at any time in credit or overdrawn.

The House of Lords did state that a charge over book debts could be a fixed charge if restrictions existed which prevented the book debts being disposed of before collection and if, on collection, the proceeds were required to be paid to the chargee itself (for the credit of an account of the chargor with the chargee which was then blocked for the benefit of the chargee's security, with the proceeds unavailable to the chargor without the chargee's prior consent) or paid into a separate account with a third-party bank over which the chargee took an effective fixed charge.

In fact, there are passages in *Spectrum* that would seem to suggest that if the fixed charge on book debts is to be upheld, payment into something akin to a blocked account is a prerequisite. For example, Lord Hope put it like this:[34] "Was the account one which allowed the company to continue to use the proceeds of the book debts as a source of its cash flow or was it one which, on the contrary, preserved the proceeds intact for the benefit of the bank's security? Was it, putting the point shortly, a blocked account?"

Again, he said:[35] "In my opinion the company's continuing contractual right to draw out sums equivalent to the amounts paid in is wholly destructive of the argument that there was a fixed charge over the uncollected proceeds because the account into which the proceeds were paid was blocked."

As far as concerns *Siebe Gorman*, Lord Hope said[36] that Justice Slade's finding that the bank could assert a lien under the charge on the proceeds of the book debts overlooked the fact that the account into which the proceeds were paid was the company's current account with the bank which the company was to be free to operate for its own business purposes within the agreed limit of its overdraft. He

34 *Ibid*, paragraph 55.
35 *Ibid*, paragraph 61.
36 *Ibid*, paragraph 58.

added that the decision should be overruled. Lord Scott pointed out that Justice Slade's remarks were strictly *obiter* and also said that it was very difficult to see what feature of the arrangement would have justified his conclusion.[37] Lord Walker respectfully suggested that Justice Slade did not make any significant error in stating the general principles which apply, but he did not correctly construe the debenture that was before him.[38] The other law lords agreed.[39]

The same respect was not afforded to the decision in *New Bullas*. Lord Millett in *Brumark* had challenged the notion that the security rights granted over a book debt could be any greater than the rights, if any, granted over the money received in payment of the debts. Since the essential value of a book debt as a security lies in the money that can be obtained from the debtor in payment, Lord Millett said[40] that the security in *New Bullas* should have been categorised as floating. This was a view with which Lords Scott and Walker agreed, Lord Scott describing the thinking in the *New Bullas* case as "heresy":[41] "If part of the arrangement is that the chargor is free to collect the book debts but must pay the collected proceeds into a specified bank account, the categorisation [of the charge on book debts] must depend on what, if any, restrictions there are on the use the chargor can make of the credit to the account that reflects each payment in."[42]

## 5. *Spectrum:* application of the third characteristic

As mentioned above, it is far from clear to what extent the tests established by *Brumark* and *Spectrum* should be applied to assets other than book debts, particularly non-circulating assets. I say this because of the overwhelming emphasis that was placed by Lord Scott on the third characteristic identified by Lord Justice Romer in *Yorkshire Woolcombers* ("if you find by the charge it is contemplated that, until some further step is taken by or on behalf of those interested in the charge, the company may carry on its business in the ordinary way as far as concerns the particular class of assets"). He said that if this characteristic were present, he would be inclined to think that the charge must be floating, whatever might be its other characteristics.[43]

This would mean that if this characteristic were present, the charge would be floating even if the charge only purported to affect an existing identified asset and even if this were not an asset which would be circulating in the business from time to time.

It has been suggested by one commentator[44] that Lord Scott's remark was intended to apply only when the assets are to be viewed as circulating assets.

---

37 *Ibid*, paragraph 118.

38 *Ibid*, paragraph 142.

39 *Ibid*, paragraphs 43 (Lord Nicholls), 44 (Lord Steyn), 45 (Lord Hope) and 165 (Baroness Hale).

40 [2001] 2 BCLC 188, 201.

41 [2005] UKHL 41, paragraph 116. In *Re Beam Tube* (see note 33, *supra*), a charge on book debts which purported to be a fixed charge was recharacterised as floating because (following *Brumark* and *Spectrum*) the debenture only purported to create a floating charge on the moneys standing to the credit of the bank account into which the proceeds of the book debts were paid.

42 *Ibid*, paragraph 116.

43 *Ibid*, paragraph 107.

44 Nicholas Frome, "*Spectrum* – 'An End To The Conflict Or The Signal For A New Campaign?'" (2005) 11 JIBFL 433.

I am not sure that this is strictly correct unless what is meant is that the asset is *treated* as circulating. I say this because Lord Scott, having made this remark, went on to give a couple of examples; the first example concerned the express assignment of a specific debt which was accompanied by a provision that reserved to the assignor the right, terminable by written notice from the assignee, to collect the debt and use its proceeds. Lord Scott observed that this assignment by way of security would be a floating security. The debt, he says, would be "specific and ascertained". My reading of this is that the debt would not necessarily be a circulating asset but, because of the reservation in favour of the assignor, it was to be *treated* as circulating. I think this is what he meant when he said that the "assets would have the circulating, ambulatory character distinctive of a floating charge". The passage that is referred to by the commentator in support (paragraphs 138 and 139 of Lord Walker's speech) would tend to support this interpretation (the example given in paragraph 138 – a fixed charge on land – would not normally be regarded as a circulating asset, but in the example it is treated as a circulating asset because it constitutes trading stock of the company).

My interpretation of Lord Scott's remark, therefore, is that it applies to any asset which is treated in a way that demonstrates that the chargee was not intended to take an immediate proprietary interest (ie, that is treated as circulating even if, as an asset, it is not inherently of a circulating nature). The fact that the charge affects a non-circulating asset does not mean that it is fixed,[45] but in such circumstances it will no doubt be easier to establish that a fixed charge was intended.

## 6. Can a charge which is expressed to be created as a floating charge be recharacterised as a fixed charge?

There are many cases where a liquidator of a company has sought to establish that a charge which is expressed to be created as a fixed charge should be recharacterised as a floating charge. The reasons why a liquidator might seek to do this would not apply in the converse situation where a floating charge is to be recharacterised as fixed. This is the case where the security document only provides for the chargor to create a floating charge, but in carrying out the two-stage process described by Lord Millet in *Brumark*, the court reaches the conclusion that the rights and obligations which the parties intended to grant each other in respect of the charged assets are such that the intention must have been to create a fixed charge, however the parties chose to describe it.

This would seem to be carrying the *Brumark* exercise to extreme lengths. Nevertheless, there is one recent case in which the court appears to have done just that.

In *The Russell-Cooke Trust Company v Elliott*,[46] Justice Mann was required to determine whether security interests that were described as floating charges should be recharacterised as fixed charges in circumstances in which the agreements in

---

45 Nicholls LJ (as he then was) in *Re Atlantic Computer Systems PLC* [1992] Ch 505 decided that the assignment of rentals under certain sub-leases of equipment constituted fixed security on the basis that the rights assigned were rights under specific existing contracts (p 534C) – that is, the first two characteristics in *Yorkshire Woolcombers* were present.

46 [2007] All ER (D) 166 (Mar).

question placed stringent restrictions upon the ability of the chargor to deal with the charged assets. After pointing out that disputes tended to focus upon a contention that a charge described as a fixed charge was in fact a floating charge, he went on to say that the principle was the same in the converse situation because in each case it was the nature of the agreement rather than the labels assigned to the agreement by the parties that fell to be considered. He went on to find that the charges were fixed. While this decision is attractive from a legal purist's standpoint, it does not, in my view, accord with commercial good sense.

If the decision is correct, it would appear to be the case that the parties cannot contract for a floating charge in circumstances in which restrictions apply which are characteristic of a fixed charge. This would be a somewhat bizarre result. There do not seem to be any public policy reasons why a chargee should not be able to waive the benefit of security that would otherwise be fixed so that it is only floating in nature. In other contexts, the courts have been prepared to hold that a party can waive benefits that he would otherwise receive. For example, in *Maxwell Communications Corp plc, Re (No 2)*,[47] which was later approved in *Re SSSL Realisations (2002) Ltd (in liquidation)*,[48] it was held that an unsecured creditor could contractually subordinate his rights on a liquidation to those of other unsecured creditors, thereby waiving the *pari passu* distribution principle. On this analogy, it is difficult to see why parties should not be able to contract to waive the benefits of fixed security. Unfortunately, Justice Mann did not take the opportunity to consider the wider commercial issues such as how the order of priority would be affected by allowing floating security to be recharacterised as fixed. In my view, recharacterisation should not be used in order to prevent a party waiving rights which are for his own exclusive benefit; if he were so prevented, the effect would be to defeat the expectations of interested parties, such as the preferential creditors of the company, and to provide the chargee with a windfall which he had not contracted for. It should be possible to contract for a floating charge even though the nature of the rights and obligations which the parties intended to create is characteristic of a fixed charge. An alternative argument that might be available in some cases is that the chargee would be estopped from asserting that the charge was fixed in circumstances in which the security document expressly stated that it was floating and third parties had relied upon the statement to their detriment or had in some way changed their position.

My view is that *Russell-Cooke* took *Spectrum* one stage too far. It may be significant that the issue had not been considered before and Justice Mann may have felt bound by precedent to decide the case in the way he did given that all of the previous cases involving recharacterisation of fixed security as floating security focused heavily on the strict characteristics of the charges in question in determining whether the security was, in fact, classified as fixed or floating. However, it was in my view open to the judge to distinguish the previous cases, including *Spectrum*, on the basis that the previous cases all concerned charges which were expressed to be fixed in nature being recharacterised as floating charges, and that there were no public policy

---

47 [1994] 1 All ER 737.
48 [2005] 1 BCLC 1.

reasons for applying the doctrine of recharacterisation in the converse situation – that is, where the charge was expressed to be floating in nature.

In *Re Beam Tube,*[49] Justice Backburne accepted the argument made on behalf of the joint administrative receivers that the acceptance by the company four months after execution of the debenture of restrictions on the use of the moneys standing to the credit of the account into which the proceeds of the book and other debts of the company were paid could not have the effect of converting the charge over the account into a fixed charge.[50] The debenture had provided that until the security should become enforceable or the security agent had issued a direction to the company following a default, the proceeds paid into the collection account should be available to the company and be subject only to a floating charge.

*Russell-Cooke* differed from *Re Beam Tube* in that it appears that the restrictions in *Russell-Cooke* were agreed at the outset and were applied in practice. In *Re Beam Tube,* on the other hand, the agreement at the outset was that the proceeds of the debts paid into the collection account should be freely available to the chargor until the security became enforceable or there was a default and the restrictions which were subsequently agreed relating to the BLL suspense account were intended to give effect to the terms of the agreement regarding the collection of moneys belonging to the chargor.

*Re Beam Tube* does show the difficulties that will be encountered if it is necessary for the court, in categorising the nature of the rights and obligations of the parties, to look at the parties' conduct to see whether the restrictions on the chargor dealing with the charged assets have been operated in practice. If subsequent conduct is relevant, why in *Re Beam Tube* did the subsequent agreement establishing the BLL suspense account as a blocked account not convert the charge which had been expressed to be a floating charge into a charge that was fixed? It was clear from the correspondence that the parties thought that they were giving effect to the terms of the debenture. Nevertheless, the restrictions had not been operated in practice. Preferential creditors had priority over any charge which *as created* was a floating charge. The fact that the chargor had subsequently agreed that restrictions should apply to withdrawals from the collection account could not retrospectively convert the charge, which was created as a floating charge, into a charge that was fixed.

## 7. How to apply *Spectrum*

It is suggested that the issues that need to be addressed in determining whether a security interest on an asset is fixed are the following:

- Identify the asset.
- If the asset has no value apart from its proceeds, the asset and its proceeds must be treated as a single asset (this is the 'essential value test').
- What rights is the chargor given in relation to the asset?
- Are those rights inconsistent with the chargee taking an immediate proprietary interest in the asset?

---

49 See notes 33 and 42 *supra*.
50 See paragraph [49] of the judgment.

## 7.1 The market perspective

Before examining how the application of these principles may affect different asset classes, it is worth looking at the reaction of the market to the *Spectrum* decision. The decision was to a large extent foreshadowed by *Re Brightlife* and *Brumark* and should not have taken the market by surprise; nevertheless, it has caused some apprehension in the financial community, primarily reflecting concern as to the potential implications for transactions involving the taking of security over non-circulating assets.

A number of articles appeared in the legal press and law firms became much more reluctant to give opinions (including so-called 'reasoned opinions') on the likelihood of fixed security being recharacterised as floating security. Guidance was issued by one of the major rating agencies on the likely impact of the decision and what they expected the law firms to address in their legal opinions. A special report by Fitch Ratings[51] set out a number of features which were likely to be affected by the *Spectrum* decision, including the substitution of collateral and the application by a cash manager of the cash flow generated by secured assets in an agreed waterfall. These features might be said to be potentially inconsistent with the chargee taking an immediate interest in the asset. The report also pointed out that the issue was more likely to be relevant to some structures than others: for example, the issue would be likely to arise in relation to an issuer/borrower structure often used in commercial mortgage-backed securities and whole business transactions where the issuer is a bankruptcy-remote special purpose vehicle (SPV) but the borrower that provides security is not, or in relation to a structure involving the sale of revolving assets, such as credit card receivables, where collections can be applied by the servicer in the purchase of new assets.

## 7.2 Particular assets

I now intend to examine how the principles in *Spectrum* may be applied to different asset classes.

### *(a) Book debts*

Both Lord Millett in *Brumark* and Lord Scott in *Spectrum* in applying the essential value test concluded that a simple book debt and its proceeds were to be regarded as a single asset.

### *(b) Insurance proceeds and charter hire*

In aircraft and ship financing transactions, it is standard practice for the lenders to take assignments of the right to receive moneys under the insurance policies (hull, third-party liability, protection and indemnity etc) and of the right to receive charter hire under charterparties entered into with third parties. Typically, the assignment of insurances will contain provisions dealing with the insurance proceeds so that on a total loss of the aircraft or ship, the entire proceeds are applied in repayment of the loan, but proceeds in respect of other claims below a fixed amount can be paid to the

---

51 "*Spectrum Plus* – Implications for Structured Finance Transactions", December 16 2005.

assignor (which, in the case of hull insurance, allows the assignor to carry out any necessary repairs etc). The assignment of the right to receive charter moneys will contain similar provisions (but without reference to a total loss). Once an event of default occurs, all insurance and charter moneys are paid directly to the mortgagee.

It is difficult to see why the right to receive moneys under the insurance policies or the right to receive charter hire under charterparties should differ from a book debt (unless, perhaps, the assignment relates only to a specific existing policy or charterparty) and so payment into a blocked account would appear to be necessary if the assignment is to be construed as fixed security.

### *(c)* ***Rents under computer subleases***

Where an assignment by way of security is taken of rents due under agreements for the sub-letting of equipment (and not of the equipment itself), it is again thought that the rents and their proceeds will be regarded as a single asset so that if the proceeds are paid into an account controlled by the chargor, the assignment will be regarded as floating security.

This was the situation in *Re Atlantic Computer Systems PLC*[52] and *Re Atlantic Medical Limited*.[53] In the former case, there was an assignment to a bank of all the benefit of the sub-leases and all rentals under the sub-leases, and in the latter case the assignment extended to "any other sub-leases, hire purchase agreements or similar agreements from time to time entered into by [the company]", although the judge did not think that these additional words constituted a valid ground of distinction. In both cases, the court held that the assignment was in the nature of fixed security, even though the assignee had no control of the accounts into which the proceeds were paid. These decisions have been much criticised. In my view, applying the essential value test, the sub-leases and their rental proceeds would be regarded post *Spectrum* as a single asset, and as there was no control of the proceeds, the assignments would now be regarded as floating security. It is true that there is a passage in the judgment in *Atlantic Computer* which would seem to indicate that the subject matter of the security was more than just the right to receive the rental income (on p 534H it is stated that there was nothing to indicate that the company was to be at liberty to deal with its other rights under the sub-leases). On the other hand, the judge in *Atlantic Medical* described the distinction between a fixed charge on the sub-leases and a floating charge on rents and other moneys becoming payable up to the occurrence of an event of default as an "unreal one" (p 394). The fact that the assignment in *Atlantic Computer* did not include future sub-leases should not of itself under the *Spectrum* test make any difference because, if Lord Scott is right, the security is to be treated as floating if the third characteristic is present, even if the first is not.

### *(d)* ***Investment property***

Where security is on freehold or leasehold property subject to and with the benefit

---

52 Note 43 *supra*.
53 [1993] BCLC 386.

of one or more leases or sub-leases, possibly coupled with an express assignment of the right to receive the rent, the situation is on a superficial basis very similar to that which existed in *Atlantic Computer* and *Atlantic Medical*, save that the subject matter of the leases or sub-leases is real property rather than equipment. Indeed, in *Atlantic Computer* Lord Justice Nicholls (as he then was) justified his decision that the assignment of the rental income should be treated as fixed security notwithstanding that the assignor retained control of the proceeds, as follows:[54] "A mortgage of land does not become a floating charge by reason of the mortgagor being permitted to remain in possession and enjoy the fruits of the property charged for the time being. This is even so if the property is leasehold and the term is very short, and as such the term is of a wasting character."

One difference is that in *Atlantic Computer* there was no charge on the equipment itself. Beyond that, in the case of real property the lessor is endowed with a whole package of rights beyond the right to receive the rental payments. At the very least, he is entitled to repossession of the property on the expiration of the term of the lease. He is also entitled, if the lease so provides, to exercise controls over dealings by the lessee of the leased asset (controls over alienation, sub-letting etc). The reversionary interest should not be treated as circulating just because the rental income remains in the control of the lessor/chargor.

In most cases such as this the essential value of the reversionary interest is quite distinct from the rental income so that the charge on the reversionary interest will not be treated as floating merely because the chargor continues until default to be in receipt of the rent.[55] It is thought most unlikely that the House of Lords intended to rewrite the law of charges on real property. Clearly, if the only security that is taken is an assignment of the rental income, the proceeds of which are paid into an account which the assignor is free to use without restriction, the situation could well be different, as the amounts due from the lessee or the sub-lessee are analogous to book debts. However, the case would still not be on all fours with *Spectrum* because the rights that are the subject of the assignment became due under specific existing contracts and are therefore less likely to be recharacterised.

### *(e)* ***Shares and other securities***

Where a lender takes a mortgage of shares by way of security (whether a legal mortgage with the lender or its nominee being the registered holder of the shares or an equitable mortgage where the mortgagor remains the registered holder), it is very common for the mortgage to provide that unless and until an event of default occurs, any dividend or other income should (in the case of a legal mortgage) be paid to the mortgagor or (in the case of an equitable mortgage) may be retained by the mortgagor, and that the voting rights will be exercised in accordance with any directions received from the mortgagor).

It is thought that the essential value of the shares or securities comprises more than the right to the income (eg, there may be a right to a return of capital on a

---

54 [1992] Ch. 505, 534G.

55 See *Re Offshore Ventilation* [1989] BCC 160.

winding-up) and more than the temporary right to exercise or to control the exercise of the right to vote.

Accordingly, it is submitted that the inclusion of such provisions in the mortgage should not normally result in the mortgage being characterised as floating security.

In *Arthur D Little Limited (in administration) v Ableco Finance LLC*,[56] the administrators of a company sought to set aside a charge on shares in a subsidiary on the basis that it was void against them because it had not been registered as a floating charge. The charge which was expressed to be a fixed charge extended not only to the shares themselves but also to "distribution rights" (dividends). There were various restrictions on the disposal of the shares, but it was expressly provided that until an event of default occurred, the chargor should be entitled to receive all dividends and to exercise all voting rights (unless the exercise would be prejudicial to the interests of the chargee).

It was held that the charge on the shares was a fixed charge. The judge did not apply the essential value test, but reached his decision on the basis that the shares were not part of the circulating assets of the company and the chargor was not left free to withdraw them from the security. He drew the distinction that was made in *Brumark* between a power of disposition and a power of consumption; this was no more than the exercise of the power of consumption.

### *(f) Custodian accounts*

Security is sometimes taken over accounts maintained by a custodian. The security is typically expressed to relate not just to the rights of the chargor against the custodian and in and to the accounts, but also (in the case of non-cash accounts) to the underlying securities represented by entries on the custodian accounts. The securities themselves are unlikely to be physically held by the custodian, but instead are probably held in bearer or registered form as part of some larger fungible holding in Euroclear, Clearstream or the Depository Trust Company, or with some other depository or sub-custodian.

Any charge on the rights that the chargor may have against the custodian confers a purely personal right. Insofar as an attempt is made to take a charge on the securities themselves, this may confer a proprietary right, although it is recognised that there could well be difficulties in asserting that right if the securities were located in a foreign jurisdiction that did not recognise the proprietary claim.

In a typical collateralised debt obligation (CDO) transaction, an SPV raises funds in the capital markets which are then invested by the SPV in the purchase of bonds and other securities, subject to specified eligibility criteria. The securities are held by a custodian on behalf of the SPV; the custodian will establish at least one cash account and one securities account for the SPV. The SPV creates a charge (which is expressed to be a fixed charge) on the cash and securities accounts held with the custodian in favour of a security trustee as security for its obligations to the noteholders. The SPV will have entered into an investment management agreement under which the investment manager is appointed to manage the SPV's cash and

56 [2002] 2 BCLC 799.

securities. In some cases (eg, in a transaction involving a structured investment vehicle), the investment manager will have a wide discretion to buy and sell securities, subject to specified eligibility criteria. In a conventional CDO, the investment manager may only have authority to substitute securities whose credit quality is declining, but may not have general authority to trade the securities. In most CDOs, therefore, the investment manager has authority, within the parameters set out in the investment management agreement, from time to time to buy and sell securities and to give instructions to the custodian for such purpose. The investment manager acts as agent for the SPV unless and until notified of the occurrence of a default, at which point it acts as agent of the security trustee. The SPV assigns to the security trustee its rights under the investment management agreement and the custodian agreement, and notice is given to the investment manager and custodian of such assignments.

While the investment manager has the right to buy and sell investments on behalf of the SPV, neither the SPV nor the investment manager has the right to authorise the release of the cash or the securities to anyone other than the security trustee.

The essential value of the security on the custodian securities accounts lies in the underlying investments. As the investment manager acts on behalf of the SPV/chargor in switching the investments and in doing so acts, prior to a default or wind-down event, without reference to the security trustee, there is obviously some risk that the charge on the accounts is only a floating charge. The situation is analogous to that in *Re Cosslett* where Lord Justice Millett (as he then was) in the Court of Appeal thought[57] that the chargor's unfettered freedom to deal with the plant, goods and machinery on site was inconsistent with the nature of a fixed charge. However, the risk would clearly be minimised if it could be established that the investment manager owed a duty to the security trustee equivalent to that which it owes to the SPV/chargor so that it could be said that in taking the decision to switch investments it was also acting on behalf of the security trustee. The assignment by the chargor in favour of the security trustee of its rights under the investment management agreement clearly helps in this respect, but it would obviously be safer if the investment manager could be appointed to act as agent of the security trustee before as well as after default.

Some of the disadvantages of recharacterisation do not apply if the charge on the custodian account can be classified as a security finance collateral arrangement.[58]

### *(g)* *Goods and chattels*

The essential value of goods or chattels is normally not limited to the proceeds of sale. Unlike a book debt, they can be used and enjoyed before, and independently of, any sale. Accordingly, it should be possible to obtain fixed security on, for example, a piece of equipment if it can be shown that the mortgagor does not exercise any

57 [1999] 1 BCLC, 205, 218. On this point, the House of Lords did not disagree [2002] 1 AC 336, 357G.

58 See above. However, a right of substitution may mean that the charge cannot be so classified because of the unsatisfactory definition of 'equivalent financial collateral' in the Financial Collateral Arrangements (No 2) Regulations 2003.

rights in relation to the equipment itself which are inconsistent with the mortgagee having an immediate interest. A right of substitution would normally be inconsistent (see *Re Cosslett* above), but probably not a right to effect repairs.

It is not necessary that the mortgagee should have possession of the asset. If his title depended upon possession, he would have a pledge. A mortgage or charge is a security interest that is not dependent upon possession. It is for that reason that a mortgage or charge, whether created by a company or an individual, would normally require registration either under Section 395 of the Companies Act 1985 or under the Bills of Sale Acts.

### *(h) Securitisation waterfalls*

In the traditional securitisation structure, an SPV is set up to raise funds in the capital markets by the issue of debt securities ('notes'). A second entity which wishes to securitise its assets (the 'originator') sells a portfolio of assets to the SPV. The portfolio generates an income or other payment stream. The payment stream (which may be the proceeds of receivables) is applied by the SPV in making payments of interest and principal on the notes. The SPV grants security over all or substantially all of its assets, including the receivables and the bank accounts into which the proceeds of the receivables are paid, to a security trustee to be held on behalf of the secured parties, which would normally include the security trustee itself and the noteholders.

Securitisation structures generally require that the proceeds in the bank SPV's accounts be applied at agreed intervals (eg, monthly) in accordance with a mandatory payment waterfall. The only amounts permitted to be removed from this 'closed system' are amounts required to be paid representing certain key expenses of the SPV, which will normally be capped in order that the rating agencies can model the cash flows. The remaining funds are applied to pay interest and principal on the notes.

The documents normally provide for two waterfalls of payment, one of which applies before enforcement of the security and the other after enforcement. The pre-enforcement waterfall often provides for payments to be made from the bank accounts to particular unsecured creditors of the SPV, such as to Her Majesty's Revenue & Customs (HMRC) in respect of tax, before payments are made to service interest or repay principal on the notes. In almost all financings, the company must be in a position to pay its operating expenses from its cash flow, but with a securitisation the cash flow generated by the charged assets is likely to be the only cash flow available to the SPV to pay these expenses.

The bank accounts into which the proceeds of the receivables or other payment stream is paid are held with the 'account bank' (which might or might not be the security trustee) in the name of the chargor and within the control of the 'cash manager'. The cash manager normally acts as agent of the chargor until notified of a default, at which point it acts as agent of the security trustee. There are provisions in the cash management agreement for the replacement of the cash manager if it becomes insolvent or commits a breach of the agreement. There is no independent audit or verification of the actions of the cash manager by or on behalf of the SPV or the security trustee, although it is usual for reports to be provided to the security trustee at regular intervals in arrears, detailing the movements of cash that have taken place.

Where trade receivables are securitised, it is not usually practicable to have the proceeds of the receivables paid directly into the bank accounts of the SPV. This may be because the redirection of payments into the SPV's accounts (even if not disclosed to the debtors) might be considered by the originator to be harmful to the commercial relationship between the originator and its customers. Alternatively, the originator may simply take the view that it would be an administrative nightmare to try and redirect the payments, especially if there is a multiplicity of customers in different jurisdictions.

The usual solution is to allow for the 'intermingling' of moneys in the originator's bank accounts so that payments are made into these accounts of the proceeds of securitised receivables and receivables or other moneys that are not securitised. The originator then declares a trust of the moneys in the accounts so that if the originator enters liquidation, the proceeds of the receivables that are securitised do not form part of the liquidation estate. Reconciliations are carried out at regular intervals and at the end of each period the balance on the trust account which represents the securitised receivables is transferred to the accounts of the SPV.

The credit rating agencies accept the risk that it might not be possible for the issuer/security trustee to trace the moneys in the trust accounts and they model their cash flows on that basis.

The question has been raised whether the charge created by the SPV on the receivables or other assets producing the payment stream might be recharacterised as no more than a floating charge following the decisions in *Brumark* and *Spectrum*. The main concern arises from the use of the pre-enforcement waterfall, but some concern also arises from the inter-mingling of the proceeds of the receivables with the originator's own moneys in the trust accounts.

The pre-enforcement waterfall will typically provide that the proceeds of the receivables should be applied at specified intervals (perhaps monthly) in the payment of, or in the establishment of a reserve for, certain of the secured liabilities (eg, payments due under an interest rate swap or payments of principal and/or interest due on notes, or on particular classes of notes, in accordance with their agreed ranking).

There would be no problem if the pre-enforcement waterfall ended there. However, it is normally necessary to make provision for the payment of certain necessary expenses because the SPV will have no other means by which they can be satisfied. These expenses may include payments of tax to HMRC.

Where the asset producing the payment stream is trade receivables, *Brumark* and *Spectrum* tell us that it is not sufficient that there are restrictions on dealing with the trade receivables – the security trustee must also control the proceeds. The essential value of a trade debt lies in the right to payment so the trade debt cannot be distinguished from its proceeds. As mentioned earlier in this chapter, there are certain passages in *Spectrum* which indicate that nothing short of a blocked account will suffice. This implies that the proceeds credited to the account cannot be released to anyone other than the secured creditor(s) unless consent is given by the secured creditor(s) or the security trustee on their behalf at the time of the release; a prospective general licence to deal with the proceeds in the future will generally be inconsistent with the existence of a fixed charge.

Nevertheless, it has been suggested that it should not be necessary that the entire proceeds should be applied in discharge of the secured debt. Any suggestion as to what limitations there should be on the uncompromising position adopted by Lord Hope in *Spectrum* that the entire proceeds either should be retained by the chargee in a blocked account or should be applied in or towards the discharge of the secured debt is necessarily speculative – no limitations were mentioned in either *Brumark* or *Spectrum* – but common sense dictates that there should be some.

While each case will depend on its own facts, it has been suggested that the following factors (or a combination of these factors) may be relevant:

- quantum;
- purpose; and
- control devices.

On quantum, if the amount released to the chargor or to unsecured creditors in the pre-enforcement waterfall can be classified as *de minimis*, then it should be ignored. It is not possible to say what quantum of the proceeds would be regarded as *de minimis*, but it is suggested that this factor on its own should be relied upon with a degree of caution.

On the question of purpose, it could be argued that the application of the proceeds or part of the proceeds in a manner calculated to preserve or enhance the value of the security is not inconsistent with the chargee taking an immediate interest in the asset. For example, where there is an assignment by way of security of rent arising from the lease of real property, the application of the rental payments in paying rent due under the head lease or in complying with the obligation of the chargor under the lease to maintain the buildings on the property should be not be inconsistent with the chargee's rights to the rental payments.

It is more difficult to justify in this way the payment of tax due from the chargor to HMRC. On the one hand, if the tax is not paid, HMRC will no doubt serve a winding-up petition upon the chargor, thus forcing the security trustee to enforce the security earlier than was expected – something that is unlikely to be in the interests of the secured creditors. It is for this reason that, if tax liabilities are expected, a reserve will always be created and the establishment of the reserve will rank at a higher level in the waterfall than the payments of interest and the repayments of principal in respect of the notes. On the other hand, the payment of tax is less obviously a payment to preserve or enhance the value of the security than, say, the payment of rent due under a head lease. The connection with the preservation of the charged asset is less direct. It remains to be seen whether the courts will regard a waterfall which allows the proceeds of the charged asset to be applied in payment of, or in establishing a reserve for, tax as a hallmark of security which is floating in nature. Each case will turn on its own facts, but what can be said with certainty is that it will be relevant to the analysis which the court is required to make following the *Brumark* decision.

Turning to control devices, it is thought unlikely that the preparation of an indicative budget of expenditure or the monitoring of the expenses as and when they are incurred will be sufficient to indicate that the chargee has retained sufficient control of the proceeds, particularly if the budget is prepared or the expenses are monitored by the chargor or its agent (eg, the cash manager), even if there is provision for the budget or report to be delivered to the security trustee. Likewise, it is unlikely that an automated transfer from the blocked account to an operating account to allow the expenses to be paid would be sufficient. It is possible that a provision for 'negative control' whereby, for example, the security trustee would be notified of the proposed expenditure and would be deemed to have consented if it did not object within a specified period might be enough, but only if the right to refuse consent was real and both parties understood that the objection could in practice be made.

### *(i) Assignment of rights under the transaction documents*

In securitisation transactions, it is common for the issuer SPV and sometimes other parties to assign by way of security all of their rights and benefits under the transaction documents. These rights may include, among others:

- the right to receive certain payments;
- the benefit of undertakings from the liquidity facility providers, the cash managers, the swap providers, the corporate services providers etc;
- the right to damages for breach of contract; and
- the right to serve notices.

It is not uncommon for the assignment to be coupled with a proviso that the assignor can continue to exercise the rights (or certain of the rights) under these transaction documents until default.

The question in such cases is whether the continued exercise of the rights in question by the chargor is inconsistent with the chargee taking an immediate interest in the rights. Depending upon the facts, it may be possible to argue on the basis of the factors described above (quantum, purpose, control devices) that the security (despite the proviso) remains fixed.

Alternatively, where the chargor is entitled to exercise only certain of the rights under the relevant transaction document, it may be possible to sever these rights from the other rights so that only the charge on the former would be liable to be recharacterised as floating.

## 8. Conclusion

It should not be assumed that a security interest is fixed merely because it is described as such in the security document. Nor should it be assumed that it will be fixed because that appears to be the intention of the parties based upon the language of the security document. It is necessary, as Lord Millett said in *Brumark*, to ascertain the nature of the rights and obligations and to ask whether they are inconsistent with the nature of a fixed charge. Put another way: are they inconsistent with the chargee taking an immediate interest in the asset? Each asset must be looked at separately and, in deciding what is a separate asset, the courts will apply what I have called the 'essential value test'.

The risk of recharacterisation is not confined to security interests on circulating assets, although if the asset is non-circulating, there is perhaps a presumption that the asset is not intended to be dealt with in the ordinary course of business and is therefore less likely to be recharacterised.

The importance of *Spectrum* was the emphasis that was given to the third characteristic in *Yorkshire Woolcombers* and the need for the secured creditor to control not just the asset itself, but also the proceeds or fruits of the asset if they formed part of its essential value.

In many ways, the parties are trying to have their cake and eat it: they want to give the chargor the maximum flexibility to deal with the asset as if the security interest were floating while at the same time maintaining the minimum level of control that is required in order to be able to assert that the security is fixed.

When these principles are applied to different transactions and different asset classes, it is apparent that many of the financing structures commonly used by investment bankers and law firms may need to be scrutinised more thoroughly in the future and the consequences of potential recharacterisation more carefully assessed.

# Security trustees

**Paul U Ali**
University of Melbourne

Security trusts are encountered in a wide variety of financing transactions, including secured syndicated loans, project finance, secured corporate bond and medium term note programmes and securitisation.[1] In each of these cases, the assets held by a borrower or issuing vehicle are charged in favour of a security trustee for the benefit of the borrower's lenders or investors.[2] This arrangement is depicted in the following diagram.

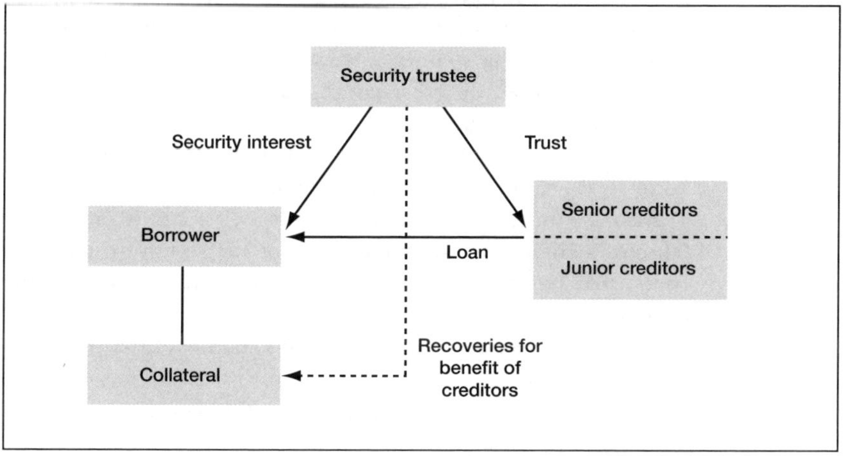


The appointment of a security trustee is administratively convenient. Changes to the composition of the class of creditors beneficially entitled to the security interest – for example, when lenders sell down portions of a secured syndicated loan made to the borrower or when investors trade the debt securities issued by the borrower as part of a secured bond programme or securitisation – do not require changes to be made to the registration of the security interest, as the security trustee remains the holder of record in relation to the security interest.

1 See Financial Markets Law Committee, "Issue 62 – Trustee Exemption Clauses" (May 2004), Ch 2.

2 The characterisation of the security trust as a 'trust' is straightforward – the trust property comprises the security interest or interests granted by the borrower to the security trustee – compared to the case of the note trustee, as it is uncertain whether the payment obligations of the borrower to the creditors can properly be said to constitute the trust property held by the note trustee for the benefit of the creditors, as it is the creditors that are taken to hold those obligations: see A Hudson, *The Law on Investment Entities* (Sweet & Maxwell, London, 2000), pp 170-171; SL Schwarcz, "Commercial Trusts as Business Organizations: Unraveling the Mystery" (2003) 58 *Business Lawyer* 559, at 569-570.

More importantly, only the security trustee is entitled to enforce the security interest against the borrower and the individual creditors of the borrower – despite holding secured claims against the borrower – are precluded from taking independent action against the borrower in respect of their claims.[3] However, this enforcement power is not exercisable at the sole discretion of the security trustee; if the borrower defaults in the performance of the obligations secured by the security interest or becomes insolvent, the security trustee will normally be able to enforce the security interest only if it has been directed to do so by a stipulated majority of the creditors. This creation of a single avenue for the enforcement of the security interest, coupled with the provision for the security trustee to act on the direction of a majority of creditors, means that the borrower is not exposed to the prospect of multiple enforcement actions and also that the creditors are protected against collective action problems and opportunistic behaviour by individual creditors.[4]

The perception – encouraged, unsurprisingly, by security trustees themselves – is that the security trustee is merely the repository of the security interest held over the borrower's assets and, due to contractual stipulations requiring it to act only when directed, is merely a passive conduit for the will of the majority of the creditors for whose benefit it holds the security interest. The passive nature of the security trustee's role is reinforced by other contractual terms normally encountered in security trusts, such as the following:

- The security trustee may assume, unless notified to the contrary, that the borrower is performing all of its obligations;
- The security trustee is not required to keep itself informed or inquire as to the borrower's compliance with the terms of the security trust or any other contractual terms relating to the borrower's financial obligations to the creditors;
- The security trustee is not required to take any steps to ascertain whether an event of default has occurred in relation to the borrower (eg, including a failure to make a payment when due on the part of the borrower or the borrower's insolvency);
- The security trustee is taken not to have knowledge of an event of default in relation to the borrower unless actually notified by a creditor or the borrower (or one of the other transaction parties, such as a separate note trustee or a servicer);
- The security trustee need not act in the absence of directions from a stipulated majority of creditors; and
- The security trustee is under no obligation to enforce the security interest following an event of default in relation to the borrower, pending the receipt of directions from a stipulated majority of creditors.

---

3 The creditors – or, invariably, a stipulated majority of the creditors – will normally be permitted to take independent action against the borrower where the security trustee has failed to act within a reasonable time or is unable to act (eg, due to the creditors and the security trustee failing to agree to the terms on which the latter should be indemnified in relation to any personal liability incurred as a result of its enforcement of the security interest).

4 See G Fuller, *Corporate Borrowing: Law and Practice* (Jordans, Bristol, 3rd ed, 2006), p 194; P Rawlings, "The Changing Role of the Trustee in International Bond Issues" [2007] *Journal of Business Law* 43, at 46-47.

Normally, the only discretion permitted a security trustee is the ability to grant a waiver, without the need for the prior consent of the creditors, of a breach by the borrower of the terms of the security trust or any other contractual terms relating to the borrower's financial obligations to the creditors, where the security trustee is of the opinion that such a breach is not materially prejudicial to the interests of the creditors. In addition, while the terms of the security trust will, as noted above, normally be carefully drafted to relieve the security trustee of any positive obligation to make inquiries or monitor the borrower, the security trustee may nonetheless be contractually obligated to pass on to the creditors any non-confidential information that comes into its possession in the ordinary course of its administration of the security trust as regards an event of default. However, even where such a modest requirement is imposed on the security trustee, it will not be required to act on any such information unless directed to do so by a stipulated majority of creditors.

The role of the security trustee at the heart of many secured financing structures, in particular relatively complex financing structures such as securitisation, is likely to be subjected to more exacting scrutiny than that to which security trustees have become accustomed, due to increasing delinquency and default rates in the US sub-prime residential mortgage market[5] and the exposure to that market of many sub-prime residential mortgage-backed securities (RMBS) and collateralised debt obligations (CDO) transactions.[6] Investors in both US and non-US synthetic CDOs are now confronting the risk of sizeable losses on their investments due to their assumption of credit risk on US sub-prime residential mortgage loans via their holdings of the riskier tranches of synthetic CDOs referencing US sub-prime RMBS.[7] In many of these structures, the security trustee is the party most proximate to the investors, lying as it does between the issuing vehicle and the investors. Moreover, as the one party – or one of the few parties (eg, where there is a separate note trustee) – that is clearly in a fiduciary relationship with the investors, the security trustee is an obvious target for investors seeking to recoup losses on their investments.[8]

At issue here is the extent of the security trustee's duties to the creditors for whose benefit it holds the security interest.

It is possible to argue against the imposition of broader responsibilities on the security trustee by reference to:

---

5 See Moody's Investors Service, "Challenging Times for the US Subprime Mortgage Market" (March 7 2007).

6 See D Evans, "Toxic Debt: The Ratings Charade", *Bloomberg Markets*, July 2007.

7 See Citigroup Global Markets, "A Simple Guide to Subprime Mortgages, CDO, and Securitization" (April 13 2007); Fitch Ratings, "Global US Subprime Exposure in Synthetic Collateralised Debt Obligations" (April 16 2007); D Evans, "Toxic Debt: The Poison in your Pension", *Bloomberg Markets*, July 2007.

8 See JE Spiotto, "Theories of Liability which have been Raised Against the Indenture Trustee" in *The Problems of Indenture Trustees and Bondholders* (Practising Law Institute, New York, 1995), 409 PLI/Real 671, pp 673-674; NERA Economic Consulting, "The Subprime Meltdown: A Primer" (June 21 2007). It is, in contrast, doubtful whether fiduciary duties are owed to the creditors by a corporate issuing vehicle or borrower: see GS Corey, MW Marr and MF Spivey, "Are Bondholders owed a Fiduciary Duty?" (1991) 18 *Florida State University Law Review* 971, at 984; TR Hurst and LJ McGuinness, "The Corporation, the Bondholder and Fiduciary Duties" (1991) 10 *Journal of Law and Commerce* 187, at 206; RD Ellis, "Securitization Vehicles, Fiduciary Duties, and Bondholders' Rights" (1999) 24 *Journal of Corporation Law* 295, at 311-313.

- the contingent nature of the security trustee's rights under the security trust;[9] and
- the contractual terms of the security trust.

As regards the former, it is only after an event of default has occurred in relation to the borrower and the security trustee has been directed to enforce the security interest by a stipulated majority of creditors that the security trustee will obtain control over the assets of the borrower subject to the security interest.[10] On this basis, one might contend that – as is the case with a note trustee in the United States[11] – duties should be imposed on the security trustee only following an event of default.[12] The note trustee is described as holding the benefit of the borrower's payment and other obligations on behalf of the creditors but there is ambiguity as to what the trust property is.[13] Also, until an event of default occurs, the note trustee's role as depicted in the terms of the note trust is merely 'ministerial' in nature. Until that time, the note trustee is responsible only for passively monitoring the borrower's compliance with its obligations to the creditors and has no control rights in respect of the borrower's business or any right to interfere in the borrower's management of its business.[14]

In contrast, in the case of a security trust, there is no ambiguity as to the trust property. The trust property is the security interest (or interests) over the secured assets and the security trustee enjoys control rights over that security interest from the inception of the security trust, even though the security trustee's control is sharply constrained by the contractual terms of the security trust and may be viewed, in common with the pre-default role of a note trustee, as essentially ministerial in relation to the security interest. The security trustee's duties should, consequently, not be limited to post-default situations.

---

9 The points made in this paragraph are made by way of analogy with the position of note trustees which may not necessarily hold a security interest over the borrower's assets. The role of the security trustee may be conflated with that the note trustee in some structures. Where a separate note trustee has been appointed, it will, in common with the borrower's creditors on whose behalf it acts, be a beneficiary of the security trust.

10 See JH Langbeinn, "The Secret Life of the Trust: The Trust as an Instrument of Commerce" (1997) 107 *Yale Law Journal* 165, at 173-174.

11 See MC Cohen and HL Kaplan, "The Role of the Trustee in Securitization Transactions" in JHP Kravitt (ed), *Securitization of Financial Assets* (Aspen Law & Business, New York, 2nd ed, 2004), §9.02[C]; M Riger, "The Trust Indenture as Bargained Contract: The Persistence of Myth" (1991) 16 *Journal of Corporation Law* 211, at 218-219; SL Schwarcz and G Sergi, "Bond Defaults and the Dilemma of the Indenture Trustee" (Duke Law School Working Paper, June 2007). Cf MD Sklar, "The Corporate Indenture Trustee: Genuine Fiduciary or Mere Stakeholder?" (1989) 106 *Banking Law Journal* 42, at 43, 50 and 53-55 where the imposition of duties from the inception of the trust is argued for. The distinction between the pre- and post-default position of the note trustee is a creation of the US Trustee Indenture Act of 1939, and it can be argued that this distinction cannot be attributed to the contingent nature of the rights held by the note trustee or the absence of control rights prior to an event of default as the original draft legislation actually provided for the imposition of duties on the note trustee from the inception of the trust: see SM Robertson, "Debenture Holders and the Indenture Trustee: Controlling Managerial Discretion in the Solvent Enterprise" (1988) 11 *Harvard Journal of Law and Public Policy* 461, at 473-474.

12 Neither English nor Australian law differentiates between the pre- and post-default position of the note (or security) trustee. The trustee is considered to owe duties to the creditors from the inception of the trust, to the extent that those duties have not been modified by contract: see Fuller, above n 4, pp 199-206.

13 See above n 2.

14 See Langbeinn, above n 10, at 174.

In addition, the value of the security interest is dependent upon the extent to which that security interest grants rights of recourse to the assets of the borrower, the priority ranking of such rights relative to other claims against the borrower and its assets and, ultimately, the value of the assets over which that security interest has been taken. The imposition of duties on the security trustee, beyond the narrow duties detailed in the contractual terms of the security trust, in relation to preserving or maintaining the value of the security interest will thus necessarily entail imposing additional duties in relation to preserving the value of the secured assets.[15]

The duties to which a security trustee (in common with other trustees) is subject can be divided into the duty of good faith, on the one hand – which, as it constitutes what is considered to be the minimum necessary obligation to give effect to a trust, cannot be contracted out – and other duties, including the duty of care, which are considered to be susceptible to contractual modification.[16] The latter raises the second of two possible constraints mentioned above, namely the efficacy of the terms of the security trust in narrowly framing the duties of the security trust and, by so doing, excluding or restricting the duties – and liability for breach of those duties – to which the security trustee would otherwise be subject.

For creditors – whether lenders to the borrower or investors in debt securities issued by the borrower or an interposed issuing vehicle – the critical duty is likely to be the duty of care, which requires security trustees to act prudently as regards their administration of the trust property.[17] For example, the security trustee's failure to act expeditiously on information provided to it or in enforcing the security interest following an event of default may lead to the creditors incurring a loss on their claims. In such a situation, the creditors may seek to recoup that loss from the security trustee on the grounds that the trustee has failed to act with due care.[18] The standard against which a security trustee's conduct, as that of a party whose profession or business is or includes acting as a security trustee, is measured is the care, skill and diligence that a prudent person engaged in that profession or business would exercise when acting on behalf of others.[19]

This duty which has, as is the case in the United Kingdom, been restated in Australian trustee legislation can be modified by the terms of the security trust.[20] However, both statute and the general law impose limits on the extent of such contractual modification.[21] Where, for instance, the security trust secures a retail

---

15 It is arguable that the duties of the trustee may extend beyond merely acting to preserve the trust property to attempting to secure repayment of the obligations to the creditors: see Schwarcz and Sergi, *ibid*, on the difficulties of applying the traditional formulation of the duty to act prudently (acting to preserve the value of the trust property) to note (and thus also security) trustees.

16 *Armitage v Nurse* [1998] Ch 241, at 253-254.

17 See Schwarcz and Sergi, above n 11.

18 See, for example, *Concord Trust v Law Debenture Trust Corp Plc* [2005] 1 WLR 1591 (as regards the mandatory obligation of a note trustee to accelerate the borrower's payment obligations following an event of default and being directed to do so by a stipulated majority of creditors).

19 *Bartlett v Barclays Bank Trust Co Ltd* [1980] 1 Ch 515, at 534. See also J Benjamin and M Yates, *The Law of Global Custody* (Butterworths, London, 2nd ed, 2002), p. 90; PU Ali, G Stapledon and M Gold, *Corporate Governance and Investment Fiduciaries* (Lawbook Co, Sydney, 2003), p. 30; Fuller, above n 4, p. 199.

20 See, for example, Trustee Act 1925 (NSW), s 14B(1) and (3); Trustee Act 1958 (Vic), s 7(1) and (3).

21 See Benjamin and Yates, above n 19, pp. 89-90; Fuller, above n 4, pp. 200-202.

issue of debentures,[22] it will not be possible, due to statutory provisions regulating debentures in Australia, for the terms of the security trust to exempt the security trustee from certain statutory obligations, including the requirement to:[23]

- exercise reasonable care and skill to ascertain whether the secured assets are sufficient to meet the claims of the creditors;
- exercise reasonable care and skill to ascertain whether the borrower has breached the terms of the security trust or debentures;
- do everything in its power to ensure that the borrower remedies any breach of the terms of the security trust or debentures known to the security trustee; and
- comply with the directions given by a stipulated majority of creditors.

Despite the licence that has seemingly been given to security trustees (and other trustees) to limit their obligations, and any liability for breach of those obligations, to what the courts have termed the 'irreducible core' of trustee obligations (ie, the duty to act in good faith for the benefit of the beneficiaries), it is likely that a court will, in interpreting any contractual modification of duties and liability, draw a distinction between the duties of traditional, gratuitous trustees on the one hand, and the duties of professional trustees on the other, such as security trustees, which are being remunerated for their services and profess to have special knowledge or experience as regards the role that they perform.[24] Such an approach is consistent with the higher standard of care, skill and diligence expected of security trustees.[25]

In addition, where a trustee such as a security trustee has been appointed for the express and limited purpose of holding a security interest for the benefit of the creditors, and that trustee is a professional trustee and is charging a fee for the limited services that it provides, there is a risk that a court may view attempts to curtail the managerial responsibilities of the trustee (eg, as regards the monitoring of the trust property or otherwise acting to preserve the value of the trust property) as undermining a fundamental requirement for the careful and diligent management of the trust property and thus the very trust itself.[26] Should a court take the view that the irreducible core obligations contemplated by a security trust embrace certain

---

22 The securities issued in many securitisations are not debentures under Australian law: see B Salter, "The Law of Securitization in Australia" in PD Dolan and CV Davis (eds), *Securitizations: Legal and Regulatory Issues* (Law Journal Press, New York, 2006), §25.03[2][a].

23 Corporations Act 2001 (Cth), ss 283DA and 283DB. The trust deed can, however, provide for a majority of at least 75% of the debenture holders (by face value) to release the security trustee for liability to show the requisite care and skill.

24 See, for example, *Target Holdings Ltd v Redferns* [1996] AC 421, at 435: "it is important if the trust is not to be rendered commercially useless, to distinguish between the basic principles of trust law and those specialist rules developed in relation to traditional trusts which are applicable only to such trusts and the rationale of which has no application to trusts of a quite different kind." See also Law Commission, "Trustee Exemption Clauses: A Consultation Paper" (Consultation Paper 171, December 2002), paras 4.33-4.40 and 4.84; Law Commission, "Trustee Exemption Clauses" (Cmnd 6874, July 2006), paras 4.6, 4.17, 4.26 and 4.29.

25 See above n 19. Moreover, this distinction is contemplated in *Armitage v Nurse* [1998] Ch 241, at 256: "trustees who charge for their services and who, as professional men, would not dream of excluding liability for ordinary professional negligence should not be able to rely on a trustee exemption clause excluding liability for gross negligence."

26 See J Getzler, "Equitable Compensation and the Regulation of Fiduciary Relationships" in P Birks and F Rose (eds), *Resulting Trusts and Equitable Compensation* (LLP, London, 2000), p 256.

minimum requirements of care, skill and diligence, and that the attempt, under the terms of the security trust, to define narrowly the duties of the trustee runs counter to those core obligations, the security trustee will find itself – despite the terms of the security trust – subject to broader duties to preserve the value of the trust property. This, as noted above, will necessarily involve the security trustee being subject to more onerous requirements to monitor the secured assets and act to preserve the value of those assets.

Moreover, where the conduct of a security trustee is considered to be so unreasonable that no trustee engaged in a similar business or profession would have considered that such conduct was in the best interests of the beneficiaries, it is likely that a court will characterise that conduct not as negligence, but as deliberate or reckless indifference to the beneficiaries' interests and thus a breach of good faith for which the trustee clearly cannot, by contract, relieve itself of liability.[27] A court could well take that view of a situation where the security trustee receives information from a source other than the borrower or a creditor (or other transaction party) that a possible event of default may have occurred in relation to the borrower and does not investigate that information or even pass that information on to the creditors.[28] A court may thus have considerable sympathy for the view expressed by Moody's that a security trustee (or note trustee) that is unresponsive to credible indications that the borrower is in default has left the creditors in a situation where "the integrity of the transaction depends entirely on the willingness of transaction participants to report [to the trustee] their own failures to act in accordance with transaction documentation".[29]

27 See, for example, *Walker v Stones* [2001] QB 902. See also D Hayton, "The Irreducible Core Content of Trusteeship" in AJ Oakley (ed), *Trends in Contemporary Trust Law* (Clarendon Press, Oxford, 1996), p 59; M Bryan, "Contractual Modification of the Duties of a Trustee" in S Worthington, *Commercial Law and Commercial Practice* (Hart Publishing, Oxford, 2003), pp 524-526; Rawlings, above n 4, at 53.

28 See Moody's Investors Service, "Moody's Re-examines Trustees' Role in ABS and RMBS" (February 4 2003); SD Gibson, "The Case for the Expanded Role of Trustees in Securitizations" (2004) 121 *Banking Law Journal* 387, at 402 and 405.

29 See Moody's Investors Service, *ibid.*

# Reform

**Gerard McCormack**
University of Leeds

The easy availability of credit is often considered to be one of the cornerstones of a modern market economy. Conventional wisdom suggests that the possibility of securing credit promotes the availability of credit. 'Security' may be defined broadly as a right over property to ensure the payment of money or the performance of some other obligation. Security is said to encourage lenders to make loans that they would not otherwise make, to lower the cost of credit and to serve as fair exchange for the credit. Creditors often wish to take security to give them priority over other creditors in the event of the debtor becoming insolvent, and also to provide them with a measure of control over the secured assets and more generally over the debtor's business. A debtor is perhaps more likely to pay a secured creditor because otherwise it would risk losing assets that may be crucial to the carrying on of its business. Moreover, the taking of security opens up the possibility of the creditor exercising self-help remedies and it may also shorten a credit inquiry, in that a creditor might focus its investigations on the value of the secured assets.

It is also conventional wisdom, particularly among international financial institutions, that a modern law of secured credit should embody certain fundamental principles, including the principle that the law should provide for the granting of security in the widest possible range of circumstances. In other words, it should be possible to take security over all sorts of property to secure all sorts of credits. Moreover, all types of debtor should be free to grant security, and in favour of all types of creditor. Another fundamental principle is that security rights over property should be effectively publicised.

This chapter focuses primarily on the 'publicity' aspects of security and examines the issue of personal property security law reform in the common law developed world, particularly in England.

## 1. The English publicity system for company security interests and certain points of comparison

In England, details of the main types of charge created by companies must be registered at the companies registration office, Companies House. There is the possibility of a fine on the company for failure to register, but the main consequences of non-registration are visited on the charge holder, which loses its priority where the company goes into administration or liquidation. The registration obligation is now laid down in Part 25 of the Companies Act 2006. The obligation applies only to charges strictly so called and does not cover 'quasi-securities'. The latter are functionally equivalent legal devices such as finance leases, retention of title clauses in sale of goods contracts or factoring arrangements (ie, the absolute assignment of receivables). Quasi-securities may involve many of the same economic consequences as charges, but have different legal characteristics and effects.

The company charge registration system does not apply to security agreements executed by individuals, but there is a parallel system in place: the Bills of Sale Acts. Basically, this legislation requires that chattel mortgages and other similar security agreements created by individuals be in a particular statutory form and also registered in court offices. Failure to comply with the statutory requirements results in invalidity of the security. In fact, the requirements are so cumbersome and difficult to comply with that the Bills of Sale Acts are effectively bypassed in practice. Consumer purchases in England are often funded through hire purchase agreements which, technically speaking, are an agreement for the hire of goods coupled with an option to purchase the goods at the end of the hire period.

The Bills of Sale Acts have a consumer protection aspect to them, albeit one which is imperfectly and inappropriately realised. However, the company charge registration system has a different orientation. Its main rationale is the provision of information for persons such as credit reference agencies and prospective charge holders that wish to assess the creditworthiness of the company. For instance, prospective charge holders can ascertain from the register whether security has already been created over the assets of the company. In consequence, they are better informed about making a lending decision and structuring the terms of any loan.

The English system is essentially a transaction-based system of registration and should be contrasted with the notice filing system under Article 9 of the US Uniform Commercial Code and the Canadian and New Zealand Personal Property Security Acts.

> *The most characteristic difference between notice filing and traditional systems of registration is that notice filing is parties-specific rather than transaction-specific. What is filed are not the details of a particular security but notice that certain parties have entered into, or may in future enter into, a secured transaction in relation to specified property. This approach has certain implications. A notice may be filed in advance of the transaction and the proposed transaction may never take place. The same notice may serve a series of connected transactions. And the information given on the register is necessarily rather general in character, being an invitation to further inquiry rather than a full account of the right in security.*[1]

Article 9-style regimes also apply to all security interests, regardless of whether the security provider is an individual or a business entity. The main points of comparison between the English system and Article 9/Personal Property Security Act regimes are outlined in the following table.

---

1 Scottish Law Commission discussion paper, "Registration of Rights in Security by Companies" (October 2002), at p 8.

| Features | English-style registration | US-style notice filing |
|---|---|---|
| What is registrable/ fileable? | • Certain categories of charge<br>• Grantor - companies | • Transactions that are security in a functional sense (save certain excepted ones)<br>• Grantor – not limited to companies |
| Obligation | On the charge giver | Not an obligation, but an available means of perfection |
| Priorities | Strictly no, but failure to register means charge holder loses priority | Date of filing is reference point for settling order of priorities |
| Non-registration | Void against liquidator and other creditors | May lose priority<br>Can also be avoided by a company's trustee in bankruptcy (equivalent to an English liquidator) |
| Timing | • Prescribed time to register<br>• After creation of charge<br>• Extension by court | No prescribed time<br>May be filed in advance of transaction |
| Particulars filed | • Details of transaction<br>• Particulars such as date of creation of charge, amount secured, property charged, names of charge holders<br>• Instrument of charge | • Financing statement with name of debtor and secured party and indication of collateral<br>• May cover a series of connected transactions<br>• Security agreement not filed |
| Certificate of due registration | • Issued by registrar<br>• Conclusive evidence requirements met | None – filing office does not check accuracy of information |

While, unlike Article 9, the English system does not require the registration of quasi-securities, in some respects it is more comprehensive. In the main, Article 9 and systems based upon it do not apply to security over land or to security over certain types of property that may be registrable in specialist property registers (eg, security over intellectual property rights and ship and aircraft mortgages). These exclusions are difficult to justify rationally. Pressure group politics and lobbying by vested interest groups undoubtedly have a part to play as well. They are perhaps explicable on the basis in particular that land tends to have its own distinctive legal regime. Also, in federal jurisdictions, land law is often considered to be a matter within the exclusive competence of the state or provincial legislature, as distinct from chattel mortgage law, which has a more cross-territorial reach.

## 2. More details on the English registration system

While there have been variations in procedure, the essential features of the registration scheme has remained the same for over 100 years.[2] To be registrable, a security interest must constitute a 'charge', be created by a company and come within the statutory list. If the security interest does not meet all of these criteria, then it is not registrable. It is fair to say that the registration requirement is imposed only in respect of a limited category of enumerated charges. In England, the company charge registration was first introduced by Section 14 of the Companies Act 1900[3] and applied to four categories of charge:

- a charge for the purpose of securing any issue of debentures;
- a charge on uncalled capital of the company;
- a charge created or evidenced by an instrument which, if executed by an individual, would require registration as a bill of sale; and
- a floating charge on the undertaking or property of the company.

The categories have been extended over the years. Charges on land and charges on book debts became registrable in 1907.[4] In 1928 the list was extended to charges on unpaid calls, to ship mortgages and to charges on goodwill, patents, trademarks and copyright.[5] Charges on aircraft were added by the Mortgaging of Aircraft Order 1972.

Certain particulars of the charge - such as the date of creation, amount secured, property charged and persons entitled thereto - together with the instrument of charge, must be delivered to the companies registrar within 21 days of the date of creation of the charge. The registrar compares the instrument of charge with the filed particulars and, once satisfied that everything is in order, issues a certificate of due registration which is stated by statute to be conclusive evidence that all requirements as to registration have been complied with. There is a procedure whereby a charge may be registered out of time, but this requires a court application.

An unregistered but registrable charge becomes void against a certain stated class of persons: the liquidator, administrator and creditors of the company. This provision has been interpreted as meaning that an unregistered charge becomes void

---

2 For a detailed historical account of the development of the company charge registration provisions see De Lacy, "Reflections on the Ambit and Reform of the Part 12 of the Companies Act 1985 and the Doctrine of Constructive Notice" in De Lacy, ed, *The Reform of UK Company Law* (London, Cavendish, 2002).

3 This follows the recommendations of the 1895 Davey Committee on Company Law Amendment. Chapter 25 of the Companies Act 2006 replaces Part 12 of the Companies Act 1985.

4 Section 10 of the Companies Act 1907.

5 Section 43 of the Companies Act 1928.

only against unsecured creditors in a liquidation or administration According to Lord Hoffmann in *Smith v Bridgend County Borough Council*: "The plain intention of the legislature was that property subject to a registrable but unregistered charge should be available to the general body of creditors (or a secured creditor ranking after the unregistered charge) as if no such charge existed."[6]

However, an unregistered charge is still valid towards the company and, outside liquidation or administration, the charge holder can exercise all remedies conferred by the charge through exercising a power of sale over assets covered by the charge etc. The charge, though, is invalid against another person with property rights in these assets (eg, a secured creditor) and therefore the unregistered charge holder would have to hand over the proceeds of sale of the assets to such a person. While registration is not *per se* a reference point for determining priorities, the holder of an unregistered but registrable charge is reduced to the rank of an unsecured creditor in the event of the company that created the charge going into liquidation.

Many common law countries still follow the broad outlines of the English approach towards registration of company charges, including Ireland, Singapore and Hong Kong. However, there are some differences in detail. For instance, in Ireland and in Singapore there is no obligation to submit the instrument of charge along with the prescribed particulars to the registrar of companies. Because of the absence of the instrument of charge itself, the registrar does not, as a matter of course, check whether the particulars are a full and accurate description of the charge. Nevertheless, interestingly enough, in both countries the registrar is still required to issue a certificate of due registration.

## 3. Article 9-style notice filing

Under Article 9, the security agreement itself is not filed but rather a simple record - a financing statement – that provides a limited amount of information.[7] The financing statement may be filed either before or after the security agreement is drawn up. The filed notice merely indicates that a person may have a security interest in the collateral (property) concerned, but to ascertain the complete state of affairs it is necessary to make further inquiry from the parties. There is a statutory procedure under Article 9-210 whereby a secured party, at the debtor's request, may be required to make disclosure. In many cases, however, the debtor or another prospective financier may be able to obtain the requisite information without the need to invoke the compulsory features of Article 9-210.

Notice filing under an Article 9 regime removes the need to make a number of repeat filings where there is a series of transactions between the parties.[8] The financing statement is effective to cover transactions under a security agreement that was not in existence and not even contemplated by the parties at the time that the financing statement was filed, provided that the indication of collateral in the financing statement is sufficiently broad to cover the collateral concerned. Similarly,

---

6 [2002] 1 AC 336 at para 68.
7 Article 9-502, Official Comment.
8 See generally Article 9-502, Official Comment.

a financing statement is effective to cover after-acquired property of the type indicated and to perfect future advances under security agreements, irrespective of whether after-acquired property or future advances are mentioned in the financing statement and even though they may not have been contemplated by the parties at the time that the financing statement was drawn up.[9]

In simple terms, a financing statement may cover the entire credit relationship of the parties. Therefore, a seller which is contemplating the supply of goods to a buyer over an extended period of time may take a security interest in all the supplies by filing a simple financing statement instead of having to register each contract of sale separately, which would be the case if a retention of title clause were held to constitute a registrable charge under present English law.[10] The creditor may state simply that it is taking security in certain collateral to cover advances made to the debtor, including future advances, irrespective of whether there is any commitment on the part of the creditor to make the advance.[11]

There are simple formal requirements for an effective financing statement:

- the debtor's name;
- the name of a secured party or representative of the secured party; and
- an indication of the collateral.

A financing statement must reasonably identify the collateral; alternatively, it is permissible to state that the financing statement covers all assets or all personal property.[12] However, a broad statement of this kind (eg, all the debtor's personal property) would not be a sufficient description for the purposes of a security agreement.[13] Article 9, in fact, lays down fairly strict requirements for the description of collateral in the security agreement. These requirements are stricter than for the description of property in an English-style floating charge.

Article 9-506 provides that a financing statement substantially satisfying the formal requirements is effective, even if it has minor errors or omissions, unless the errors or omissions make the financing statement seriously misleading.[14] Records filed in the filing office do not require signatures for their effectiveness, although there is a requirement that the debtor authorise the filing in an authenticated record.[15] A person who files an unauthorised record is liable for damages.[16] Article 9-516 provides that communication of a record to a filing office and tender of the filing fee or acceptance of the record by the filing office constitutes filing.

In the United States, the complete divorce between security agreement and financing statement means that there is no scope for a conclusive evidence certificate issued by the filing office. A financing statement may be filed long before a security

9 Article 9-204.
10 See generally *Clough Mill Ltd v Martin* [1985] 1 WLR 111.
11 See Article 9-323.
12 Article 9-504.
13 Article 9-504, Official Comment.
14 Article 9-506(c). In an English-style registration system, the certificate of due registration issued by the registrar means that the registration can be accepted as valid even though the particulars registered were not an accurate description of the charge.
15 Article 9-509.
16 Article 9-625.

agreement is executed; moreover, the financing statement may be intended to cover more than one security agreement. In the United States, the filing office performs a purely ministerial function. It is not the function of the filing office to check the accurateness of the information provided:[17] "A filing office may not reject...an initial financing statement indicating that the debtor is a State A corporation and providing a three-digit organizational identification number, even if all State A organizational identification numbers contain at least five digits and two letters." Article 9-516 provides an exhaustive list of grounds upon which the filing office may reject a record. Some of these are grounds that have the effect of rendering the financing statement itself ineffective, but some are not grounds that would have this effect. The latter include the failure to provide a name and mailing address for the secured party of record. If the filing office improperly rejects a financing statement that complies with all the requirements of Article 9, then the financing statement is still regarded as effective,[18] except as against a purchaser of the collateral which gives value in reasonable reliance upon the absence of the record from the files.

## 4. The general features of Article 9

Apart from notice filing, there are many other significant differences between Article 9 and the current law relating to security interests in England. Article 9, for example, contains a comprehensive set of priority rules and makes quasi-securities registrable. The Canadian and New Zealand Personal Property Security Acts follow Article 9 in this regard. Article 9 abandons the old distinctions that are still prevalent in English law between creating security over an asset and the use of absolute title to achieve the same economic objective. Article 9 adopts the universal, generic concept of a security interest. All the old terminology of the law still found in England - such as 'pledge', 'mortgage', 'conditional sale' and 'trust receipt' - has been replaced by the unitary concept of a security interest. Article 9 makes no distinction between legal and equitable security interests or between fixed and floating security interests.

Article 9-109 applies Article 9 to any transaction, regardless of form, that creates a contractual security interest in personal property and to a sale of accounts, chattel paper, payment intangibles or promissory notes.[19] 'Security interest' is defined in Article 1-201(37) as meaning an interest in personal property or fixtures that secures either payment or else the performance of an obligation. The term also includes any interest of a buyer of accounts, chattel paper, payment intangibles or promissory notes . The special property interest of a buyer of goods on identification of those

17 See Article 9-516, Official Comment.

18 Article 9-516(d). The effect is somewhat similar in an English-style registration system, although in the latter there is no protection for purchasers that acquire property in the reasonable but mistaken belief that the property is unsecured. The crucial issue is whether the particulars have been delivered to the registrar of companies within the prescribed period and not whether the particulars appear on the register during that period or even at all.

19 However, Article 9 does not apply to a sale of accounts, chattel paper, payment intangibles or promissory notes as part of a sale of the business out of which they arose or to an assignment of the same which is for the purpose of collection only. Neither does it apply to an assignment of a right to payment under a contract to an assignee that is also obligated to perform under the contract, nor to an assignment of a single account, payment intangible or promissory note to an assignee in full or partial satisfaction of a pre-existing indebtedness.

goods to a contract for sale[20] is not characterised as a 'security interest', but a seller may also acquire a security interest by complying with Article 9. In other words, even a 'simple' retention of title clause is transformed by statutory language into the taking of a security interest.[21] Article 9 applies irrespective of whether title to the collateral is with the secured party or the debtor, though there are special rules, for example, for the sale of accounts.[22]

### 4.1 Attachment and perfection of a security interest

The central concepts of Article 9 are attachment and perfection. A security interest is said to attach when it becomes enforceable between creditor and debtor (ie, it creates an obligation).[23] Article 9-203 lays down that a security agreement attaches if:

- value has been given;
- the debtor has rights in the collateral; or
- the power to transfer rights in the collateral to a secured party and one of a number of other alternative conditions are fulfilled, including that the debtor has authenticated a security agreement that provides a description of the collateral.

However, the parties may agree to postpone the time for attachment, in which case the security interest attaches at the agreed time. Article 9-204 specifically states that a security agreement may cover after-acquired property, but the security agreement will not attach unless and until the debtor has rights in the collateral. The concept of 'rights in the collateral' is not free from controversy, although it clearly connotes something less than full ownership.

Perfection, on the other hand, refers to the process whereby the security interest becomes effective against third parties (ie, it creates a property right).[24] Perfection generally occurs through filing and the date of filing is the reference point for settling the order of priorities between competing security interests in the same collateral. Article 9-308 states that a security interest is perfected:

- when it has attached; and
- when all the steps required for its perfection have been complied with.

A security interest is perfected when it attaches, if the applicable requirements are satisfied before the security interest attaches.[25] Although filing a financing statement is the standard way of perfecting a security interest, other methods of perfection are permissible in certain circumstances.[26] For example, security over investment property may be perfected by the secured party taking control of the collateral. In the case of intermediated securities, this will occur if the securities intermediary agrees

---

20 See Section 2-401 of the Uniform Commercial Code.

21 For a description of the different forms of retention of title clause see G McCormack, *Reservation of Title* (London, Sweet & Maxwell, 2nd ed, 1995) at p 2.

22 A 'payment intangible' is defined in Article 9-102(61) as meaning a general intangible under which the account debtor's principal obligation is a monetary obligation. General intangibles are the residual category of personal property.

23 Articles 9-203(f) and 9-315.

24 See generally Article 9-308.

25 Article 9-308(a).

26 Article 9-310.

to respond to instructions from the secured party rather than from the debtor. Moreover, certain security interests are perfected automatically upon attachment.[27]

## 4.2 Treatment of the floating charge

One of the fundamental features of Article 9 systems is to assimilate the treatment of fixed and floating charges. In other words, the fixed/floating charge distinction is abolished and replaced by the single unitary notion of a security interest. In fact, pre-Article 9 US law did not recognise the equivalent of the floating charge. The leading authority is *Benedict v Ratner*,[28] where the US Supreme Court had to decide on the legal implications of a purported assignment of account receivables under which the assignor went on collecting the receivables from the debtors, which had not been notified of the assignment. The assignors continued to use the proceeds in the ordinary course of business without accounting in any way to the assignee. In England, an arrangement of this kind would be categorised as a floating charge and upheld on this basis, but the US Supreme Court held that the transaction was void against the assignor's trustee in bankruptcy as a fraudulent conveyance under the state law of New York. The court said:[29] "Under the law of New York a transfer of property as security which reserves to the transferor the right to dispose of the same, or to apply the proceeds thereof, for his own uses is, as to creditors, fraudulent in law and void."

It is perhaps not surprising that lawyers in a country as legally sophisticated and commercially pragmatic as the United States sought to get around the limitations of the decision and a sophisticated avoidance industry developed.[30] As a result of pre-Article 9 legislative developments in the United States, most types of personal property, whether tangible or intangible, became available as collateral to secure loans.[31] Often change came as the result of particular legislation passed at the behest of finance companies. Special interest groups might plead for a particular legislative initiative and the result was a mismatch of complex and interlocking statutes, with intricate registration requirements, that lacked overall coherence and uniformity – "half a dozen filing systems covering chattel security devices might be maintained within a state, some on a county basis, others on a state-wide basis, each of which had to be separately checked to determine a debtor's status".[32]

Article 9 brought rationality and coherence, and one of the ways it did this was by recognising the functional equivalent of the floating charge.[33] Legal subterfuge

---

27 Article 9-309. These exceptions appear to be essentially pragmatic, based on industry need or lobbying by pressure groups.
28 (1925) 268 US 353.
29 (1925) 268 US 353.
30 See generally Grant Gilmore, *Security Interests in Personal Property* (Boston, Little Brown, 1965) vol 1, chapters 1-8.
31 Article 9 has been described as "an anthological collection of the most celebrated security law controversies of the preceding forty years" in Grant Gilmore, "Security Law, formalism and Article 9" (1968) 47 Nebraska LR 659 at 671.
32 See the official comment attached to the 1972 version of Article 9-101.
33 Grant Gilmore has said in "Security Law, formalism and Article 9" (1968) 47 Nebraska LR 659 at 672: "Article 9 draftsmen argued from the premise that, under existing security law, a lender could take an enforceable interest in all of a debtor's present and future personal property to the conclusion that the new statute should provide for the accomplishment of this result in the simplest possible fashion."

was rendered unnecessary by a provision allowing for the creation of a 'floating' security interest on shifting collateral.[34]

## 4.3 Priorities

Article 9-322 determines priorities among conflicting security interests in the same collateral and applies a basic principle that the first secured party to file a financing statement should have priority over competing security interests in the same collateral. The revised version of Article 9 which came into force in 2001 introduces additional variants on the basic priority position. This is done most notably by permitting perfection by control and providing this method of perfection with a status superior to that of perfection by filing.

Under the primary rule, priority dates from the earliest time that a security interest is first perfected, provided that the security interest does not become unperfected at any stage thereafter. A perfected security interest has priority over a competing unperfected security interest.[35] The first security interest to attach has priority if competing security interests are unperfected.[36] However, Article 9 does not preclude a secured party from voluntarily giving up priority.[37]

The central importance of the 'first to file or perfect' priority rule should be emphasised. The secured party that first registers a financing statement obtains priority even though it is not the first in terms of executing a security agreement with a debtor or indeed acquiring an attached security interest in the collateral. Consequently:[38]

> *Once a financing statement is registered any person who is planning to deal with someone named as debtor in the financing statement has the ability to determine whether or not the interest he intends to acquire will be subject to a security interest having a prior status. If such a person goes ahead and acquires an interest in the personal property described in the financing statement without making some accommodation with a registering party or without obtaining a discharge of the financing statement, there is no reason to give his interest priority over a subsequent security interest acquired by the registered party.*

There is an exception to the general priority rule in the case of purchase-money security interests[39] (PSMIs) which will rank ahead of a prior security interest containing an after-acquired property clause. The PMSIs favours creditors that extend credit on the understanding that the debtor will use it to acquire collateral[40] and

34 Article 9-205.
35 Article 9-322(a)(2).
36 Article 9-322(a)(3).
37 Article 9-339. The Official Comment makes it clear that a person's rights cannot be adversely affected by an agreement to which the person is not a party. On debt subordination agreements under English law, see *Re Maxwell Communications Corp* (No 2) [1993] 1 WLR 1402; *Re British & Commonwealth Holdings plc (No 3)* [1992] 1 WLR 672.
38 See R Cuming and R Wood, "Compatibility of Federal and Provincial Personal Property Security Law" (1986) 65 Canadian Bar Review 267 at 285.
39 Article 9-324 deals with the priority of purchase-money security interests.
40 One of the justifications given for recognising purchase money super-priority is that whereas a general financier takes account of average risk, the PMSI lender may have particular skills and is able to lend on particularly advantageous terms because of its special knowledge of the collateral – see generally A Schwartz, "The Continuing Puzzle of Secured Debt" (1984) 37 Vanderbilt Law Review 1051.

there is a complex definition in Article 9-103 which requires a close nexus between the acquisition of the collateral and the security interest. What is required is the giving of value that enables the debtor to acquire rights in or the use of the collateral, if the value is in fact so used.

Article 9 distinguishes between PMSIs and general security interests, awarding the PMSI a kind of super-priority status that has traditionally been enjoyed by retention of title claimants. The possibility of enjoying super-priority status has been extended to other financiers in certain circumstances. If a debtor has granted an all-assets security interest that extends over future property, then notwithstanding the general 'first to perfect' priority rule, a creditor whose advances funded the acquisition of 'new property' in the debtor's hands outranks the earlier financier in respect of this property.[41]

PMSI super-priority may be justified on the basis that the release of funds by the creditor increases the debtor's total pool of assets. The debtor is enabled to acquire new assets as distinct from merely rolling over existing debt with the debt representing the purchase price of the assets being offset by the additional property. If the new property helps the debtor's business to earn extra profits, it may even improve the position of existing creditors by swelling their security interest. Further, if an earlier creditor could rely on an after-acquired property clause to the detriment of a PMSI holder, the earlier creditor would obtain an unjustified windfall at the expense of the PMSI holder whose advance facilitated the acquisition of the property.[42] On the other hand, according super-priority privileges to the PMSI makes the assumption that the provision of funds which is tied to the acquisition of 'new' assets is more beneficial in a business sense than more general loans which can be used to pay the wages of employees.[43] One advance may not necessarily carry any greater social benefit than the other.

However, it is necessary to comply with special requirements to obtain super-priority status. Article 9-324, for instance, distinguishes between inventory and other goods, and a claim to PMSI status in inventory is more difficult to establish. 'Inventory' is defined as meaning goods that:

- are held by a person for sale or lease;
- have been leased;
- are to be furnished or have been furnished under a contract of service; or

41 Under Article 9-324(g), the holder of a purchase money security interest that secures the unpaid purchase price of collateral will prevail over the holder of a conflicting purchase money security interest that enables the collateral to be acquired. This means that a retention of title seller has priority over a lender that makes an enabling loan. There is some possible inconsistency with Article 9-328, which deals with investment property. Priority in investment property is given to the secured party which has control. Article 9-328(2) provides that if two or more secured parties have control, priority is determined by which obtained control first.

42 For a law and economics perspective on this view, see H Kanda and S Levmore "Explaining Creditor Priorities" (1994) 80 Va LR 2103 at 2138-2141.

43 See the comments in WJ Gough, *Company Charges* (London, Butterworths, 2nd ed 1996) at p 436: "It assumes that financial accommodation for the purpose of, for example, paying wages and salaries through cheques drawn on an overdrawn account is less important than for the purchase of stocks or plant and equipment. This is not a real world distinction. Credit, as a matter of business need, is indivisible in the sense that all business inputs, including wages, overheads, equipment and supplies are all vital to an ongoing business."

- are raw materials, work in progress or materials used or consumed in a business or profession.

Before a security interest in inventory can qualify as a PMSI the secured party must, before the debtor receives possession of the inventory, give notice in writing to every other secured party which has already registered a financing statement over the same collateral. The notice is required to state that the person has acquired, or expects to acquire, a PMSI in inventory of the debtor and also to describe the inventory.[44]

In the case of capital equipment rather than inventory, the qualifications necessary for obtaining PMSI status are somewhat less demanding. Automatic super-priority over prior secured lenders is gained if the PMSI is registered within 20 days of the debtor acquiring possession of the collateral.[45] "The rules intimate that the acquisition of new inventory and its associated debt is more threatening to earlier creditors than the debt-financing of new equipment but that debt tied to new inventory is still less threatening than new money unlinked to particular assets."[46]

## 5. The English Law Commission reform proposals

In England, the Law Commission has suggested replacing the existing transaction-based system of company charge registration with a notice filing system[47] in keeping with the North American and New Zealand models. The decision to use overseas legislation as a guide was taken partly because of time constraints, but also because the Law Commission saw "no need to re-invent the wheel"[48] and recognised that "the fact that Article 9 and the PPSAs have been so successful means that they deserve very careful consideration".[49]

### 5.1 Initial proposals

The Law Commission suggested that the notice filing system could be applied to a broader range of security interests and also include 'quasi-security' – such as the assignment of receivables (factoring) and retention of title clauses in sale of goods contracts. There might be a comprehensive restatement of the law of security interests and, in time, the scheme could be extended to non-corporate legal actors. In the first instance, however, it was suggested that the reform would involve the introduction of notice filing for an amended list of company charges and possibly also for 'quasi-interests', as well as rules on attachment, perfection and priorities of security interests.

The Law Commission suggested that a notice filing scheme would have the

---

44 Article 9-324, Official Comment explains the purpose of the notification requirement as being to protect a non-purchase money inventory secured party which, under an arrangement with the debtor, is typically required to make periodic advances against incoming inventory or periodic releases of old inventory as new inventory is received. If the inventory secured party receives notice, it may not make an advance. While the notification requirement is not the same as imposing a consent requirement before a PMSI over inventory can take priority, through the mechanism of an inventory secured party exerting pressure on the debtor it may function in roughly the same way.

45 Article 9-324(a).

46 See H Kanda & S Levmore, "Explaining Creditor Priorities" (1994) 80 Virginia Law Review 2103 at 2139.

47 See generally the Law Commission Consultative Report "Company Security Interests" (September 2004) at para 2.46.

48 Law Commission Consultative Report, para 1.20.

49 Law Commission Consultative Report, para 1.5.

following principal advantages:[50]

- Electronic online filing would be fast, simple and cheap in the long run.
- In a companies-only scheme the risk of an error that might invalidate a filing would be very small, since companies have a unique registration number.
- A simple description of the secured property (collateral) would suffice. This would reduce the risk of inaccurate descriptions and also protect third parties because a security interest would not be effective as regards collateral that falls within the description in the financing statement.
- Advance filing would be permissible so that a lender's priority position could be protected while negotiations over security are continuing.
- Dual registration of charges over land, ships, aircraft and intellectual property rights in the companies register, as well as in specialist property registers, would generally no longer be necessary.
- The time of filing would generally determine priorities between competing security interests in the same collateral, with an exception for PMSIs, which would enjoy priority over pre-existing security interests, subject to certain conditions. "The rules of priority will be more rational and better suited to modern conditions, for example in relation to assignments of receivables. They will still be complicated but they will be significantly clearer than under current law."[51]
- The distinction between fixed and floating charges and the associated uncertainty over the boundary between them would disappear. The floating charge would be superseded by a single type of security interest that has all the advantages of a floating charge but fewer disadvantages to the lender.

> The Law Commission suggested that its recommendations provided
> *significant improvements and cost-savings in secured finance for companies. The use of technology can made the registration of company charges much easier, cheaper and quicker. The low cost of registration makes it feasible to provide lenders with a wide range of useful information about a company's property. The law on the priority of competing interests and the remedies available in the case of default can be made simpler, clearer and better suited to the needs of modern business finance.*[52]

### 5.2 Final Report on Company Security Interests

In the Law Commission's Final Report on Company Security Interests the original reform agenda was watered down considerably.[53] The report proposed a new system of electronic notice filing that would apply to traditional security interests (essentially mortgages and charges) and also to sales of receivables. The new scheme would not extend to title retention techniques such as finance leases and simple reservation of title under sale of goods contracts. The scheme included specific proposals on

50 CR, para 2.43.

51 CR, para 2.43.

52 Press release "Law Commission consults on Provisional Recommendations on Company Security Interests", August 16 2004.

53 For a synopsis of the revised proposals, see "Company Security Interests: Developing a Final Scheme" (May 2005), available on the Law Commission website at www.lawcom.gov.uk/. The final report was published at the end of August 2005 – Law Com 296.

financial collateral,[54] and while priority would be linked to the date of registration, the scheme would also preserve the fixed/floating charge distinction, particularly in the context of insolvency. The proposals are said to "make the floating charge simpler and more effective as a security", with the opportunity being taken to deal with various problems under current law and "generally to clarify and simplify it".[55] With title retention devices now excluded from the reform package, the Law Commission ruled out giving super-priority to PMSIs. It also finally decided against a statutory statement of the rights and remedies of the parties to a security agreement and the imposition of obligations on secured parties to disclose information about the charge.

The general thrust of the notice filing proposals is preserved from the original consultation documents, but there are very considerable variations in detail. For example, in the revised proposals it was suggested that ships, aircraft and intellectual property rights should still be registrable for validity purposes at Companies House and, for priority purposes, under the specialist asset registers. In the original scheme, registration with the specialist asset registers was all that was required. Persons consulted on the proposals were of the view that double registration was worthwhile because of the advantages in finding information at one source. As far as land is concerned, Companies House would simply serve as a reception point for information transmitted from the Land Registry, with the validity and priority of charges over land being dependent solely on rules of land law.

## 5.3 Reactions

On the whole, there has been a considerable amount of practitioner resistance to the proposals, particularly from capital markets lawyers. Leading lawyers have warned of the dangers of 'throwing out the baby with the bathwater' and have suggested that there is nothing fundamentally wrong with the present system that a bit of incremental amendment cannot mend:[56] "The Law Commission's imperative seems to be to introduce a US style functional system as a wholesale replacement for our current system." On a cost-benefit analysis, this seems difficult to justify. The implementation costs will be very large, and it is difficult to see what material benefits will result from it." It might be argued on the basis of empirical evidence from New Zealand that these fears are somewhat exaggerated. In New Zealand, implementation costs do not appear to have been a major issue and the new system is widely considered a success.

However, critics have also suggested that divorcing registration from the actual conclusion of a security agreement opens up the possibility that the register may become a less reliable source of information about the state of a company's secured borrowings.

---

54 See Regulations 36-41 of the draft Company Security Regulations 2006.

55 "Company Security Interests: Developing a Final Scheme" at para 1.3. See also "Regulatory Impact Assessment on Proposals for the Registration of Companies' Security Interests" (July 2005) at p 66: "The effectiveness of floating charges will be enhanced…[I]t will no longer be necessary to employ negative pledge clauses to preserve the priority of a floating charge against subsequent charges. Nor will it be necessary to use automatic crystallisation clauses to prevent seizure of the property by other [execution] creditors. Both types of clause are unreliable in their operation and add significantly to the complexity of the current law." On the latter points see regulations 24 and 45 of the draft Company Security Regulations.

56 See R Calnan "The Reform of the Law of Security" [2004] Butterworths Journal of International Banking and Financial Law 88.

A notice on the register may relate not to an actual transaction, but to one of a multitude of possible transactions that never in the event materialised. It has also been argued that fewer details of a security interest will appear on the register in a notice filing system than under transaction filing, and that there is no justification for this in the modern information age. This perspective has appealed to the Scottish Law Commission, which suggested making a security agreement itself registrable. In its view:[57]

> *by making the security document publicly accessible, the proposed system would provide those searching the register with precisely the information they would wish to have, namely the nature and extent of the security. From the point of view of a third party, a copy of the deed itself is almost always better than an abbreviated summary.... In any event it may be assumed that existing creditors would prefer to consult a public, and online, register than to have the inconvenience, and possible embarrassment, of making an approach to the company itself.*

There are two potential problems with this proposal. The first is that the instrument of charge may contain commercially sensitive information, though this problem might be dealt with in practice if the sensitive material were hived off into a separate document. The second difficulty lies in the fact that requiring registration of the instrument of charge may not be very compatible with modern systems of electronic registration, though difficulties may not be insurmountable and Part 2 of the Bankruptcy and Diligence etc (Scotland) Act 2007 makes provision for registration of a security instrument.

Another point of criticism is that the Law Commission may have over-egged the pudding somewhat in playing up the advantages of Article 9-style notice filing. While notice filing may be more convenient and flexible than transaction filing, it is also easy to overestimate these advantages. For example, after-acquired property clauses, future advances clauses and 'floating' security interests are fully recognised by English substantive law, and although registration must relate to a particular instrument of charge rather than the entire credit relationship of the parties, the registered particulars can capture the full flexibility of the legal provisions. In addition, some of the claimed advantages bear no necessary relationship with notice filing. Although the New Zealand system is fully electronic, the original notice filing systems were paper-based. Moreover, some jurisdictions such as Singapore have online English-style company charge registration regimes.[58]

Article 9 allows filing/registration in advance of the conclusion of a security agreement. This may carry significant practical advantages in particular cases. For example, if multiple parties are involved in the security agreement, then advance registration avoids any delays stemming from difficulties in arranging execution of the agreement by all the relevant parties. It also allows a secured party to confirm that

57 "Registration of Rights in Security by Companies" (October 2002) at p 47.

58 See the UK Companies House Strategy document (April 2003) "Strategic Direction 2003/2006: The Future for Companies House" at pp 6–7: "[W]e will investigate the potential to develop an on-line service for the registration of mortgages and charges. However, as both company and land registration law is changing over the life of this plan we need to make a careful assessment of when it would be appropriate to invest in the delivery of this new service."

registration has occurred correctly before advancing any funds under the secured loan. However, the advantages of advance registration might be achieved by a variant of the present system rather than by full-blown notice filing. For instance, the draft Irish Companies Bill suggests a scheme under which a filing can be submitted prior to completion of a transaction, provided a further filing evidencing the actual creation of a security interest is filed with the registrar within 21 days of the first filing of the intention to create a security interest. In these circumstances the security would take effect as to priority from the date of the first preliminary filing. On the other hand, in the absence of the second filing within 21 days of the preliminary filing, the preliminary filing would lapse.[59] The 2007 Scottish Bankruptcy and Diligence Act includes a similar provision.

## 6. Conclusion

Even a betting person would hesitate before laying any money on the wager that England will get personal property security law reform in the near future. In fact, what Part 25 of the Companies Act 2006 does is to re-enact the existing registration of company charge provisions with some differences in legislative language, but no changes in substance. However, the very act of legislative enactment in the area may exhaust what is already a weak appetite for reform. In is Final Report on Company Security Interests the Law Commission tried to appease its critics by watering down some of its earlier reform proposals, but to no avail. In particular, City of London lawyers could not be convinced as to the virtues of the reform proposals. Bankers seem to dismiss security as an extremely important but technical area best left to their City lawyers in terms of mastering the intricacies. If the lawyers say no, then the bankers will not come to a different conclusion.

One might dismiss the reaction of the City lawyers as that of dyed-in-the-wool reactionaries; but this would be grossly unfair. The lawyers have their precedent banks and acquired knowledge and expertise. These are not to be discarded lightly. Moreover, a full-blown Article 9 would involve rewriting the Insolvency Code in terms of assimilating and accommodating the floating charge. Doing so risks reopening a hornets' nest of vested interests.

While it seems almost an article of faith among certain academic lawyers that Article 9 is the only way forward, Article 9 itself is not beyond criticism. Article 9 is now more than 50 years old and is showing signs of middle-age spread in terms of size and complexity. The language and concepts of Article 9 often appear obscure compared with the facility and comprehensiveness of the floating charge. Moreover, with the greater ease of internet registration, there seems less justification for comparatively sparse details appearing on the register than is the case with Article 9-style notice filing. Perhaps the fate of the Law Commission proposals will spur debate about the fundamentals of personal property security law.

*The author would like to thank Dr. Maisie Ooi of the National University of Singapore for helping to clarify his thinking on many of the points raised in this paper.*

---

59 See the provisions of the draft Bill and explanatory notes from the Irish Company Law Review Group at www.clrg.org/.

# Collateral

**Christian Johnson**
Loyola University Chicago

In contrast to exchange traded derivatives such as futures, credit risk has been a key concern with over-the-counter (OTC) derivative transactions since they became popular in the early 1980s.[1] The key approach to minimising credit risk has been to require parties to post collateral, with over $1 trillion in collateral being posted in 2006 alone.[2] As the use of OTC derivatives has grown and the industry has become more sophisticated, collateral has become an integral part of the OTC derivatives market.

Historically, collateral has been pledged since the market's inception; however, it use was minimal due to a limited understanding of the credit risks in the OTC derivatives market, non-standardised collateral documentation and operational difficulties in transferring and holding collateral. For example, it was estimated that only $200 million of collateral was transferred in 2000,[3] with only a fraction of that amount being pledged in earlier years. As parties have grown in sophistication and understanding of the risks involved in trading OTC derivatives,[4] the use of collateral has grown by leaps and bounds. Most importantly, however, the global OTC derivatives market has exploded, growing from a notional amount of $865 billion in 1987 to over $300 trillion at the end of 2006,[5] forcing participants to try to minimise the credit risks involved in the market.

## 1. Credit risk

The efforts to reduce credit risk in the OTC derivatives markets could be considered Herculean. 'Credit risk' is typically defined as "the risk of loss in the event the counterparty fails to perform under the terms of a contract".[6] It is important to understand, however, that credit risk in the OTC derivatives area is created and is the end result of a party's efforts to reduce and hedge market risk through transactions

1 The first publicly announced OTC derivative transaction is considered to be a cross currency swap entered into by the World Bank and IBM. See "The IBM Deal That Opens a Cash Source", *Business Week*, September 7 1981, at 48.

2 International Swaps and Derivatives Association Inc (ISDA) Margin Survey 2006, at 2, available at www.isda.org.

3 *Id* at 3.

4 One of the most well-known failures in the area was that of long-term capital management. See Lowenstein, *When Genius Failed: The Rise and Fall of Long-Term Capital Management* (2000).

5 ISDA Market Survey, available at www.isda.org. Notional amount is not the amount at risk, but is used to determine the amount of payments to made under a transaction. See the interest rate swap example below.

6 Board of Governors of the Federal Reserve System, Federal Deposit Insurance Corporation, Office of the Comptroller of the Currency, Derivative Product Activities of Commercial Banks 12 (January 27 1993).

such as a plain vanilla interest rate swap.[7]

For example, assume that Commercial Corporation (ComCo) has borrowed $10 million at a variable interest rate equal to LIBOR.[8] Concerned about the market risk that LIBOR will increase beyond its ability to meet its interest payments, ComCo enters into an interest rate swap with Derivative Dealer (DerivDealer) to hedge that market risk. Parties in an interest rate swap agree to swap payment obligations based upon a specified notional amount. Although the notional amount is used to calculate the payment amounts, it is never exchanged between the parties. Because ComCo wants to hedge its entire interest rate risk under its loan, ComCo and DerivDealer have agreed to use $10 million as the notional amount. ComCo would make a fixed rate payment to DerivDealer and DerivDealer would make a variable

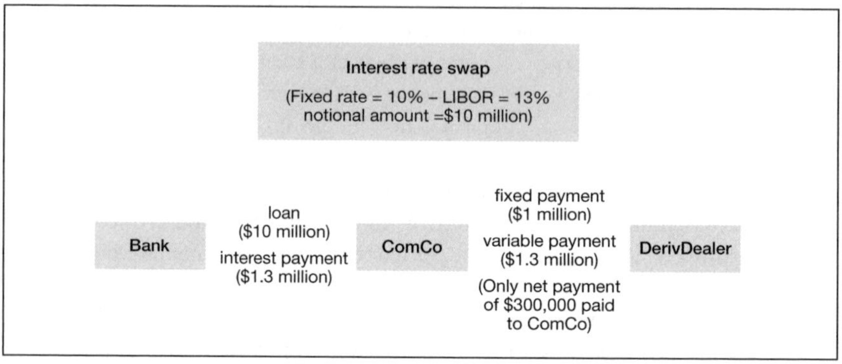


rate payment to ComCo. In our example, assume that ComCo agrees to make annual payments on the last day of each year for three years to DerivDealer equal to a fixed interest rate payment of 10%. DerivDealer agrees to make similar annual payments to ComCo equal to LIBOR.

If LIBOR were 13% at year end, DerivDealer would make a payment to ComCo equal to $1.3 million (13% multiplied by $10 million). ComCo in turn would make a simultaneous payment to DerivDealer in the amount of $1 million (10% multiplied by $10 million). Payments in an interest rate swap are always made on the same day and are netted against each other. In our example, DerivDealer would make a $300,000 payment to ComCo.

ComCo has limited its variable interest rate risk because it has avoided paying more than an effective interest payment amount of 10% on its variable rate loan. ComCo uses the $300,000 that it received from DerivDealer to meet its variable interest rate payment of 13%. If LIBOR had gone down to 8% instead, ComCo would still have had an effective interest rate cost of 10%. Its effective interest costs under the loan would equal $800,000 (8%) plus the net $200,000 payment that it would have paid to DerivDealer for a total of $1 million.

From this example, it is apparent that although ComCo no longer has any market

7 For an additional discussion of interest rate swaps, see Gooch and Klein, *Documentation for Derivatives* 421-38 (2002); Frank Meigs, "Managing the Credit Risk of Interest Rate Swaps", 77 *Journal of Commercial Lending* 8, April 1995, at 11.

8 LIBOR is the London Inter-Bank Offered Rate. For a discussion of LIBOR, see www.bba.org.uk.

risk of LIBOR rising above 10%, it has credit risk that DerivDealer will not make its net payment. Conversely, DerivDealer also is exposed to the credit risk that ComCo will fail to make its net payment to DerivDealer. Both parties also have credit risk in the event that the interest rate swap is terminated prematurely and one party is required to make an early termination payment to the other, as will be explained below.

The process of quantifying the amount of credit risk for OTC derivatives is a two-step process. The first step is to determine the credit risk for a particular transaction. The next step is to determine, assuming that the transactions between the parties were terminated early, the net early termination amount for all of the transactions to be terminated with respect to the relationship between the two parties. This process is typically referred to as 'close-out netting'.

The amount of credit risk for a particular OTC derivative transaction is generally understood to mean the replacement cost for a transaction were it to be terminated prior to maturity. Replacement cost is understood to mean how much a party would have to pay to (or be paid by) a derivative dealer to assume the obligations of the defaulting party.[9] Using their own computer models, dealers typically calculate that replacement cost daily for each transaction in order to determine the amount of credit risk and whether its counterparty needs to post collateral.[10]

For example, assume in the above swap example that LIBOR is currently 8% and ComCo is making payments to DerivDealer. Using its computer models, DerivDealer would calculate a hypothetical early termination based on the present value of ComCo's future obligation to make swap payments to DerivDealer. If the result of the calculations were an amount equal to $600,000, that would be the amount of credit risk for DerivDealer with respect to its swap payment with ComCo. If instead ComCo were in-the-money because LIBOR was above 10%, ComCo would have credit risk.

After the replacement cost for each transaction is determined, these amounts are then netted together to arrive at what is commonly referred to as the 'early termination amount'.[11] This contractual netting that occurs upon termination is commonly referred to as 'close-out netting' and can result in a much smaller net amount payable than would be payable if the early termination amount were calculated on a gross basis.

For example, assume in the above swap example that DerivDealer was in-the-money with respect to its swap with ComCo in the amount of $600,000. Assume further that there was a second swap outstanding between the parties and ComCo was in-the-money with respect to the second swap in an amount equal to $400,000. The early termination amount (ie, the close-out netting amount) would be equal to $200,000 owing by ComCo to DerivDealer.

9 Parties almost always enter into an ISDA Master Agreement (either the 1992 or 2002 version) prior to trading. The methodologies used to determine the replacement cost are referred to as 'market quotation' and 'loss' in the 1992 Master Agreement and the 'close-out amount' in the 2002 ISDA Master Agreement.

10 Joseph Levie and David J Yeres, "Mark-to-Market Arrangements", *New York Law Journal*, April 7 1994, at 5.

11 See ISDA Master Agreement, Section 6 and ISDA 2002 Master Agreement, Section 6 for the contractual provisions for calculating the early termination amount. For a discussion of calculating the early termination amount, see Gooch & Klein, *Documentation for Derivatives* 857-866 (Euromoney Books, 4th Ed 2002); Johnson, *A Guide to Using and Negotiating OTC Derivatives Documentation* 80-89 (Institutional Investor Books 2005).

To minimise this credit risk, a counterparty can pledge collateral, provide a third-party guaranty or provide a letter of credit. Market participants, however, agree that pledging collateral is the best method to reduce credit risk. The other methods are often less effective or are more cumbersome and expensive. For example, a third-party guaranty lessens the credit risk to the dealer from the counterparty, but then exposes the dealer to credit risk from the guarantor. Letters of credit can be expensive and time consuming to obtain, and may provide practical difficulties for the dealer attempting to collect under them. In contrast, pledged collateral can be transferred easily, is directly held by a party or by its custodian and can be easily liquidated.

In addition to minimising credit risk, collateral serves other important purposes for both dealers and customers. Collateral may permit less creditworthy counterparties access to the derivatives market; parties that would otherwise be prohibited by their internal policies from dealing on an unsecured basis with less creditworthy counterparties may trade with those that are willing to pledge collateral. Second, a counterparty pledging collateral might receive better pricing from a party simply because of the existence of security. Finally, collateral can be important for regulatory reasons, allowing a party such as a commercial bank to reduce the capital that it is required to hold against certain OTC derivative transactions.

## 2. Documentation

The documentation used to collateralise OTC derivative obligations has evolved significantly over time. Currently, the vast majority of collateral documents in the interdealer and large institutional sector are documented using standard credit support documents developed by the International Swaps and Derivatives Association (ISDA), as will be explained below. Outside of this market, there may be significant limitations on the type of documentation that can be used.

For example, a counterparty may be prevented in some situations from pledging collateral because it has entered into negative pledge or lien provisions with its other creditors. In these situations a counterparty is contractually prohibited from pledging collateral to secure its derivative obligations.[12] There are also situations in which a counterparty has given its lender a blanket lien on all of its assets. This would also prevent a counterparty from pledging collateral to any party other than the lender. Oftentimes, however, the documents do permit the counterparty to include any derivative obligations to the lender as secured by the blanket lien. In rare circumstances, a lender may permit its borrower to pledge a certain amount of collateral to another derivative dealer in order to facilitate its borrower's derivative trading activities.

Prior to the standardised ISDA documentation developed in 1994, a dealer used its own form of collateral agreement with its customers. Although these agreements generally served their purpose, they tended to be highly stylised and led to delays while parties negotiated each agreement's terms. ISDA's development of the

12 For a discussion of the negative pledge issue, see Johnson, "At the Intersection of Bank Finance and Derivative Transactions: Who has the Right of Way", 66 *Tennessee Law Review* 1 (Fall 1998).

standardised collateral documentation has reduced the length of the negotiation process and associated transaction costs.

Because of the bilateral nature[13] of derivative obligations, collateral documentation has unique characteristics in this area. At the inception of a swap, for example, it is unclear who will be in-the-money or out-of-the-money with respect to a particular transaction. This is because the obligations to make payments in a swap will depend upon whether a particular rate, index or price goes up or down. In order to deal with this uncertainty, the collateral documentation typically imposes an obligation to pledge on the party that is out-of-the-money at that particular point in time. This is in contrast to a pledge agreement in loan documentation in which only one party is contractually obligated to pledge collateral.

## 3. ISDA credit support documentation

ISDA has developed several forms of standardised credit support documents to provide for collateralising derivative obligations. The most common documents in use are the 1994 ISDA Credit Support Annex (Security Interest – New York Law) and the 1994 ISDA Credit Support Annex (Transfer – English Law).

In addition to these documents, ISDA has developed the following forms:

- 1995 ISDA Credit Support Deed (Security Interest – English Law);
- 1995 ISDA Credit Support Annex (Security Interest – Japanese Law); and
- 2001 ISDA Margin Provisions

The actual use of these documents, however, has been relatively limited.[14]

An important resource for understanding the reach and enforceability of these agreements are the collateral opinions that ISDA has solicited on behalf of its members in 38 different jurisdictions.[15] These opinions are provided by various legal counsel in these jurisdictions and are typically entitled "Validity and Enforceability of Collateral Arrangements under the ISDA Credit Support Documents". These opinions provide sophisticated legal analysis as to the enforceability of these different credit support documents in each particular jurisdiction. Although these opinions are invaluable, they are unfortunately made available only to members of ISDA.

Both the New York annex and the English transfer annex are bilateral agreements.[16] As such, they impose a duty on either party to transfer collateral, depending upon which party is in-the money or out-of-the-money on a hypothetical close-out netting basis under the ISDA Master Agreement. The two annexes are also substantively identical with respect to the majority of the provisions. The important exception is that the New York annex relies on one party granting a security interest

13 Barry Taylor, "Revolving Bilateral Collateral", 815 PLI/Corp 55, June 3-4 (1993).

14 See Johnson & Harding, *Mastering Collateral Management: a Practical Guide to the ISDA Credit Support Documents*, Chapters 7 and 8 (Financial Times/Prentice Hall November 2002).

15 For a list of these jurisdictions, see www.isda.org (status of collateral opinions).

16 For a detailed discussion of the ISDA Credit Support Annex, see Gooch & Klein, *Documentation For Derivatives*, Volume 2, Part 5 (Euromoney 2002); Johnson & Harding, *Mastering Collateral Management: a Practical Guide to the ISDA Credit Support Documents*, Chapters 5 and 6 (Financial Times/Prentice Hall November 2002; ISDA, "User's Guide to the 1994 ISDA Credit Support Annex" (1994).

approach, while the English transfer annex relies on a transfer of title and ownership approach.

The New York annex is a pledge agreement governed by New York state law. The pledgor (the party out-of-the-money) grants a security interest to the secured party (the party that is in-the-money). Although the collateral is actually transferred to the secured party, it is not a transfer of title like the English transfer annex. The secured party's exercise of its remedies is governed by the secured transaction provisions of the New York version of the Uniform Commercial Code and federal law.

The English transfer annex, in contrast, does not create a security interest in transferred collateral, but instead relies upon a title transfer approach, resulting in a transfer of outright ownership of the collateral. Upon the early termination of an ISDA Master Agreement, the transferee of the collateral relies upon the close-out netting provisions by offsetting its obligation to return the collateral to the transferor against the early termination amount owing to the transferee. In fact, the English transfer annex should be treated as a confirmation to the ISDA Master Agreement.[17]

Similar to the ISDA Master Agreement pre-printed form, both the New York annex and the English transfer annex consist of 10 pre-printed pages and a schedule, referred to as Paragraph 13 in the New York annex and Paragraph 11 in the English transfer annex. Paragraphs 11 and 13 are used to supplement or amend the terms of their respective annex. Consistent with the Schedule to the ISDA Master Agreement, all elections, information and amendments to an annex are made through its respective paragraph.

In the relevant Paragraph 11 or Paragraph 13, the following should be addressed:

- threshold;
- independent amount;
- minimum transfer amount;
- eligible collateral (New York) or eligible credit support (English);
- rehypothecation (New York); and
- notice information and other appropriate elections and amendments.

## 4. Threshold

The bilateral nature of an OTC derivative may cause the obligation to transfer collateral to shift between the parties. For purposes of this discussion, the party transferring collateral will be referred as the 'transferor' (although it is referred to as the 'pledgor' in the New York annex) and the party receiving collateral will be referred to as the 'transferee' (although it is referred to as the 'secured party' in the New York annex).

The amount of the transferor's obligation to the transferee is the transferee's credit 'exposure' to the transferor. The transferee is exposed because of the possibility that the transferor will default on its payment obligation to the transferee. Under the respective annex, exposure is the amount that the transferor would owe the transferee in the event that the ISDA Master Agreement were terminated on a

17 See Johnson & Harding, *Mastering Collateral Management: a Practical Guide to the ISDA Credit Support Documents* 85 (Financial Times/Prentice Hall November 2002).

particular date, computed using a 'mid-market calculation' (the midpoint of a bid ask spread).

The transferor will need to transfer collateral in the event that the exposure of the transferee to the transferor exceeds a certain amount, referred to as the 'threshold' in the annexes. The threshold essentially represents the amount of unsecured credit that the transferee is willing to extend to the transferor. The amount of the threshold will vary depending upon the credit quality of the party and is often negotiated. The parties are required to designate a threshold with respect to each other in Paragraph 11 or 13. If the parties fail to designate an amount, it is deemed to be zero. The threshold could vary from zero up to tens of millions of dollars. Between parties that have credit ratings, the threshold is often based upon such party's credit rating at the time of transferring collateral. A party, for example, that was rated AA by Standard & Poor's could be given a threshold of $25 million. A party related below investment grade (ie, BBB-) would probably have a zero threshold.

The annex requires only that the exposure in excess of a party's threshold be collateralised. For example, if a transferor's threshold were $10 million and the transferee's exposure to the transferor were $15 million, the transferor would be required to transfer $5 million. If the transferee's exposure to the transferor were to drop to $13 million, the transferee would be required to return $2 million. Typically, the threshold for the transferor will equal zero upon the occurrence of an event of default with respect to the transferor.

## 5. Independent amount

One party may have particular concerns about the creditworthiness of the other. To further secure its exposure to a counterparty, a party may require that its counterparty post an 'independent amount'. The independent amount is similar to what is commonly referred to as 'margin' that is posted for exchange-traded products such as futures contracts. A party may require an independent amount to be posted regardless of whether the counterparty is in-the-money or out-of-the-money with respect to that particular transaction. The independent amount is often calculated on a transaction-by-transaction basis as opposed to an aggregate number like the threshold.

The parties are required to designate an independent amount with respect to each other in Paragraph 11 or 13. If the parties fail to designate an amount, it is deemed to be zero. Independent amounts will vary both in amount and in how they are calculated depending upon the type and size of the transaction. For example, an independent amount could be a fixed amount that would range from $50,000 or less to millions of dollars. It could also be calculated as a percentage of the notional amount for a particular transaction. For example, for an interest rate swap which is liquid and easily valued, the independent amount could equal 1% of the notional amount. For more volatile and less liquid transactions such as equity, commodity or credit derivatives, the independent amount could be between 5% and 15% of the notional amount. The independent amount is typically returned to the transferor upon the maturity of the relevant transaction.

## 6. Minimum transfer amount

The minimum transfer amount is often characterised as the nuisance amount. This is the amount that the exposure must change before a transferor is required to transfer collateral. For example, if the transferee's exposure increased after the transferor had already posted collateral, the exposure amount would have to increase in an amount greater than the minimum transfer amount before the transferor would be required to transfer additional collateral. The same concept applies to the return of collateral. The exposure would need to drop by an amount greater than the minimum transfer amount before collateral would be required to be returned to the original transferor.

The parties are required to designate a minimum transfer amount with respect to each other in Paragraph 11 or 13. If the parties fail to designate an amount, it is deemed to be zero. The minimum transfer amount can vary from as little as $100,000 up to millions of dollars. Typically the minimum transfer amount for the transferor will equal zero upon the occurrence of an event of default with respect to the transferor.

## 7. Eligible collateral

Although any type of collateral or credit support could be eligible to be posted by the parties under the annexes, parties usually insist on designating only collateral that is highly liquid, easily valued and easily transferred. Under the annexes, the parties must designate in Paragraph 11 or 13 the types of collateral that constitute 'eligible collateral' or 'eligible credit support'. Based upon the ISDA Margin Survey 2006, the most popular forms of eligible collateral or eligible credit support were cash, government securities and a combination of government agency securities, bonds, letters of credit, equities and commodities.[18]

ISDA has developed the Collateral Asset Definitions[19] in an effort to provide standardised definitions of the various types of collateral similar to the definitions that it has developed for confirmations that document the economic terms of a transaction. Although the incorporation of the short-hand terms as defined terms in collateral documentation appears not to have caught on to any large extent, it has provided at least an authoritative list and description to help negotiate documentation. ISDA has provided tables on 22 different jurisdictions (eg, the United States and New Zealand) that each provide a description and other commentary on the most frequently used types of collateral.

It is important to appreciate that many counterparties are either unable or unwilling to accept certain types of collateral. The most common concern is that a counterparty is unable operationally to accept particular types. For example, a counterparty may not have established or have access to the type of accounts necessary to hold certain types of collateral, especially cross-border collateral. For example, a US counterparty may not have accounts at the various banks and clearinghouses necessary to hold non-US cash or securities issued outside of the United States.

Counterparties may also object to certain types of collateral for credit reasons. For

---

18 ISDA Margin Survey 2006 at 4, available at www.isda.org.
19 Available at www.isda.org.

example, some types of collateral may be either too volatile or difficult to value. This difficulty may be compounded if the collateral was not issued in the counterparty's jurisdiction. A counterparty might also have concentration limits, limiting the amount of certain types of collateral that it is permitted to hold under its credit policies. In addition, it may have percentage limitations on the amount of a particular issue that it is permitted to hold.

## 8. Valuation percentage ('haircuts')

One method to minimise the risk of holding collateral that may fluctuate or decrease in value is to specify a valuation percentage in Paragraph 11 or 13 of the respective annex. The valuation percentage is commonly referred to as a 'haircut' and is used for purposes of calculating the 'value' of posted collateral. For example, if a party has specified a valuation percentage of 97% and the fair market value of the collateral is 100, the value of the collateral would equal 97 (100 x 97%). Valuation percentages can vary from 98% to 100% for high-quality liquid collateral to much lower percentages for illiquid collateral such as thinly traded equity securities. This is to prevent a transferee from becoming under-collateralised in the event that the collateral were to fluctuate in value.

## 9. Cash

Many parties prefer to pledge cash over other types of collateral. Cash can be transferred easily between the parties and typically does not fluctuate as much in value as other forms of collateral. It is generally easy to set up deposit accounts to hold the type of cash being transferred. In addition, transferring cash can eliminate other concerns associated with transferring other forms of collateral. For example, a security may mature or go into default while it is pledged. It may also be difficult to track the payment of interest or principal, both of which can affect the value of the collateral. Many parties may not hold other forms of eligible collateral such as government securities and only have cash to transfer. The ISDA Margin Survey shows US dollars and euros as being the predominant forms of cash transferred. In addition, significant amounts of British pounds sterling and Japanese yen were also transferred.[20]

When cash is transferred as collateral, the parties generally designate that interest should be paid by the transferee to the transferor on any cash balances. For US dollars, interest on any cash balance is usually paid at a rate equal to the Federal Funds (Effective) rate published in NY Federal Reserve Statistical Release H.15(519) for that day. Interest on euro balances is usually paid at a rate equal to the EONIA rate (the overnight rate as calculated by the European Central Bank) for that day. Interest on balances of British pounds sterling is often paid at a rate equal to the SONIA (the Sterling Overnight Index Average) published by the British Bankers' Association. SONIA benchmarks the cost of funds in the overnight sterling market.

## 10. Government securities

Due to their liquidity, ease of transferability and lack of volatility, government

---

20 *Id.*

securities are also extremely popular as eligible collateral. The ISDA survey shows that the lion's share of government securities being transferred as collateral are issued by the United States, certain members of the European Union, the United Kingdom and Japan.[21] Many dealers also prefer to receive government securities over cash since the securities can be used or rehypothecated as described below.

## 11. Other types of collateral

Less liquid forms of collateral are also considered as eligible collateral from time to time. These would include quasi-government agency securities, corporate bonds, letters of credit, equities and commodities. All of these different types of collateral are less liquid, more volatile and present operational difficulties that are not present for transfers of cash or government securities.

Posting letters of credit can be especially problematic. Letters of credit must be monitored carefully by the transferee to ensure that they do not expire and that any draws made under them are presented properly.[22] In addition, the annexes were not drafted with the intention that letters of credit would be eligible collateral. It is thus necessary to do a significant amount of drafting and revising of the annex to conform the annex language to include letters of credit.

## 12. US collateral

The most typical forms of US collateral are US government securities, agency notes and obligations and mortgage-backed securities. The US government securities market is one of the most liquid and creditworthy in the world, with over $3.1 trillion outstanding.[23] US government securities are comprised of US treasury bills, treasury notes and treasury bonds. As a general rule, US government securities that have been carved up into principal only or interest only obligations are considered unacceptable as eligible collateral due to possible volatility in their valuation.

Quasi-government agency notes and obligations are also important types of US collateral. These would include notes issued Fannie Mae (the Federal National Mortgage Association) and Freddie Mac (the Federal Home Loan Mortgage Corporation) and Federal Home Loan Banks, as well as other quasi-government agencies.[24] It is estimated that there are over $2.3 trillion of these securities currently outstanding.[25]

Mortgage-backed securities are also frequently acceptable as collateral. Acceptable mortgage-backed securities are generally securities issued or guaranteed by Fannie Mae, Freddie Mac or the Government National Mortgage Association (Ginnie Mae), but could also include securities issued without these guarantees,

---

21 *Id.*

22 For a discussion of issues in drawing upon letters of credit, see Moses, "The irony of international letters of credit: they aren't secure, but they (usually) work", *Banking Law Journal* 479 June, 2003

23 Securities Industry and Financial Markets Association, at www.investinginbonds.com/marketataglance.asp?catid=31.

24 Other quasi-government agencies would include Federal Farm Credit System Banks, Student Loan Marketing Association (Sallie Mae) and Tennessee Valley Authority. See Securities Industry and Financial Markets Association, at www.investinginbonds.com/marketataglance.asp?catid=31.

25 Securities Industry and Financial Markets Association, at www.investinginbonds.com/marketataglance.asp?catid=31.

frequently referred to as private-label issuances. These securities are backed by residential home mortgages. Holders of the securities receive payments from the interest and principal paid on the underlying mortgages. Mortgage-backed securities are also considered to be highly liquid and high quality, with approximately $4 trillion outstanding in agency and government-sponsored enterprises-backed mortgage pools.[26]

## 13. Calls for collateral

The Credit Support Annex provides detailed rules as to how collateral calls are to be made and when collateral is to be transferred. Calls for the transfer of collateral are made by the transferee, while calls for the return of collateral are made by the original transferor. Because the obligation to make payments under the ISDA Master Agreement can fluctuate, it is possible that a party may be the transferee at one point and then become the transferor as the markets move against it.

The party calling for either the delivery or return of collateral will make a demand for collateral by giving notice to the other party. The calculations of exposure and value of the posted collateral are typically based on the preceding local business day values. Collateral is typically transferred on the next local business day following a call for collateral, although the parties could agree to accelerate or extend those delivery times.

## 14. Rehypothecation

The New York annex provides that the secured party holding pledged collateral has almost unlimited rights to use that collateral, unless otherwise specified in Paragraph 13. This right of the secured party to use posted collateral is commonly referred to as a 'right of rehypothecation' or 'use rights'.[27] Rehypothecation permits the secured party to sell, pledge, rehypothecate, assign, invest, use, commingle or otherwise dispose of posted collateral, subject only to a duty to return the pledged collateral pursuant to the terms of the Credit Support Annex. The transferee under the English transfer annex enjoys similar freedoms to use the collateral given that the transferee is treated as the owner of the collateral. Both the secured party and the transferee, however, have a contractual obligation to return the collateral upon the counterparty satisfying its contractual obligations under the annex.

Many large institutions such as dealers and hedge funds aggressively seek the right to rehypothecate or use collateral. One common use is to repo the collateral to a third party in a repurchase transaction. The posted collateral, however, could be used for almost any other purpose, including pledging the collateral for its own derivative obligations with other parties. Although the right is mutual, it is unlikely that a less sophisticated counterparty would have the sophistication to take full advantage of the right.

---

26 Board of Governors of the Federal Reserve, L.3 Credit Market Debt Owed by Financial Sectors, March 8 2007, available at www.federalreserve.gov/.

27 For a discussion of rehypothecation, see Johnson, "Derivatives and Rehypothecation Failure – It's 3:00pm, Do You Know Where Your Collateral Is?", 39 *Arizona Law Review* 949 (1997); Kettering, "Repledge Deconstructed", *University of Pittsburgh Law Review*, 61 U Pitt L Rev 45 (Fall 1999).

The pledgor is subject to certain legal risks if it agrees to rehypothecation. By agreeing to rehypothecation, the pledgor faces the possibility that the secured party may be unable to return the posted collateral after the pledgor has fulfilled its payment obligations under the ISDA Master Agreement because the secured party has become insolvent or has otherwise failed. A pledgor risks paying twice with respect to the same obligation upon such a failure; once it satisfies its payment obligation to the secured party; and then indirectly when the secured party fails to return the posted collateral.

Upon the failure of a secured party, a pledgor can minimise some of this by exercising its right to offset any payment obligation to the dealer against any collateral that it has pledged to the secured party. The true danger, however, is that the pledgor would become an unsecured creditor with respect to any collateral that it was unable to offset – that is, any excess of collateral value pledged over its payment obligation to the secured party.

There is some question whether jurisdictions outside of the United States would enforce or recognise rehypothecation. Some common-law jurisdictions, such as England and Australia, may find that a rehypothecation right would violate the equity of redemption enjoyed by the transferor or would violate the duty of the transferee to ensure safe custody of the transferred collateral.[28] It is thought that a right of rehypothecation would not be consistent or compatible with the rights traditionally granted in these jurisdictions under a security interest such as that granted in the New York annex or the English deed.

The issue appears to still be a concern under Australian law. Under English law, however, this concern has been dealt with by regulation. Specifically, new English regulations would permit a right of rehypothecation provided that the collateral agreement specially provides for such rights.[29] This new regulation would therefore provide that rehypothecation rights would be enforceable under the English deed if the ISDA preprinted form were amended to provide for such a right.

In addition, the concern in both jurisdictions applies only if the collateral agreements are governed by the laws of such jurisdiction (eg, Australian law) as opposed to New York law. Many practitioners believe that if a New York annex were governed by New York law, a foreign jurisdiction would probably not interfere with rehypothecation rights granted under that agreement, subject to any relevant conflict of laws analysis.

---

28 A thorough discussion of the equity of redemption is beyond the scope of this analysis.

29 Financial Collateral Arrangements (No. 2) Regulations 2003, 16(1), available at www.opsi.gov.uk/si/si2003/20033226.htm#16#16. The regulations were adopted to implement the EU Financial Collateral Directive (2002/47/EC).

# Intellectual property

**Paul U Ali**
University of Melbourne

## 1. Introduction

Businesses in industrialised countries, as well as those in the technology hubs of emerging markets, are increasingly unlikely to conform to the conventional conceptualisation of businesses as both the owners and managers of manufacturing or other income-producing assets. In an environment where more and more businesses are tenants, rather than proprietors, of their office and industrial premises, lessees of their plant and equipment, and have been supplied raw materials and inventory on a title-retention basis, the business model that emerges is one that is no longer characterised by a preponderance of tangible assets on the balance sheet. Instead, one can view the modern business as essentially a manager of human capital and the cash flows generated by the deployment of that human capital.

The key assets available to such a business for the raising of funds are thus its intangible assets, in particular:

- the receivables created by the sale of inventory or the provision of services;
- the cash into which those receivables have been converted through the process of collection or realisation;
- security holdings (shares in related or affiliated businesses, as well as portfolio investments); and
- the intellectual property of the business.

The last-named item encompasses disparate proprietary rights, including:

- the brand name and logos of the business;
- copyright in radio and television broadcasts, films, music CDs and other creative works produced, broadcast or published by the business;
- pharmaceutical, technology and, increasingly, business plan patents;
- trade secrets;
- customer databases; and
- websites and domain names.

The role of intellectual property as an important source of collateral for secured finance has recently been formally recognised by the United Nations Commission on International Trade Law (UNCITRAL). The primary focus of UNCITRAL, in the field of secured finance, has to date been on inventory, equipment and receivables, and to that end UNCITRAL has produced a draft legislative guide on secured finance transactions. It has now embarked upon a study of how security interests over intellectual property can be more fully incorporated in that guide.[1]

## 2. Security interests over intellectual property

To date, issues relating to the efficacy of security interests over intellectual property as a fundraising mechanism have been masked by the 'bundled' approach towards secured finance. First, it is not usually the case that a business will raise funds on the security of its intellectual property, in isolation to the other assets of the business.[2] Secured finance, especially in common law jurisdictions that permit the creation of enterprise-wide security interests, typically involves a lender taking either:

- a single security interest over all assets of the business (as is the case in the so-called 'Article 9' jurisdictions); or
- a series of equitable mortgages or fixed charges over specific asset classes (land and buildings, plant and equipment – and, if possible, receivables and their cash proceeds), coupled with a floating charge over all assets of the business.[3]

Second, the intellectual property of a business is usually an intrinsic part of other assets of the business, such as inventory that is branded with the brand name and the logo of the business and inventory whose manufacture and sale represents the commercialisation of the patents held by the business.[4] As the value of the intellectual property is directly linked to the cash flows generated from its commercialisation and those cash flows are integral to the borrower's capacity to service its obligations to a lender, the lender, if providing funds on a secured basis, would be unlikely to rely solely on security interests over the intellectual property, but would also demand security interests over any inventory derived from the intellectual property or in which the intellectual property has been incorporated and, more particularly, security interests over the receivables and the cash proceeds generated from the commercialisation of the intellectual property (whether through the sale of inventory, the provision of services or the licensing of the intellectual property to third parties).

---

1 UNCITRAL, "Possible Future Work on Security Rights in Intellectual Property" (A/CN9/632, April 25 2007), paras 1-5.

2 I Davies, "Secured Financing of Intellectual Property Assets and the Reform of English Personal Property Security Law" (2006) *26 Oxford Journal of Legal Studies* 559, at 560.

3 Although a single floating charge is, on its own, sufficient to create a secured claim against all of the borrower's assets, a claim secured only by a perfected floating charge is vulnerable to being deferred to claims under subsequently perfected fixed charges and to the claims of preferential creditors. A lender providing funds on a secured basis, in the United Kingdom and Australia, for example, would normally seek to bolster its floating charge with perfected fixed charges (which would enjoy priority over subsequently perfected fixed charges other than earlier created fixed charges of which the lender had notice when its own fixed charges were granted, and the borrower's preferential creditors): see PU Ali, *The Law of Secured Finance* (Oxford University Press, Oxford, 2002), pp 209-211. However, the efficacy of fixed charges over circulating assets (eg, receivables and their cash proceeds) has been sharply reduced in the United Kingdom as a result of the House of Lords' decision in *Re Spectrum Plus Ltd* [2005] AC 680. In contrast, there is no need, in the United States, Canada and New Zealand, for a lender to take a package of security interests over the borrower's assets: a single, perfected security interest is capable of conferring a first-ranking claim against the borrower's assets and thus absolute priority over the claims under any subsequently perfected security interests, whether or not such security interests were created earlier (and also all unperfected security interests).

4 UNCITRAL, above n 1, para 9.

A typical 'security package' over intellectual property would involve – as distinct from and, invariably, in addition to a floating charge over all of the assets of the business – the creation of specific security interests over each type of intellectual property held by the business,[5] the goodwill associated with the intellectual property (in the case of trademarks and service marks)[6] and the benefit of any licences of the intellectual property.

A lender seeking to accomplish this under Australian law would be confronted by:

- the existence of separate statutory regimes for each of the different types of intellectual property held by the business;
- the incomplete coverage of those regimes insofar as security interests are concerned; and
- the inconclusive nature of the registration requirements applicable to the majority – but not all – of the various types of intellectual property.[7]

This last issue is compounded, in the case of corporate borrowers, by the need for concurrent registration under the Australian companies legislation for, again, some but not all of the different types of intellectual property. It is readily apparent that this state of affairs is not conducive to the efficient utilisation of intellectual property as collateral in secured finance.

However, the problems identified in this chapter are not unique to Australia. They are, in fact, a direct consequence of the model for regulating security interests over personal property that Australia has inherited from the United Kingdom – a model that is characterised by the regulation of security interests according to their legal form, multiple and overlapping registration regimes (where some security interests must be registered on more than one register and others not at all), and a complex body of rules of priority which, among other things, vary from asset to asset.[8]

## 3. Application of intellectual property statutes to secured finance transactions

The principal statutes governing intellectual property in Australia are the Copyright Act 1968, the Designs Act 2003, the Patents Act 1990 and the Trade Marks Act 1995.

---

5 As regards security interests over intellectual property under Australian law, see generally JD Lipton, *Security over Intangible Property* (Lawbook Co, Sydney, 2000), Chs 7, 9 and 11; JV Swinson, "Security Interests in Intellectual Property" in Mallesons Stephen Jaques, *Australian Finance Law* (Lawbook Co, Sydney, 5th ed, 2002), Ch 21.

6 Not all types of goodwill are capable of supporting a security interest. In addition, the utility of taking a discrete security interest over goodwill is questionable, given that those types of goodwill (ie, 'premises', 'competition' and 'name' goodwill) that can support a security interest are capable of transfer only in conjunction with the intellectual property with which that goodwill is associated. However, it is not necessary for a security interest over a trademark or service-mark to be accompanied by a security interest over the associated goodwill: Trade Marks Act 1995 (Cth), s 106(3).

7 Ali, above n 3, pp 148-149.

8 The comments of law reform bodies in Australia and the United Kingdom are instructive in this regard: for example, Law Commission, "Company Security Interests" (Consultation Paper 176, 2004, London), paras 1.4, 2.5 and 2.70; Law Commission, "Company Security Interests" (Law Com 296, 2005, London), paras 1.7, 1.48 and 3.145; Australian Attorney-General's Department, "Review of the Law on Personal Property Securities" (Discussion Paper 1, 2006, Canberra), paras 5 and 7.

In addition, there is separate legislation – the Circuit Layouts Act 1989 and the Plant Breeder's Rights Act 1994 – governing intellectual property in integrated circuits and in relation to the propagation of new plant varieties respectively.

The above statutes, with the exception of the Trade Marks Act, stipulate that an assignment of intellectual property must be recorded in writing and signed by the assignor of the interest (and also the assignee in the case of interests acquired in registered designs, patents and plant breeder's rights) for the assignment to be effective.[9] In addition, the above statutes – with the exception of the Copyright Act and the Circuit Layouts Act – provide for the registration of such transactions.[10]

However, each of these acts, as regards the acquisition of interests in intellectual property, in referring only to an 'assignment' of intellectual property, is arguably confined to mortgages (legal and equitable).[11] Such a restrictive reading of the acts is controversial (and the implications of a broader reading for the priority-ranking of security interests over intellectual property are discussed below), with lenders in Australia operating on the assumption that the registration provisions are sufficiently broad to permit the registration of other types of security interest.[12] In addition, this apparently restrictive language can readily be dealt with in practice: where a lender is providing funds on a secured basis to a borrower, it will very likely have sufficient bargaining power to insist upon a mortgage, as opposed to a charge, over the borrower's intellectual property being created (should the lender wish to have absolute certainty that its secured status is capable of being recorded under the various intellectual property statutes).

This lack of uniformity as to the registrability of security interests over intellectual property and also the arguably incomplete coverage of security interests are further compounded by:

---

9 Copyright Act 1968 (Cth), s 196(3); Designs Act 1906 (Cth), s 25C(3); Patents Act 1990 (Cth), s 14(1); Circuit Layouts Act 1989 (Cth), s 45(3); Plant Breeder's Rights Act 1994 (Cth), s 20(2). In contrast, the Trade Marks Act 1995 (Cth) does not impose an explicit writing requirement for assignments of trademarks or service marks, although written evidence would be required for the registration of such an assignment under the act and it would, in practice, be unusual for such a transaction not to be evidenced by writing. For a discussion of the corresponding statutory regimes in the United Kingdom, see H Beale, M Bridge, L Gullifer and E Lomnicka, *The Law of Personal Property Security* (Oxford University Press, Oxford, 2007), pp 474-479.

10 An assignment of a patent, trademark or service mark must be registered: Patents Act, s 187; Trade Marks Act, ss 107(1) and 109(1). Non-registration also carries priority consequences which are discussed below in the body of this chapter: Patents Act, s 189; Trade Marks Act, s 22 (as amended by the Trade Marks Amendment Act 2006 (Cth)). Also, unregistered interests are not admissible in court as evidence of an interest in a patent: Patents Act, s 196. Assignments of plant breeder's rights must also be registered (and a time limit of 30 days after the acquisition of the interest is specified): Plant Breeder's Rights Act, s 21(1). The act does not specify the consequences of a failure to register, but non-registration is likely to affect the ability of the assignee under Section 53 of the act to enforce its interest in the plant breeder's rights in relation to infringement of those rights. In contrast, registration of assignments of registered designs is voluntary: Designs Act, s 114. However, unregistered interests are not admissible in court as evidence of an interest in a registered design: s 119.

11 A mortgage, whether legal or equitable, involves title to the intellectual property (or other secured property) being assigned from the mortgagor to the mortgagee, with the consequential division of the equitable estate and the retention of a residual equity of redemption in respect of the intellectual property by the mortgagor. A fixed charge, in contrast, is created via an encumbrance of the equitable estate and does not involve a division of that estate: see Ali, above n 3, pp 112-114. See also Beale *et al*, above n 9, pp 96-97. Further support for the application of these provisions to mortgages can be found in the fact that the Patents Act and the Patents Regulations 1991 (Cth) expressly contemplate the registration of mortgages of patents under that act: Patents Act, s 103; Patents Regulations, Reg 19.1(a).

12 See also Lipton, above n 5, pp 114-115 and 180.

- the rules contained in two of the intellectual property statutes (the Patents Act and the Trade Marks Act);
- the fact that registration under those two acts is not conclusive of the priority position of a registered security interest; and
- uncertainty as to the relationship between those two acts and the Australian companies legislation in relation to security interests granted by a company over its intellectual property.

## 4. Priority rules under intellectual property statutes

Of the four statutes that provide for the registration of interests arising by way of assignment, only two, the Patents Act and the Trade Marks Act, address priority issues. Under those two acts, failure to register an assignment of a patent, trademark or service mark means that the borrower, as the registered owner of the intellectual property, can deal with that property as if it were the absolute, unencumbered owner of the property.[13] The borrower's dealings with its intellectual property are, under the two acts, stated to be subject only to "rights appearing in the Register to be vested in another person".[14] The two acts also provide that a 'purchaser' of the intellectual property in good faith for valuable consideration and that does not have notice of the unregistered interest will take the property free of any 'equities' constituted by that unregistered interest.[15]

A lender whose security interest over intellectual property is registrable[16] under either of these acts (a status arguably restricted, at least in principle, to mortgages in the context of secured finance transactions) but has not been registered is thus at risk of having that security interest defeated not only by a subsequent purchaser of the intellectual property, but arguably also by a subsequent secured party capable of being brought within the term 'purchaser' (namely, a secured party that, like the lender, holds a mortgage of the intellectual property).[17]

This latter point leads possibly to a curious result.[18] The lender's mortgage, as a registrable but an unregistered assignment, is capable of being defeated by a

---

13 Patents Act, s 189(1); Trade Marks Act, s 22(1).

14 *Ibid.*

15 Patents Act, s 189(2) and (3); Trade Marks Act, s 22(2) and (3).

16 Legal mortgages require a transfer of legal title. Accordingly, for a lender to obtain a legal mortgage of the intellectual property, it is necessary for the assignment of title to the intellectual property to be registered, with the lender being recorded as the proprietor of the intellectual property. Equitable mortgages, in contrast, involve a transfer of equitable, not legal, title and registration is not necessary to create an equitable mortgage of the intellectual property in favour of the lender. The question arises as to whether registration under the Patents Act or Trade Marks Act of an assignment by way of security denotes a legal mortgage, so that only two states are possible: registered (legal) mortgages and unregistered (equitable) mortgages. Registration of an equitable mortgage would thus entail its conversion into a legal mortgage, with the lender being recorded as the proprietor of the intellectual property. However, both acts recognise, in their priority provisions, that a party other than the proprietor can have its interests registered – as the proprietor's dealings with the intellectual property are made subject to the rights of other registered parties: Patents Act, s 189(1); Trade Marks Act, s 22(1). In addition, the Patents Act clearly envisages that the mortgagee of a patent may be a party other than the proprietor of the patent: s 103. On this basis, it is possible to conceive of both legal mortgages and registered equitable mortgages of patents, trademarks and service marks.

17 See above n 11.

18 For a discussion of this and other conundrums concerning the priority ranking of security interests over patents (and also, since the 2006 amendment, trademarks and service marks), see Swinson, above n 5, pp 526-527.

subsequently created mortgage even if that later mortgage is not registered, as the term 'purchaser' does not appear to be restricted to registered purchasers under either the Patents Act or the Trade Marks Act (if the holder of that mortgage did not, at the time the mortgage was created, have notice of the lender's earlier mortgage).[19] Accordingly, in the absence of notice on the part of the holders of subsequently created security interests of the earlier security interests, priority, insofar as those unregistered security interests are concerned, would be conferred in reverse order to the time of creation of the security interests[20] – as each secured party would have left the borrower, as the registered holder of the intellectual property, in a position to create security interests capable of ranking ahead of all existing, unregistered security interests.[21]

It is possible to avoid this result by confining the term 'purchaser' to parties that have acquired title absolutely to the intellectual property and excluding parties whose interest in the intellectual property has been obtained under an assignment by way of security (ie, a mortgage) or which hold some lesser interest (if one takes the view that the two acts apply to mortgages as well as other security interests).

Registration of a security interest under the Patents Act or the Trade Marks Act means that all subsequent dealings by the borrower with the intellectual property will be subject to that security interest, preventing the borrower from subsequently creating security interests over the intellectual property ranking ahead of the registered security interest. The rule conferring priority on subsequent purchasers (regardless of the view taken of the scope of this rule) would have no application in this situation as registration would confer notice of the security interest.

However, registration under the Patents Act or the Trade Marks Act does not entail absolute priority over all competing security interests, even if that security interest is the first to be registered over the intellectual property. A registered security interest held by a lender will be subordinated to any earlier created security interest (whether this security interest was registered after the lender's security interest or is unregistered), of which the lender had notice when its security interest was created,[22] as the lender will not be able to avail itself of the priority rule that protects purchasers without notice.[23]

## 5. Relationship of intellectual property statutes with companies legislation

A further complicating factor is the relationship between the intellectual property statutes and the more generalised regime governing the registration of security

19 It is possible that a similar result will be arrived at under the UK patents legislation, whose priority provisions are similar to those in the Australian Patents Act: see Beale *et al*, above n 9, p 476.

20 The lender can reverse this order of priorities by registering its security interest before the holder of the subsequently created security interest registers that interest: Patents Act, s 189(1); Trade Marks Act, s 22(1).

21 The potential for this priority rule to apply to security interests that are not registrable under the Patents Act or the Trade Marks Act is discussed in the next section of this chapter, in the context of the relationship between these two acts and the Corporations Act 2001 (Cth).

22 An equivalent rule applies to security interests over patents in the United Kingdom: see R Calnan, *Taking Security: Law and Practice* (Jordans, Bristol, 2006), p 254; Beale *et al*, above n 9, p 476.

23 Patents Act, s 189(3); Trade Marks Act, s 22(3).

interests granted by companies contained in the Corporations Act 2001.[24]

There are two aspects to this relationship. The first concerns the need for security interests granted by companies over their intellectual property to be registered in more than one register, and the second concerns the uncertainty as to the interaction of the priority rules in the Patents Act and Trade Marks Act with the priority rules in the Corporations Act.

Charges (this concept under the Corporations Act also extends to mortgages)[25] created by a company over its copyright, patents, registered designs, trademarks, service marks (and licences to use any of these) and goodwill must be registered under the Corporations Act within 45 days of their creation.[26] Failure to comply with this requirement will render the charge void against a liquidator or administrator (including a receiver) of the company.[27] However, there is no provision in the Corporations Act for the registration of security interests over the intellectual property in integrated circuits (assuming that such intellectual property is not also the subject of a patent) or plant breeder's rights. Moreover, of the types of intellectual property covered by the charge registration provisions of the Corporations Act, registration of security interests is also mandatory under the statutes governing patents, trademarks and service marks.[28]

This requirement for dual registration under the relevant intellectual property statute and the Corporations Act is complicated by the different consequences that flow from non-registration.

Insofar as the Corporations Act is concerned, a lender that holds a registrable but unregistered security interest over a borrower's intellectual property will be unable to enforce that security interest against a liquidator or administrator of the borrower (the very situations in which a lender is likely to be most desirous of being able to utilise its security interest). In addition, that unregistered security interest will be postponed to:

- all registered security interests over the intellectual property (except for a registered security interest that was created after the lender's unregistered security interest and of which the holder of the registered security interest had notice when its security interest was created);[29] and
- all earlier created unregistered (registrable) security interests.[30]

However, the lender's unregistered (registrable) security interest will have priority over all subsequently created unregistered (registrable) security interests.[31]

Failure to register a security interest under the intellectual property statutes may render the security interest inadmissible as evidence in court[32] and, in the case of the

24 The company charge provisions of this act are modelled on the UK version but, unlike the latter, also include a statutory code of priorities for contests between registrable security interests: Corporations Act, s 279(1).
25 Corporations Act, s 9.
26 Corporations Act, ss 262(1)(e) and 263(1).
27 Corporations Act, s 266(1)(c)(i).
28 See above n 10.
29 Corporations Act, ss 280(2)(b) and 281(a).
30 Corporations Act, ss 278(1)(c) and 281(b).
31 *Ibid*.
32 See above n 10.

Patents Act and the Trade Marks Act, has, as discussed in the previous section of this chapter, explicit priority consequences. First, an unregistered security interest held by a lender will be postponed to all registered security interests over the intellectual property (except for a registered security interest that was created after the lender's security interest and of which the holder of the registered security interest had notice when its security interest was created).[33] This is equivalent to the position under the Corporations Act regarding the relative priority rankings of registered and unregistered security interests.

However, in contrast to the position under the Corporations Act, a lender that holds an unregistered security interest over intellectual property may be postponed to a subsequently created unregistered security interest, but may enjoy priority over all earlier created unregistered security interests (provided that in both instances the holder of the later security interest did not, when its security interest was created, have notice of the earlier unregistered security interest).

Second, there is an issue of which rules of priority should apply as regards contests between competing security interests over patents, trademarks and service marks.

The Corporations Act states that the rules of priority contained in that act which apply to contests involving registrable charges[34] "do not apply so as to affect the operation of" the Copyright Act, the Designs Act, the Patents Act or the Trade Marks Act.[35] As noted above, of these acts, only the Patents Act and the Trade Marks Act are concerned with priority contests. Accordingly, the rules of priority under the Corporations Act would apply to their fullest extent to registrable charges over copyright and registered designs, but only to the extent to which the Patents Act and Trade Marks Act are silent on matters affecting the priority-ranking of registrable charges over patents, trademarks and service marks.[36]

The scope of the priority rules contained in the Patents Act and Trade Marks Act – and thus the scope for the application of the priority rules in the Corporations Act – is unclear. The priority rules in those acts state, as has been discussed in the previous section of this chapter, that the registered owner of the intellectual property must deal with the intellectual property subject to "rights appearing in the Register to be vested in another person" and provide for the primacy of the claim of a 'purchaser'[37] in good faith for value and without notice over unregistered interests.[38] Assignments of intellectual property are registrable under the two acts and,

33 Registration under the Corporations Act also carries the benefit of giving constructive notice of the existence of the charge to the entire world: s 130(2). This should provide some measure of protection to the holder of a registrable security interest that has not been registered under the Patents Act or Trade Marks Act (or where registration under that act is completed after registration under the Corporations Act). However, Swinson, above n 5, p 530 is of the view that registration under the Corporations Act should not give constructive notice of the existence of a charge over patents as the patents register should be the authoritative register for determining interests in patents. It is equally unclear whether registration under the intellectual property statutes would constitute constructive notice for the purposes of the priority rules contained in the Corporations Act.

34 Corporations Act, s 279(1). For a discussion of these priority rules, see Ali, above n 3, pp 213-214.

35 Corporations Act, s 279(5).

36 See Lipton, above n 5, p 183; Swinson, above n 5, pp 529-530.

37 That is the term employed: Patents Act, s 189(2) and (3); Trade Marks Act, s 22(2) and (3).

38 Patents Act, s 189; Trade Marks Act, s 22.

accordingly, one can argue that at the very least, the priority rules contained in the acts should apply to contests between an assignee (including a mortgagee) and a purchaser. On a narrow reading of 'purchaser', this would limit the application of the priority rules to contests involving an absolute assignee, leaving room for the application of the priority rules in the Corporations Act, to their fullest extent, to competing registrable charges over patents, trademarks and service marks.

A broader reading of the priority rules in the Patents Act and Trade Marks Act would extend their application to contests between competing assignees, as the concept of a registrable assignment under the two acts extends to mortgages and, as discussed in the previous section of this chapter, the concept of purchaser is capable of being applied to any party that acquires title to the intellectual property.[39] In that case, the priority rules in the Corporations Act would apply only to contests other than one between mortgagees (despite the registrable status of the competing mortgages under the Corporations Act) potentially leading to the outcome of a priority contest in relation to patents, trademarks and service marks being determined by the legal form of the security interests involved. A contest between two unregistered mortgages could, under the priority rules contained in the Patents Act and Trade Marks Act, lead to the subsequently created mortgage having priority over the earlier created one (if the second mortgagee did not, at the time its mortgage was created, have notice of the first mortgage).[40] However, that is not the case under the Corporations Act, where an unregistered (registrable) charge has absolute priority over all subsequently created unregistered (registrable) charges.[41] One would therefore be left with a situation where an unregistered mortgage could be subordinated, under the Patents Act or the Trade Marks Act, to all subsequently created, unregistered mortgages but would enjoy absolute priority over all other unregistered (but registrable under the Corporations Act) security interests created after it.

An even broader reading of the priority rules in the Patents Act and the Trade Marks Act is possible due to potentially expansive reference to 'equities' in those rules. A 'purchaser' of patents, trademarks or service marks in good faith for value and without notice of an equity to which that property is subject will prevail over that equity.[42] If, as considered above, the term 'purchaser' is confined to absolute assignees, then the scope of 'equities' is not relevant and this rule of priority will apply only to contests involving an absolute assignee of the intellectual property, leaving the application of the priority rules in the Corporations Act unhindered. However, if the term 'purchaser' extends to all assignees, whether absolute or by way of security, then the scope of the term 'equities' is critical to understanding the scope of the priority rules in the Patents Act and Trade Marks Act. Those rules provide, as noted above, that the registered owner of intellectual property will, in terms of its freedom to deal with the intellectual property, be constrained by interests that have

---

39 See above n 11.

40 The priority rankings of the two mortgages should be reversed if the earlier created mortgage had been registered under the Corporations Act: see above n 33.

41 Corporations Act, ss 278(1)(c) and 281(b).

42 Patents Act, s 189(3); Trade Marks Act, s 22(3).

been registered in respect of the intellectual property but may otherwise deal with the intellectual property as if it were the absolute owner. Read, in conjunction with the priority rule dealing with the right of a purchaser to prevail over 'equities' in relation to the intellectual property, it is arguable that the term 'equities' is referable to interests that are registrable but which have not been registered under the Patents Act or the Trade Marks Act. On this basis, the priority rules in the two acts would be limited to contests involving mortgages.

However, the acts provide no other guidance as to the scope of 'equities' and it can be argued that that term should be accorded its generally accepted legal meaning,[43] If so, that term will be sufficiently wide so as to extend beyond registrable security interests (mortgages) to all security interests which, if granted over intellectual property, would give rise to 'equities' in relation to that property.[44] Such an interpretation would encompass the entire category of registrable charges over intellectual property under the Corporations Act, meaning that the priority rules in that act would then be confined to contests between registrable charges over patents, trademarks and service marks, where none of the competing charges is a mortgage.[45]

Despite the uncertain contours of the priority rules contained in the Patents Act and Trade Marks Act, and the scope they leave for the application of the priority rules contained in the Corporations Act, the matter is capable of a practical resolution – namely, by ensuring that the security interest is registered[46] – as the key area of difference between the two sets of priority rules relates to their treatment of contests between unregistered security interests.

The above analysis illustrates the formal legal issues with which borrowers seeking to raise funds on the security of their intellectual property – and prospective lenders – must grapple under Australian law.[47] The following part of this chapter briefly examines the characteristics of intellectual property that distinguish it as an asset class from other types of intangible property and which may further undermine

---

43 Such an interpretation is supported by the Trade Marks Act, which states that "equities in respect of a registered trade mark may be enforced in the same way as equities in respect of any other personal property": s 21(2).

44 This would clearly embrace fixed charges. The exact nature of the interest in property conferred by an uncrystallised floating charge remains debatable (see Ali, above n 3, pp 119-121; Beale *et al*, above n 9, p 105), but whether this interest is a present equitable interest, a defeasible equitable interest or a suspended equitable interest constituting a mere equity, that interest will be caught by this interpretation of 'equities'.

45 Swinson, above n 5, pp 529-530, takes the view that the priority rules in the Patents Act should apply ahead of the priority rules in the Corporations Act to contests between security interests derived from the registered owner of the patent, but that contests between security interests that have not been registered under either of those acts should be determined by the priority rules in the Corporations Act.

46 Dual registration is the preferred course of action due to the Corporations Act precluding unregistered (registrable) charges from being enforced against a liquidator or administrator of the borrower, and the uncertainty as to whether registration under the Corporations Act alone constitutes notice for the purposes of the priority rules under the Patents Act and Trade Marks Act: see above n 33.

47 The co-existence of federal laws governing intellectual property (which, like their Australian – and UK – counterparts, are sufficiently broad so as to encompass assignments of intellectual property by way of security) and state or provincial laws governing security interests over personal property has also created considerable legal complexity in relation to the use of intellectual property as collateral for secured finance in the United States and Canada: see, for example, B Clark and B Clark, *The Law of Secured Transactions under the Uniform Commercial Code* (AS Pratt & Sons, Arlington, VA, 2002), paras 1.08[1][e]-[h]; JR Sandrelli, CJ Ramsay and AI Bahadoorsingh, "Remedies under Security Interests in Canada: An Overview" in IM Fletcher and O Swarting (eds), *Remedies under Security Interests* (Kluwer Law International, The Hague, 2002), pp 67-69.

the ability of a borrower to use intellectual property as collateral for secured finance.[48]

## 6. Intellectual property as collateral

Intellectual property is fundamentally different from the other types of intangible that are routinely employed as collateral in secured finance. There are three characteristics of intellectual property that need to be borne in mind when considering its use as collateral.[49]

### 6.1 Fundamental characteristics of intellectual property

First, intellectual property can be characterised as 'non-rivalous', meaning that the use of intellectual property by one party does not detract from the ability of other parties to use that intellectual property simultaneously; the mere fact that one party is currently in possession of and enjoying the use of intellectual property is not, of itself, a bar to other parties possessing or using that very same property. Second, intellectual property is infinitely replicable. The derivation of products from intellectual property or the incorporation of intellectual property in products does not preclude the party having possession of that property from repeating this creation process indefinitely. Both of these characteristics contribute substantially to the commercialisation of intellectual property and the capacity of intellectual property to generate substantial cash flows for a borrower.

However, the third characteristic of intellectual property – which is a natural corollary of the first two characteristics – concerns the level of control that can be exerted by a borrower and, ultimately, its lenders over intellectual property. Because intellectual property can be enjoyed simultaneously by an infinite number of parties and because it can be replicated an infinite number of times, it is far less susceptible to control than other types of intangible property, leading to the prospect of unauthorised use (eg, piracy or passing-off) of the intellectual property with adverse consequences for the value of that property and the cash flows that can be generated from its commercialisation.

In addition to these fundamental characteristics of intellectual property, there are a number of legal risks affecting intellectual property that need to be considered as part of any assessment of the suitability of intellectual property as collateral.

### 6.2 Validity of intellectual property

A successful challenge to the validity or scope of the borrower's intellectual property may result in the cessation of, or a sharp reduction in, the cash flows generated from the commercialisation of the intellectual property. A lender may need to consider requiring the borrower to insure the intellectual property, by taking out patent validity insurance for example.

---

48 The discussion that follows is based on PU Ali and ACH Chang, "Fund-Raising for High-Technology Companies: The Intellectual Property Securitisation Option" in JJ de Vries Robbe and PU Ali (eds), *Innovations in Securitisation* (Kluwer Law International, The Hague, 2006), pp 216-220.

49 See KE Maskus, *Intellectual Property Rights in the Global Economy* (Institute for International Economics, Washington, DC, 2001), p 146.

## 6.3 Infringement and enforcement

The value of intellectual property depends upon it not being infringed upon and the extent to which the borrower is prepared to defend it against infringement and challenge competing intellectual property. Again, a lender may wish to consider requiring a borrower to obtain infringement insurance covering lost profits and royalties attributable to infringement of the borrower's intellectual property.

In addition, the value of the borrower's intellectual property may be eroded by third parties 'designing around' that property without overtly infringing upon the property. For instance, it is common practice for technology companies to design around not-so-strong patents or poorly drafted patents held by their competitors.

Enforcing intellectual property against alleged infringers is also not without risk. An attempt by the borrower to enforce its intellectual property is likely to draw a legal challenge to the validity and scope of that intellectual property as a response. It is important to note, in this context, that intellectual property does not absolutely preclude infringement (in the analogous sense that ownership of other property precludes trespass or conversion), but merely comprises 'probabilistic' rights to try to prevent infringement and, moreover, that the scope of protection provided by intellectual property is imprecise.[50] In the United States, roughly half of the patents that have been litigated have been invalidated by a court (with the attempt to enforce the patent resulting in its extinguishment).[51]

Accordingly, to address the related risks of infringement and invalidation, companies now routinely apply for multiple patents on closely related technologies, such as in relation to the re-invention of the originally patented technology or the invention of improvements, even if incremental, to such technology.[52] Cross-licensing agreements and patent validity insurance may also be used to supplement the company's strategy of applying for multiple patents.

## 6.4 Cross-licensing agreements

Cross-licensing agreements are often used as a mechanism to resolve or even forestall patent infringement disputes between the holders of competing intellectual property.[53] Such an agreement typically provides for the mutual release of all pending

---

50 See JP Choi, "Patent Litigation as an Information Revelation Mechanism" [1998] *American Economic Review* 1249; C Shapiro, "Anti-Trust Limits to Patent Settlements" (2003) 34 *Rand Journal of Economics* 391.

51 See MA Lemley and C Shapiro, "Probabilistic Patents" (2005) 19 *Journal of Economic Perspectives* 75, at 79-80. While only a small minority of patents are litigated, those that are litigated are significant patents. As the authors note (*ibid*, at 79): "The patents involved in litigation are those that are important enough commercially to justify the costs of litigation and for which the parties were unable to reach a mutually attractive settlement."

52 See C Shapiro, "Navigating the Patent Thicket: Cross-Licenses, Patent Pools, and Standard-Setting" in A Jaffe, J Lerner and S Stern (eds), *Innovation Policy and the Economy* (National Bureau of Economics, Cambridge, MA, 2001); J Lerner and J Tirole, "Efficient Patent Pools" (2004) 94 *American Economic Review* 691; G Clarkson and D DeKorte, "The Problem of Patent Thickets in Convergent Technologies" [2006] *Annals New York Academy of Sciences* 180; PB Nelson, "Patent Pools: An Economic Assessment of Current Law and Policy" (2007) 38 *Rutgers Law Journal* 539. This multiplicity of patents also leads to 'royalty stacking', where a single product may potentially infringe a large number of patents resulting in liability to pay multiple royalties: see further MA Lemley and C Shapiro, "Patent Holdup and Royalty Stacking" (2007) 85 *Texas Law Review* 1991.

53 See JP Choi, "Patent Pools and Cross-Licensing in the Shadow of Patent Litigation" (CESifo Working Paper, November 2003).

litigation and claims in relation to designated intellectual property, and for each party to grant to the other a non-exclusive licence to manufacture, use or sell products in which that intellectual property is incorporated. Accordingly, a company may wish to ensure that it retains unencumbered ownership of its intellectual property so that the intellectual property can be utilised in future cross-licensing agreements, and for that company the costs of restricting its ability to cross-license freely its intellectual property may outweigh the benefits to be obtained for using its intellectual property as collateral for secured finance.

### 6.5 Obsolescence

Although intellectual property has a relatively long legal life (as constituted by the period of statutory protection afforded to it) compared to other types of intangible property, the commercially exploitable life of a borrower's intellectual property may fall short of its formal legal life. In particular, advances in technology may result in the development of superior substitutes or more cost-effective technologies, rendering the borrower's intellectual property obsolete and therefore making it no longer economically feasible for the borrower to continue the commercialisation of its intellectual property.

## 7. Conclusion

Intellectual property is potentially an important source of collateral for companies seeking to raise funds on a secured basis. This is especially so for technology companies, for which intellectual property may be their most valuable asset or, in the case of new ventures, their only substantial asset. It is therefore important that the legal framework for secured finance transactions involving intellectual property permits those transactions to be implemented efficiently. That is not the case in Australia.

However, an efficient legal framework will not, on its own, bring about an increase in the use of intellectual property as collateral for secured finance. Lenders will need to be satisfied that the security structure used adequately addresses the unique characteristics of intellectual property, particularly since those characteristics make intellectual property less susceptible to the control mechanisms employed by lenders in respect of security interests over other types of intangible property. Moreover, even where a lender is prepared to advance funds on the security of intellectual property, the borrower may wish to ensure that its intellectual property remains unencumbered or that the security structure employed does not detract from the borrower's freedom to utilise the intellectual property in a cross-licensing agreement. This is likely to make it very difficult for the lender to design a security structure that is capable of delivering to the lender rights to the intellectual property superior to those that it could have obtained under an enterprise-wide floating charge.

# International receivables

**Spiros V Bazinas**
UNCITRAL
United Nations Office of Legal Affairs

## 1. Introduction

The United Nations Convention on the Assignment of Receivables in International Trade – the result of almost six years' work at the inter-governmental level by the United Nations Commission on International Trade Law (UNCITRAL) – was adopted by the United Nations General Assembly and opened for signature by states in December 2001.[1] The main objective of the convention is to facilitate international receivables financing practices, such as asset-based lending, securitisation, factoring, forfaiting and project finance relating to receivables.[2]

In this way, the convention may well promote the availability of capital and credit at more affordable rates across national borders and facilitate the cross-border movement of goods and services (Preamble, fifth paragraph).[3] With a view to meeting these objectives, the convention:

- removes legal obstacles to receivables financing practices (eg, certain statutory limitations and contractual limitations); and
- enhances certainty with respect to certain key substantive law issues (eg, effects of the assignment on the debtor) and private international law issues (eg, law applicable to conflicts of priority).

To achieve its objectives, the convention covers all types of assignment (pure outright assignments, outright assignments for security purposes and assignments by way of security).

This chapter discusses some key aspects of the convention and their value for receivables financing practices.

1 GA Resolution 56/81 of December 12 2001 (to be published in UNCITRAL Yearbook, 2001, vol XXXII; currently available on UNCITRAL's website at www.uncitral.org). It will enter into force once ratified by five states (Article 45 (1)).

2 Practices in which a related service, but no financing, is provided are also covered: see Analytical Commentary on the draft Convention on Assignment of Receivables in International Trade (A/CN 9/489), paras 7-13 (to be published in UNCITRAL Yearbook, 2001, vol XXXII; currently available on UNCITRAL's website, *supra* n 1). For a list of the *travaux préparatoires*, see footnotes 1 through 11 of A/CN 9/489. For a discussion of earlier drafts of the convention, see Spiros V Bazinas, "An International Legal Regime for Receivables Financing: UNCITRAL'S Contribution," 8 Duke J Comp & Int'l L 315 (1998); and Carsten Boehm, *Die Forderungsabtretung, in* UNCITRAL-Konventionsentwurf (Shaker Verlag, Aachen, 2000).

3 For a more detailed analysis of the general principles of the convention and its effects on domestic law, see Spiros V Bazinas, "*Le Projet de Convention de la* GNUDCI. *Ses objectifs et Ses Effets sur les Autres Lois*", 75 *Revue de Droit Bancaire et de la Bourse* 169, 171-182 (1999) [hereinafter, Bazinas, Le Projet]; and Spiros V Bazinas, "*Die Arbeit von UNCITRAL Im Bereich Der Forderungsabtretung Zur Kreditsicherung*", in *Die Forderungsabtretung, Insbesondere Zur Kreditsicherung* (Walther Hadding & Uwe H Schneider, eds, 1999).

## 2. Scope of application

### 2.1 International assignments and international receivables

The convention applies to international assignments and to the assignment of international receivables (Article 1(1)). 'International' is an assignment in which the assignor and the assignee are located in different states (Article 3). 'International' is a receivable in which the original creditor (assignor) and the debtor are located in different states (Article 3). The point at which internationality of the assignment is determined is the time of the conclusion of the contract of assignment. The internationality of the receivable is determined at the time of the conclusion of the contract from which the receivable arises. Any subsequent change of location does not affect the application of the convention.

With the exception of the debtor-related provisions, for the application of the convention, the assignor needs to be located in a contracting state (Article 1(1)). With this approach, the scope of the convention is quite broad and thus no reference is made to application of the convention by virtue of private international law rules whose application could raise uncertainty as they are not uniform (see exception below for the application of the debtor-related provisions).

For the application of the debtor-related provisions of the convention, the debtor too needs to be located in a contracting state or the law governing the original contract needs to be the law of a contracting state (Article 1(3)). This approach is premised on the assumption that, as long as the debtor is protected (ie, under the convention, can raise the lack of notification as a defence), whether the assignment is effective between the assignor and the assignee or as against third parties (other than the debtor), the debtor need not be located in a contracting state.[4] Application of the debtor-related provisions by virtue of private international law rules should create no uncertainty since they are based on a concrete uniform rule (referring to the law governing the receivable which, in the case of contractual receivables subject to the convention, is the law governing the original contract).

### 2.2 Domestic assignments of domestic receivables

The rule is that the convention does not apply to domestic assignments of domestic receivables. However, there are two exceptions to this rule.

To ensure consistent results, the convention applies to subsequent assignments (ie, an assignment from A to B, from B to C and so forth), irrespective of whether they are international or relate to international receivables, provided that any prior assignment in the chain of subsequent assignments is governed by the convention (Article 1(1)).[5]

---

4 For a detailed analysis of, among other things, the convention's applicability, see Franco Ferrari, "The Uncitral Draft Convention on Assignment in Receivables Financing: Critical remarks on Some Specific Issues", in *Private Law in the International Arena – Liber Amicorum Kurt Siehr* (Juergen Basedow et al eds, 2000, TMC Asser Press, The Hague).

5 See Uwe Schneider/Alexandra Dreibus, "*Die Kettenabtrettung*", in *Bankrecht und Perspektiven, Festschrift fuer Herbert Schimanksi* (Norbert Horn, Hans-Juergen Lwowski, Gerd Nobbe eds, 1999, RWS Verlag, Cologne).

Further, to ensure certainty as to the priority rights of assignees, the convention covers all possible priority conflicts, including a conflict between a domestic assignee of a domestic receivable and a foreign assignee of the same domestic receivable (Articles 22 and 5(m)(i)).

## 2.3 Assignment and receivable

Under the convention, 'assignment' means a transfer of a receivable by agreement (Article 2(a)). It includes pure outright transfers, outright transfers for security purposes and the creation of security rights in receivables. It also includes subrogation and pledge-type transactions. It does not include transfers by operation of law (eg, statutory subrogation) or unilateral assignments.

'Assignor' is the old creditor in the transaction giving rise to the assigned receivable (original contract), which is normally but not necessarily the borrower in the financing contract. 'Assignee' is the new creditor, the lender in the financing contract. 'Debtor' is the obligor in the original contract.

'Receivable' is defined as a contractual monetary claim (Article 2). A broad variety of receivables are included, such as receivables from the supply of goods, construction and services, whether the contracts are commercial or consumer contracts. Also included are toll road receipts, royalties, damages for breach of contract, interest, non-monetary claims convertible to money and returned goods (at least, in the relationship between the assignor and the assignee, provided that they take the place of the assigned receivables; Articles 14(1) (a) and (b)).

## 2.4 Exclusions and other limitations

Some assignments are excluded because they are insignificant in practice (eg, assignments to a consumer; Article 4(1)(a)). Other assignments are excluded because they are already sufficiently regulated and additional regulation by the convention would be unnecessary, as is the case with 'financial receivables' such as those arising from securities, letters of credit and bank deposits (Article 4(2)).[6]

In addition to exclusions, the convention contains limitations on its application to certain practices. With respect to these practices, the convention applies but does not affect the rights of certain parties. For example, the convention applies to the assignment of consumer receivables but does not override consumer protection law. Similarly, the convention applies to the assignment of receivables from negotiable instruments but does not refer the priority of a holder in due course to the law of the assignor's location, instead, for example, of the law of the instrument's location (Articles 4(3) to (5)).

---

6 For a detailed analysis of exclusions or other limitations relating in particular to securities and to real estate receivables, see Harry C Sigman and Edwin E Smith, "Toward Facilitating Cross-Border Secured Financing and Securitization: An Analysis of the United Nations Convention on the Assignment of Receivables in International Trade", in 57 *The Business Lawyer* 727, 734 (February 2002). On this matter, see also Spiros V Bazinas, "Multi-Jurisdiction Receivables Financing: UNCITRAL's Impact on Securitization and Cross-Border Perfection", 12 Duke J Comp & Int'l L (2002).

The convention also contains limitations to the scope of the provision on anti-assignment agreements between the assignor and the debtor (Article 9). This provision applies only to the assignment of receivables arising from:

- the supply or lease of goods or services other than financial services;
- construction contracts;
- contracts for the sale or lease of real property;
- credit card transactions;
- the sale, lease or licensing of intellectual property or information; and
- close-out payments under multi-party netting arrangements (Articles 9(3) and 10(4)).

As a result of these limitations, the effectiveness of an assignment, made despite an anti-assignment agreement, of a receivable to which Article 9 does not apply is left to law outside the convention. Under Article 29, that law is the law governing the receivable. If, under that law the assignment is not effective, there is no assignment to which the convention (with the exception of Article 29) can apply. As a result, for example, the assignment of the financial receivables not excluded in Article 4 (eg, sales of loans or insurance policies) would, in effect, be excluded from the scope of the convention. The convention can apply only if, under the law applicable by virtue of Article 29, the assignment is effective despite the fact that it was made in violation of an anti-assignment clause.

### 2.5 Location

Location is defined by reference to the place of business (Article 5(h)). If an assignor or assignee has a place of business in more than one state, reference is to be made to the place in which it has its central administration. If a debtor, though, has a place of business in more than one state, reference is to be made to the place which has the closest relationship to the original contract. The reason for the different approach followed with respect to the debtor lies in the need to avoid surprises to the debtor as to the law applicable to its rights and obligations. On the other hand, more certainty is needed with respect to the location of the assignor, since that location is crucial for the determination of whether the convention (with the exception of the debtor-related provisions) applies and for the identification of the law applicable to priority conflicts (Articles 1(1) and 22). If a party has no place of business, reference is to be made to its place of habitual residence (Article 5(h)).

As already mentioned, this location rule is intended to ensure certainty and predictability in the application of the convention and in the determination of the law applicable to priority conflicts. The traditional closest-connection test could not ensure that result. One of the effects of this novel location rule is that dealings of branch offices will be referred to the law of the central office. The certainty achieved with this rule, though, should outweigh the potential discomfort from this change. In addition, in view of the broad exclusions of the assignment of 'financial receivables', such as securities, letters of credit and deposit accounts (Article 4(2)), the impact of this change in particular on the banking industry should be limited (eg, to sales of loans).[7]

## 2.6 Effectiveness of the assignment

The convention deals with certain effectiveness-related issues (eg, statutory limitations and contractual limitations on the assignment of receivables) by way of substantive law rules. With respect to all other effectiveness-related issues, the convention provides the law applicable (Articles 22-23 and 26-32).

### *(a) Statutory limitations*

The convention sets aside statutory limitations on the assignment of:

- future receivables;[8]
- parts or undivided interests in receivables; and
- receivables that are not identified individually at the time of the assignment, as long as the receivables can be identified as receivables to which the assignment relates when they arise (Article 8).

Such statutory limitations are normally concerned with the impact of a bulk assignment on the economic freedom of the assignor, related specificity concerns or the priority given to financing institutions over small suppliers.[9] Limitations (eg, with respect to partial assignments) may also be concerned with debtor inconvenience and expense.[10]

The convention's approach is based on the assumption that if the assignor may assign its receivables, it may obtain access to more credit and at a lower cost, with the result that it will be able to offer better credit terms to its buyers/debtors. The convention's approach does not frustrate the objective of assignor-related limitations

---

7 At its 2001 session, UNCITRAL considered and rejected a suggestion to introduce an exception to the central administration location rule with respect to branches of banks or other financial institutions. The suggestion was that branches of banks and other financial institutions should be deemed as being located in the state with the closest connection to the assignment. The reasons for UNCITRAL's decision included that:
- exceptions would compromise the certainty achieved by the central-administration location rule, which was appropriate in the vast majority of cases;
- priority issues should be referred to the law of the state in which the bank or other financial institution would be wound up – namely, its place of central administration;
- treating branches of banks or other financial institutions in effect as separate legal entities would create confusion in practice, in particular as to where to file; and
- there was no uniform understanding of the terms 'bank' and 'financing institution', and thus use of those terms might create uncertainty and have a different effect depending on the meaning given to those terms in the various countries.

See Report of the United Nations Commission on International Trade on its thirty-fourth session, General Assembly, Official Records, Fifty-sixth session, Supplement 17 (A/56/17), paras 150-53, to be published in UNCITRAL Yearbook, 2001, vol XXXII (currently available on UNCITRAL's website, *supra* n 1). For further discussion of this matter, see Catherine Walsh, "Receivables Financing and the Conflict of Laws: The UNCITRAL Draft Convention on the Assignment of Receivables in International Trade", 106 Dick L Rev 159 (2001).

8 Under the convention, a receivable is a 'future receivable' if the contract from which it may arise does not exist at the time of the conclusion of the contract of assignment (Article 5(b)). Whether a receivable is mature or payable, or whether it has been earned by performance, is irrelevant.

9 Hein Koetz, "Rights of third parties. Third Party Beneficiaries and Assignment", in 7 *International Encyclopedia of Comparative Law*, 58-91 (1992).

10 *Id*, 105.

because it does not give priority to one or the other creditor.[11] It merely gives all creditors a rule by which they can determine which law will govern priority. Further, the convention is mindful of the need to protect the debtor and includes a number of provisions in this regard (eg, Article 17).

Apart from the statutory limitations mentioned, the convention does not affect other statutory limitations, such as statutory limitations relating to sovereign receivables (on contractual limitations with respect to the assignment of sovereign receivables, see Article 40).

#### *(b)* *Contractual limitations*

The convention validates an assignment made despite an anti-assignment agreement between the assignor and the debtor (Article 9(1)). However, it does not invalidate the anti-assignment agreement as between the assignor and the debtor, or eliminate any liability that the assignor may have for breach of contract. There are two limitations, though:

- The debtor may not avoid the original contract on the sole ground of the breach of the anti-assignment agreement; and
- The assignee is not liable towards the debtor on the sole ground that it had knowledge of the anti-assignment agreement between the assignor and the debtor (Article 9(2)).

The convention takes this approach so as to give precedence to the interest of the economy as a whole, even at the expense of inconveniencing some powerful debtors that have the bargaining power to negotiate anti-assignment agreements (consumer debtors do not have such power; in any case the convention does not override consumer protection legislation; Article 4(4)). However, if a state cannot prohibit an assignment by way of statute and can do so only by way of an agreement, that state can enter a reservation so that it will not be bound by the provision of the convention dealing with anti-assignment agreements (Article 40). A reservation was preferred to an exception to the rule, since otherwise to protect certain states, the cost of credit could be increased to all states, even though it would be not necessary or desirable. In addition, if the convention provided that in all cases contractual limitations relating to sovereign receivables were fully effective, only powerful contractors would be able to compete for public contracts.

### 2.7 Form

The convention leaves form of the contract of assignment to law applicable outside the convention, to which the convention points (for the form of the contract of assignment, see Article 27). Form of the assignment, as a condition of priority, is left

---

11 Bazinas, *Le Projet*,173 . For the convention's impact on various legal systems, see also Bruce Markell, "UNCITRAL's Receivables Convention: The First Step, But Not the Last", 12 Duke J Comp & Int'l L (2002). In fact, UNCITRAL has already taken its next step in the field by embarking on the preparation of a legislative guide on secured transactions, aimed at harmonising domestic law. A first preliminary draft of this guide will be considered by an UNCITRAL Working Group in May 2002 (A/CN.9/WG.VI/WP.2 and Addenda 1 through 12; to be published in UNCITRAL Yearbook, 2002, vol XXXIII; currently available on UNCITRAL's website, *supra* n 1).

to the law of the assignor's location (Articles 22 and 5(g)). However, to the extent that notification of the debtor is a requirement for the effectiveness of an assignment as between the assignor and the assignee, it is set aside (Article 14(1)).[12]

### 2.8 Transfer of security rights

An accessory, personal or property, security right (eg, a guarantee or a pledge), securing payment of the assigned receivable is transferred with the receivable without a new act of transfer (Article 10(1)). The assignor is obliged to transfer to the assignee an independent security or other supporting right (eg, an independent guarantee or a standby letter of credit; Article 10(1)).

With respect to contractual limitations, a security right is treated in the same way as a receivable (ie, the contractual limitation is valid between the parties thereto but does not affect the transferee; Articles 10(2) and (3)). This provision applies to 'trade receivables' defined broadly (Article 10 (4)), and does not affect any obligations of the assignor towards the debtor under the law governing the security right (eg, damages for the transfer of pledged shares to a foreign assignee; Article 10(5)). Similarly, this provision does not affect any form or registration requirement necessary for the transfer of the security right (Article 10(6)).

## 3. The relationship between the assignor and the assignee

### 3.1 Party autonomy

Under the convention, the assignor and the assignee may structure their transaction as they wish to address their particular needs. However, they may not affect the rights of third parties (Article 6). The convention also recognises trade usages agreed upon and trade practices established between the parties (Article 11).[13] In order to fill gaps left in the assignment contract and to provide a list of issues to be addressed in the contract, the convention contains a number of default rules dealing with matters such as representations, notification and payment, and contractual rights to proceeds.

### 3.2 Representations

The convention follows generally accepted principles and attempts to establish a balance between fairness and practicality. The risk of hidden defences of the debtor, for example, is placed on the assignor (Article 12(1)(c)). The reason for this approach is that the assignor is in a better position to know whether it will perform the original contract properly and will not give rise to debtor defences. If the convention provided that the risk of hidden defences were on the assignee, the assignee would include that risk in the calculation of the cost of credit. Parties are, of course, free to agree otherwise.

---

12 See also Sigman & Smith, supra n 6, at 738.

13 It is worth noting that in an international assignment, only international trade usages are binding, unless otherwise agreed by the parties (Article 11(3)).

## 3.3 Notification and payment

Under the convention, an assignment is effective as between the assignor and the assignee irrespective of whether the debtor has been notified (Article 14(1)). However, notification changes the way in which the debtor may discharge its debt, limits the debtor's rights of set-off arising from contracts unrelated to the original contract to those available at the time of notification and makes any amendment to the original contract subject to the actual or constructive consent of the assignee (Articles 17, 18(2) and 20(2)).

'Notification' means a writing that "reasonably identifies the assigned receivables and the assignee" (Article 5(d)). For a notification to be effective, it needs to be received by the debtor and be "in a language that is reasonably expected to inform the debtor about its contents" (Article 16(1)). In order to avoid invalidating notifications that do not include a payment instruction and are given, for example, for the purpose of limiting the debtor's rights of set-off, the convention does not require that a notification include a payment instruction. However, notifying parties would be well advised to include a payment instruction even if they wish the debtor to continue paying the assignor, since otherwise the debtor may not know how to discharge its debt (Articles 17(1) and (2)). In such a case, if the notification is given by the assignee, the debtor may request adequate proof (Article 17(7)) or pay into an escrow account or a public deposit fund (Article 17(8)).

The convention introduces an independent right of the assignee to notify the debtor and to request payment (Article 13(1)); and, to protect the debtor, a right to request adequate proof (Article 17(7)). Such a right is essential in situations where a notification is most needed (ie, where the assignor defaults in the financing contract and is unlikely to cooperate with the assignee).[14] In practice, parties try to address this problem by including in the financing contract an authorisation for the assignee to notify the debtor. Even if parties agree that the debtor should not be notified, the notification triggers a change in the way in which the debtor is to discharge its debt but does not have any other effects (Article 13(2)). The reason for this approach is that the debtor's discharge should not be made subject to agreements to which the debtor is not a party, while the party notifying in breach of an agreement should not unduly benefit from such a notification.

## 3.4 Contractual right to proceeds

As between the assignor and the assignee, the assignee may claim proceeds (and returned goods) if payment is made to the assignee, to the assignor or to another person over which the assignee has priority (Article 14). Whether the assignee may retain such proceeds is an issue of priority left to the law of the assignor's location (Article 22).

The term 'proceeds' means "whatever is received in respect of an assigned receivable". It includes proceeds of proceeds but not returned goods (Article 5(j)). For

14 In legal systems in which priority is based on the time of notification and notification is possible only with the authorisation of the assignor, by withholding such authorisation, the assignor may force the assignee to concessions or, by giving his authorisation to one of many assignees, the assignor may decide who has priority.

the proceeds-related provisions of the convention to apply, proceeds need to be identifiable (eg, by virtue of Article 24(2) or of the tracing-related provisions of law applicable outside the convention).

## 4. The relationship between the assignee and the debtor

### 4.1 The principle of debtor protection

The convention introduces a high standard of debtor protection. It makes debtor discharge subject to an objective criterion (ie, notification; Articles 17(1) and (2)). It allows the debtor to discharge its debt by paying the right person even under law outside the convention (Article 17(8)). Most importantly, it gives the debtor the right to seek adequate proof in case of doubt (Article 17(7)). With the exception of rights of set-off that arise from contracts unrelated to the original contract and are not available to the debtor at the time of notification, the convention preserves all the defences and rights of set-off that the debtor can raise (Article 18). The convention also introduces strict conditions with respect to waivers of defences by the debtor (Article 19), and deals with the third-party effects of contract modifications (Article 20).

Further, the convention explicitly elevates debtor protection to one of the basic principles underlying the convention (Article 15). As a result, any uncertainty or gap in the convention is to be resolved in a way that is favourable to the debtor. In any case, the assignment cannot change the currency and the country of payment. Whether the debtor can agree to such a change is left to law applicable outside the convention.

### 4.2 Discharge of the debtor by payment

#### *(a) The rule*

The debtor's discharge is based on written notification received by the debtor. Up to the time of receipt of notification, the debtor may discharge its debt by paying in accordance with the original contract. After receipt of notification, the debtor may obtain a valid discharge only by paying as instructed in the notification (Articles 17(1) and (2)).

Whether the debtor knew or ought to have known of another assignment with priority is irrelevant. It would be unfair for the debtor to be subject to constructive knowledge requirements or to have to determine who has priority. In addition, it would be very difficult for a third party to establish what the debtor actually knew. This approach does not encourage bad faith or fraud, but attempts to ensure certainty with respect to payment by and discharge of the debtor, which is an important element in pricing a transaction. Bad faith is very difficult to prove. As to fraud, the convention, on the one hand, does not override national law and, on the other hand, does not upgrade fraud to the normal circumstance that needs to be addressed expressly and specifically.

#### *(b) Multiple notifications*

The convention also deals with multiple notifications or payment instructions relating to one and the same assignment, to several assignments of the same receivables by the same assignor and to several subsequent assignments (Articles 17(3) to (6)). It may be interesting to examine briefly the approach taken in the convention with respect to notification of a partial assignment. If the debtor receives such notification by one or several assignees of parts of the receivable the debtor owes, the debtor may discharge its debt by paying in accordance either with such notification or with the convention as if no notification were received (eg, pay in accordance with the original contract; Article 17(6)).

By giving the debtor the right to determine whether the notification of a partial assignment is effective with respect to debtor discharge (it is effective for any other purpose), the convention avoids prescribing, in a regulatory manner, what the assignor, the assignee or the debtor ought to do. It also avoids creating liability for any damage or loss to the debtor. In this way, the convention does not invalidate partial assignments. It merely suggests that assignors and assignees may need to consider ensuring, at the time of the conclusion of the original contract or of the contract of assignment, the debtor's consent to notification of partial assignments. If the debtor does not consent to such notification, assignors and assignees need to structure their payments in an appropriate way (eg, by agreeing on a lock-box arrangement; Article 24(2)).

### *(c)* *Adequate proof*

One of the main debtor-protection provisions gives the debtor a right to request adequate proof of the assignment when notification is given by an assignee without the apparent authorisation of the assignor (Article 17(7)). In this way, the convention protects the debtor from having to pay twice by paying an unknown, unauthorised third party. Adequate proof includes, but is not limited to, a writing with the assignor's signature (eg, a copy of the assignment contract or an authorisation by the assignor to the assignee). If the assignee does not provide adequate proof within a reasonable period of time, the debtor may discharge its debt by paying in accordance with the convention as if no notification had been received.

The convention does not settle explicitly the question of what the debtor should do to avoid being in breach and having to pay damages plus interest, if the debt becomes payable during the time the debtor awaits to receive adequate proof. Depending on the circumstances, the debtor may have pay to an escrow account or to a public deposit fund or to court (Article 17(8)), or the payment obligation may have to be suspended if such a possibility is not available. In any case, a legitimate assignee can protect itself by providing 'adequate proof' promptly.

### 4.3 Defences and rights of set-off

The convention codifies generally accepted principles.[15] The debtor may raise against the assignee any defences or rights of set-off that the debtor could raise if the claim had been made against the assignor. Rights of set-off arising from the original contract or a related transaction may be raised against the assignee even if they become available to the debtor after notification (Article 18(1)). Rights of set-off that

15 See, for example, Article 9 of the Unidroit Convention on International Factoring (Ottawa, 1988).

arise from unrelated contracts and become available to the debtor after notification may not be raised against the assignee (Article 18(2)). After notification, the debtor is aware that the assignee is the rightful claimant and should not be subject to the separate dealings of the debtor with the assignor.

The meaning of the words 'become available' (ie, whether the right has to be quantified, mature or payable) is left to the law governing the original contract, if the right of set-off arises from the original contract (Article 29). The convention contains no rule in this respect for other types of set-off.

The convention introduces another innovation. The debtor cannot raise against the assignee the breach of an anti-assignment agreement by the assignor (Article 18(3)). This is a logical consequence of the rule in Article 9. Otherwise, although it would be valid, an assignment made despite an anti-assignment agreement between the assignor and the debtor could be deprived of any value to the assignee.

### 4.4 Waiver of defences

The debtor may, in return for some benefit (eg, a higher amount of credit or a longer repayment period), waive its defences and rights of set-off by agreement with the assignor. To warn the debtor of the consequences of the waiver, the convention requires a signed writing for a waiver or its modification (Article 19(1)). Also to protect the debtor from undue pressure by the assignor, the convention provides that defences or rights of set-off arising from fraudulent acts of the assignee or based on the debtor's incapacity may not be waived (Article 19(2)). However, defences or rights of set-off arising from fraudulent acts of the assignor may be waived. The convention does not deal with and thus does not limit any agreements between the debtor and the assignee by which the debtor may waive its defences or rights of set-off.

### 4.5 Modification of the original contract

Often, the original contract needs to be modified to meet the changing needs of the parties. The *inter-partes* effect of such modifications is a matter of the agreement. However, the third-party effects (ie, whether the debtor can pay the receivable as modified and whether the assignee can claim payment of the receivable as modified) are dealt with in the convention (Article 20).

The basic rule is that, up to notification of the debtor, any contract modification is effective as against the assignee and the assignee acquires the receivable as modified (Article 20(1)). After notification, such a modification is ineffective without the actual or constructive consent of the assignee (Article 20(2)). Any liability that the assignor may have towards the assignee under law applicable outside the convention for breach of an agreement not to modify the original contract is not affected (Article 20(3)).

## 5. The relationship between the assignee and competing claimants

### 5.1 Substantive v private international law priority rules

The main rule of the convention dealing with priority among competing claims is a private international law rule (Article 22). This reflects the fact that states were not prepared to agree on a substantive law priority rule (ie, first to conclude the contract of assignment, first to notify the debtor or first to file a notice about the assignment in a public filing office).

The value in this rule is in the fact that deviating from traditional approaches centralises all priority conflicts to the law of the assignor's location (in the case of places of business in more than one state, the law of the assignor's central administration).[16] This single, easily determinable law to govern priority issues will resolve an issue over which great uncertainly exists in law and literature. Article 12 of the Rome Convention on the Law Applicable to Contractual Obligations (1980) is a typical example of the current status of the law on this issue. It is not clear whether Article 12 governs priority questions. The *travaux préparatoires*, the letter and the spirit of Article 12 and of the Rome Convention as a whole, as well as an ample body of literature, suggest that Article 12 does not govern such questions. However, the opposite view is also represented in literature and in jurisprudence.[17]

However, even if Article 12 governs priority questions, neither of the possible answers (ie, the law chosen by the parties or the law governing the receivable) is appropriate in the increasingly common case of bulk assignments of all present and future receivables. The law chosen by the parties would result in the application of several laws (and, in any case, it would be inappropriate to submit third-party effects to the law chosen by the parties). The law governing the receivable would present the same problem. Further, it would not allow parties to determine the law applicable at the time of assignment.

The law of the assignor's central administration presents another advantage. It is likely to be the place where the main insolvency proceeding with respect to the assignor will be opened. Thus, conflicts between the rules governing priority and the applicable insolvency law rules will be reduced and, if any, will be resolved by the rules of the same jurisdiction. In the case of a secondary insolvency proceeding opened, for example, in a country where the debtor has assets, the priority rules of the law of the assignor's central administration will apply subject to the mandatory and public policy rules of the forum state (Article 23).

To supplement the private international law priority rule of Article 22, the convention includes a set of optional substantive law priority rules, from which states that wish to modernise their relevant law may choose by way of declaration (Article 42 and annex to the convention).

### 5.2 Priority

'Priority' is defined as a right of relative preference (in payment or other satisfaction of the assigned claim, such as return of the goods sold; Article 5(g)). In order to

---

16 This rule has been rightly described "as a great step forward in the development of international commercial and the harmonization of conflict-of-laws rules in the area of secured transactions" – see Jean Michel Deschamps, "The Priority Rules of the United Nations Receivables Convention", 12 Duke J Comp & Int'l L (2002).

17 See generally Eva-Maria Kieninger, "*Das Statut der Forderungsabtretung im Verhältnis zu Dritten*", 62 *Rabels Zeitschrift*, 678 (1998); see also Teun HD Struycken, "The Proprietary Aspects of International Assignments of Debts and the Rome Convention Article 12", 24 Lloyd's Marit Com LQ 345 (1998); and Walsh, *supra* n 5, at 171.

ensure that all the relevant issues are covered, the convention provides that priority includes the determination of whether the right is personal or *in rem*, whether it is a security right and any steps necessary to render the right effective against a competing claimant.

The last element is a direct reference to all effectiveness-related issues that are not governed elsewhere in the convention (Article 22 expressly excludes from its scope all such issues). In jurisdictions in which no distinction is drawn between effectiveness as between the parties and as against third parties, that would be the normal result of the wording of the definition of priority. The result would be the same for jurisdictions that do make such a distinction, but for another reason. An assignment cannot be effective against third parties if it is ineffective as between the assignor and the assignee.

### 5.3 Competing claimant

In order to ensure that all possible conflicts of priority are covered, the convention defines 'competing claimant' to refer to other assignees, even if one of the competing assignments is domestic and relates to domestic receivables. Also included are:

- creditors with a right in other property extended by law in the receivables arising from such property (eg, a seller with a retention of title extended by law to the receivable arising from the sale of the property);
- other creditors of the assignor; and
- the administrator in the insolvency of the assignor (Article 5(m)).

### 5.4 Mandatory and public policy exceptions

The convention strikes a balance between the need to preserve the certainty achieved by its private international law priority rule and the need to respect fundamental policy decisions of the forum. Thus, the applicable priority rule may be set aside if its application in a concrete case is manifestly contrary to the public policy of the forum (Article 23(1)). The attribute 'manifestly' is used to emphasise that public policy exceptions should be interpreted restrictively and be invoked only in exceptional cases of fundamental importance to the forum.[18]

Deviating from the traditional approach, the convention does not allow the substitution of the priority rules of the forum for the priority rules of the applicable law. The rationale underlying this approach is that such substitution would create uncertainty, which would negatively affect the availability and the cost of credit. Once the offensive priority rule of the applicable law is set aside, the balance of the applicable priority rules should apply (Article 23(2)). There is one exception. Super-priority rules of the forum, such as rules in favour of the state for taxes or of employees for wages, may apply in the place of the displaced applicable priority rules (Article 23(3)).

---

18 See "Guide to Enactment of the UNCITRAL Model Law on Cross-Border Insolvency", para 89, in UNCITRAL Yearbook vol XXVIII: 1997 (available also on UNCITRAL's website, *supra* n 1).

### 5.5 Law applicable to priority in proceeds

One of the legal obstacles to receivables financing is the lack of a property right in proceeds. Due to the differences among legal systems as to the nature and the treatment of rights in proceeds, the convention does not contain a general substantive or private international law rule as to priority in proceeds. However, it does contain a limited proceeds rule, according to which in certain circumstances priority in proceeds follows the priority in the receivables (Article 24). The convention refers to cases in which the assignor receives payment on behalf of the debtor and such payments are reasonably identifiable (eg, they are held in a separate deposit or securities account). This provision is intended to ensure that assignees in practices, such as securitisation or undisclosed invoice discounting, have a right in proceeds. This 'lock-box' kind of provision may well make possible receivables financing in countries in which such financing is not possible because property rights in proceeds are not recognised.

### 5.6 Optional substantive law priority rules

As mentioned, the convention offers states three substantive law priority rules to choose from by way of declaration (ie, first to conclude a contract of assignment, first to notify the debtor and first to file a notice about the assignment in a public filing office; Annex to the convention). These optional model provisions annexed to the convention may be of value to states that have no priority rules or have insufficient priority rules. The convention provides states with a choice, since no agreement could be reached on one priority rule. In any case, in an environment characterised by free competition, the system that provides the most economic benefits will prevail.[19]

It may be interesting to note that states that wish to adopt priority rules based on the registration of a notice about the assignment in a public registry are offered a choice between using an existing registration system or a new national or international registration system (Article 42). In particular as to the international registration system, the convention provides a mechanism for contracting states to designate a supervising authority, appoint the first registrar and prepare the necessary regulations (Article 42(6)).

## 6. Independent private international law rules

### 6.1 Scope and purpose

The convention contains in Chapter V a set of private international law rules that may apply if the forum is in a contracting state, whether or not the assignor or, for the purpose of the debtor-related provisions, the debtor is located in a contracting state, or the law governing the receivable is the law of a contracting state (Articles 1(3) and 26).

The purpose of these rules is twofold. With respect to transactions to which the

19 For the economic value of a filing system, see Steven L Schwarcz, "A perfection system for cross-border receivables financing", U PA J Int'l Econ L (1999). The commission's further work on security interests may provide additional guidance to states in this regard (see *supra* n 10).

provisions of the convention other than Chapter V would also be applicable, these rules may apply to fill gaps in the convention (Article 7(2)). With respect to transactions to which the provisions of the convention other than Chapter V would not be applicable (because of the lack of a territorial connection with a contracting state), these rules operate as a mini private international law convention.

However, states may declare that they do not wish to be bound by these rules (Article 39). This reservation was allowed to ensure that states that wished to adopt the convention would not be precluded from doing so just because the independent private international law rules were inconsistent with the own relevant rules. However, particular attention was given to the need to avoid such inconsistencies with texts such as the Rome Convention.

### 6.2 Form of the contract of assignment

If the contract of assignment is concluded between persons located in the same state, formal validity is subject to the law of the state which governs the contract or of the state in which it is concluded (Article 27 (1)).

If a contract of assignment is concluded between persons located in different states, the contract is formally valid if it satisfies the formal requirements of either the law which governs it or the law of one of those states (Article 27(2)).

### 6.3 Law applicable to the mutual rights and obligations of the assignor and the assignee

The mutual rights and obligations of the assignor and the assignee (eg, the interpretation of the terms and conditions, the assignee's obligation to extend credit, the existence and effect of representations) are subject to the law of their choice (Article 28(1)).

The parties' freedom of choice is subject to the public policy of the forum and the mandatory rules of the forum or a closely connected third country (Articles 31 and 32).

In the absence of a choice of law, the law of the state with which the contract of assignment is most closely connected governs (Article 28(2)). The closest-connection test was adopted in this case since it is unlikely to have much impact in view of the fact that in the vast majority of cases parties chose the applicable law.

### 6.4 Law applicable to the rights and obligations of the assignee and the debtor

The relationship between the assignee and the debtor, the conditions under which the assignment can be invoked as against the debtor and contractual limitations on the assignment are subject to the law governing the original contract (Article 29). The fact that most of these issues are covered by the substantive law rules of the convention limits the impact of this provision. However, certain issues were deliberately not covered in the substantive law rules of the convention, such as the question as to when a right of set-off is available to the debtor under Article 18. In particular, this last question is governed by Article 29, at least with respect to transaction set-off (ie, set-off arising from the original contract or another contract that was part of the same transaction).

Another question falling within the scope of Article 29 is the effect of anti-assignment clauses in the case of assignments of receivables to which Article 9 does not apply (either because they relate to assignments of non-trade receivables or because the debtor is not located in a state party to the convention).

However, statutory limitations are not covered in Article 29. While some statutory limitations are aimed at protecting the debtor, many statutory limitations are intended to protect the assignor. So in the absence of a clear way to draw a distinction between the various types of statutory limitation, it would be inappropriate to subject them to the law governing the original contract. In any case, with the exception of certain statutory limitations (Article 9(1)), the convention does not affect statutory limitations (Article 9(3)).

### 6.5 Law applicable to priority

Priority is referred to the law of the assignor's location (Article 30). The value of this rule is that it may apply to transactions to which Article 22, which it repeats, does not apply because of the absence of a territorial connection between an assignment and a state party to the convention.

## 7. Final provisions

The convention will enter into force upon ratification by five states (Article 45). States may exclude by declaration further practices, but not practices relating to 'trade receivables' as they are broadly defined in Article 9(3) (Article 41). The convention prevails over the Ottawa Convention (Article 38). However, this does not affect the application of the Ottawa Convention to the rights and obligations of a debtor if the receivables convention does not apply to that debtor (ie, if the debtor is not in a state party to the Receivables Convention or the law governing the original contract is not the law of a state party to the Receivables Convention).

## 8. Conclusion

With the right mix of substantive and private international law rules, the convention could have "a dramatic impact on removing significant legal barriers in the financing of international trade"[20] and has been rightly hailed as "the first step towards the globalization of asset-based lending".[21]

It eliminates or reduces a number of obstacles to cross-border transactions relating mainly to certain statutory limitations and to contractual limitations. The

---

20 Harry C Sigman & Edwin E Smith, "The Draft UNCITRAL Convention on Assignment of Receivables in International Trade: A Summary of the Key Provisions as Completion Draws Near," 33 UCC L J 344, 356 (2001).

21 Michael Carsella, "Uncitral Update", 5 *Secured Lender* 6 (1999). The potential of the United Nations Convention on the Assignment of Receivables in International Trade is generally recognised by commentators. See Dorothee Janzen, "*Der UNCITRAL-Konventionsentwurf zum Recht der Internationalen Finanzierungsabtretung, Symposium in Hamburg am 18. und 19. September 1998*" , 63 *Rabels Zeitschrift* 368 (1999); I Lojendio Osborne, "*Projecto de convención internacional sobre cesión de creditos, Estudios de derecho mercantil: homenaje al Profesor Justino F. Duque Dominguez*", 2 Valladolid 1251 (1998); Jean-Pierre Mattout, "*Cessions internationales de créances, Les besoins de la pratique*", 75 *Revue de Droit Bancaire et de la Bourse* 165 (1999); Schwarcz, *supra* n 19; Jean Stoufflet, "*Cessions internationales de créances, Les contraintes juridiques actuelles*", 75 *Revue de Droit Bancaire et de la Bourse* 169 (1999).

validation of assignments of future receivables, bulk assignments and assignments made despite anti-assignment clauses in the relevant original contracts is particularly significant in this regard.

In addition, the convention promotes certainty with respect to a number of substantive law issues, such as those relating to the debtor's rights and obligations. Of particular importance is the structuring of the debtor's discharge around an objective criterion (ie, written notification) and the separation of the debtor's discharge from issues of priority, as well as the preservation of the debtor's rights and defences.

Moreover, the convention breaks new ground in centralising all priority issues to the law of the assignor's location. One of the most important achievements of the convention may well prove to be the referral of priority in proceeds, covered by a so-called 'lock-box arrangement', to the law of the assignor's location. This rule may well facilitate significantly receivables financing in countries in which property rights in proceeds are not recognised.

Further, the convention's independent private international law rules provide useful guidance in filling gaps in the convention and add value to the convention to the extent they unify generally applicable private international law rules.

Finally, the optional substantive law priority rules contained in the Annex to the convention usefully supplement the private international law priority rules, referring to the law of the assignor's location, in the case of states desiring to modernise or harmonise their priority regimes.

*The views expressed in this paper are the personal views of the author and do not reflect the views of UNCITRAL or the United Nations. This paper is based on an article published in the* Uniform Law Review/Revue de droit uniforme *(Rome) 7:49- 67, 2002-2.*

# Bank accounts

**Spiros V Bazinas**
UNCITRAL
United Nations Office of Legal Affairs

## I. Introduction

The legislative guide being prepared by the United Nations Commission on International Trade Law (UNCITRAL)[1] on secured transactions, which deals with proprietary (as opposed to personal) security rights in movable (as opposed to immovable) property, is about to be completed.[2]

The main objective of the legislation recommended in the draft guide is to facilitate secured financing. On the assumption that security reduces the risk of non-payment, secured lending is considered as having the potential of enhancing the amount of credit that can be made available and of decreasing its cost. At the same time, the draft guide recognises that such an economic result cannot be reached automatically only through the enactment of appropriate legislation, but depends largely on the relevant infrastructure, judiciary and enforcement mechanisms existing in a legal system.

The current status of secured credit law in the world (in both developed and developing countries) indicates the need for reform in the area of secured credit law in general. At a time when markets have become global, secured credit law continues to remain largely territorial. The divergences among the various legal systems on fundamental issues are such that often the applicable law is set aside as contrary to the public policy of the forum state and a security right effectively created in one country may have little value once the encumbered assets move to another country. This situation can hardly be regarded as being conducive to the unhindered development of international trade.

In addition, with few exceptions, secured credit law is based on a multiplicity of statutes (or non-statutory rules) that leave gaps, present inconsistencies and, in any case, create legal uncertainty. Uncertainty in this context means credit at a high cost, less credit or no credit, depending on whether the risk can be reasonably estimated. The effect of this result on the development of national trade and the competitiveness of businesses in international markets cannot be anything but negative.

Moreover, new types of asset, such as intellectual property, are emerging as valuable sources of credit against a backdrop of legislation that can be described, at

1 For a brief description of UNCITRAL and its work, see www.uncitral.org/en-index.htm.
2 Documents relating to the draft guide (A/CN.9/631and Addenda 1 to 11) are available on the UNCITRAL website at www.uncitral.org/uncitral/en/commission/sessions/40th.html.

the very least, as outdated.[3] In many developed countries, practice relies on its own ingenuity and that of its lawyers and judges (this is true even in the most code-faithful civil law countries, such as Germany). When things go wrong and a debtor goes bust, creditors start praying. This is not a climate in which low-cost secured credit can be made available and play its role in economic development.

Each chapter of the draft guide has two parts: a commentary and a set of legislative recommendations. The commentary includes an analysis of the key issues and the ways in which they can be addressed in domestic secured transactions legislation. The recommendations are addressed to legislators and are very detailed and specific. Each chapter has a set of legislative recommendations that apply generally to all types of asset and a set of asset-specific recommendations that apply specifically to certain types of asset (eg, receivables, rights to payment of funds credited to a bank account, proceeds of independent undertakings, negotiable instruments and negotiable documents).[4]

This chapter address issues relating to security rights in rights to payment of funds credited in a bank account because of their importance (the bulk of corporate wealth is in receivables, bank accounts and securities).

## 2. Scope of the draft guide

The draft guide deals mainly with consensual security rights – that is, rights *in rem* created by agreement. 'Security right' is defined to mean "a consensual property right in movable property and attachments that secures payment or other performance of one or more obligations, regardless of whether the parties have denominated it as a security right".[5]

However, the chapter on priority deals with all possible priority contests, including contests between consensual and non-consensual security rights, such as the rights of preferential creditors or other rights, such as the rights of an enforcing unsecured creditor (Recommendations 89 and 90).[6]

Under the draft guide, in principle, all types of asset may serve as collateral ('encumbered assets', in the terminology of the draft guide) and all types of obligation (whether present or future, determined or determinable) may be secured. Any person, legal or natural, including a consumer, can act as a secured creditor and debtor or other third-party grantor. However, in the case of a conflict with consumer protection law, consumer protection law will prevail. While the focus of the draft guide is on goods, including equipment and inventory, the draft guide also deals with security rights in receivables (and, to some extent, sales of receivables), negotiable instruments, negotiable documents, rights to payment of funds credited to bank accounts and proceeds of letters of credit and independent guarantees (the draft guide uses the term 'independent undertaking'; Recommendation 2).

---

3 For a discussion of security rights in intellectual property, see document A/CN.9/632 at daccessdds.un.org/doc/UNDOC/GEN/V07/827/54/PDF/V0782754.pdf?OpenElement.

4 For a discussion of the draft guide, see *Reforming Secured Transactions, The UNCITRAL Legislative Guide as an inspiration*, Bénédict Foëx/Luc Thévenoz/Spiros V Bazinas (eds).

5 See A/CN.9/631/Add.1, para 19.

6 Recommendations referred to in this article are contained in document A/CN.9/631.

The law recommended in the draft guide does not apply to security rights in aircraft, railway rolling stock, space objects, ships and intellectual property to the extent that this is inconsistent with other law governing security rights in such assets (Recommendations 4(a) and (b)). Neither does it apply to security rights in securities (although the issue of whether the exclusion will be limited to intermediated securities only is still open; Recommendation 4(c)) or immovable property (Recommendation 5). Securities are typically subject to special legislation and to work by UNIDROIT[7] and the Hague Conference on Private International Law. Immovable property raises different issues and is subject to well-developed law.[8]

## 3. The creation of a security right in a right to payment of funds credited to a bank account

The draft guide contains a set of definitions and rules of interpretation. Definitions and rules of interpretation are not part of the legislative recommendations. They are rather indicative and are offered to the national legislature as a suggestion. However, the commentary emphasises the importance of the definitions to a full understanding of the recommendations of the draft guide and thus suggests that the national legislature uses them.

'Bank account' is defined to "mean an account that is maintained by a bank into which funds may be deposited or credited. The term includes a checking or other current account, as well as a savings or time deposit account. The term does not include a claim against the bank evidenced by a negotiable instrument".[9]

The encumbered asset is not the bank account itself or the bank-client relationship, but rather the right to payment of funds credited to the bank account. Further, to ensure that the rules applicable to receivables do not apply to rights to payment of funds credited to bank accounts, the definition of the term 'receivable' provides that the term "means a right to payment of a monetary obligation excluding rights to payment evidenced by a negotiable instrument, the obligation to pay under an independent undertaking and the obligation of a bank to pay funds credited to a bank account".[10]

The main differences in the treatment of rights to payment of funds credited to bank accounts lie in:

- the consequences of an assignment made despite an anti-assignment agreement (this binds a debtor of a receivable, but not a depositary bank);
- the way in which a security right is made effective against third parties (by registration in the case of a receivable; by registration or control in the case of a bank account);
- priority (in the case of a bank account, control beats registration); and
- applicable law issues (in the case of a receivable, the law of the grantor's

---

7 The International Institute for the Unification of Private Law.

8 Intermediated securities are the subject of work by UNIDROIT (see www.unidroit.org/english/workprogramme/study078/item1/archive/s-78-18.pdf). The Hague Conference on Private International Law also prepared the Hague Convention on the Law Applicable in Respect of Certain Rights in Securities (http://hcch.e-vision.nl/index_en.php?act=conventions.text&cid=72).

9 See A/CN.9/631/Add.1, para 19.

10 *Id.*

location; in the case of a bank account, the law of the relevant branch or the law specified in the account agreement).

Like a security right in any other type of movable property, a security right in a right to payment of funds credited to a bank account is created by agreement between the grantor and the secured creditor (Recommendation 12). For a security agreement to be effective, "it must reflect the intent of the parties to create a security right, identify the secured creditor and the grantor, and describe the secured obligation and the encumbered assets. A generic description of the encumbered assets is sufficient (e.g. 'all present and future assets' or 'all present and future inventory')" (Recommendation 13).

The security agreement may be oral if accompanied by transfer of possession of the encumbered asset. In the case of a security right in a right to payment of funds credited to a bank account or other intangible asset, "the agreement must be concluded in or evidenced by a writing that in conjunction with the course of conduct between the parties indicates the grantor's intent to create a security right" (Recommendation 14). The intention is to introduce a very low threshold for a written form requirement. Further, the draft guide provides that an electronic communication meets the written form requirement (Recommendation 11).

If the right to payment of funds credited to a bank account asset exists and the grantor has rights in it at the time of conclusion of the agreement, the security right is created at that time. If the asset to be encumbered does not exist at that time or if the grantor acquires rights thereafter, the security right is created when the asset comes into existence or the grantor acquires rights in the asset (Recommendation 12).

Once a security right is created, it is effective as between the grantor and the secured creditor. Effectiveness as against third parties is in principle, subject to further requirements (see section 5).

By splitting effectiveness in such a way and establishing the notion of priority, the draft guide makes it possible for more creditors to obtain a security right in the same asset, while regulating their priority. As a result, debtors may use the full value of their assets to obtain credit from more than one creditor by creating more than one security right in the same assets, while they remain in possession of their assets to generate the income necessary to pay their debts. At the same time, creditors are provided with an objective way to determine their priority before they extend credit, thus being able to structure their credit agreements accordingly.

Further, as the draft guide introduces further requirements for a security right to become effective against third parties, treating effectiveness against all as a single issue would inadvertently result in unnecessarily making the creation of a security more burdensome. Registration or control is not necessary for a security right to become effective as between the grantor and the secured creditor. And registration as a method of creation would be particularly burdensome for acquisition financing transactions, such as retention-of-title sales, hire-purchase agreements and financial leases.

As, upon its creation, a security right in a right to payment of funds credited to a bank account is effective only as between the grantor and the secured creditor (and the grantor's unsecured creditors), it is effective even if it is created despite a contrary agreement between the grantor account holder and the depositary bank. This result does not affect the rights or obligations of the depositary bank, as the depositary bank is not bound by this security agreement and has no obligation whatsoever towards the secured creditor, unless it consents to the creation of a security right (Recommendation 27).

## 4. The third-party effectiveness of a security right in a right to payment of finds credited to a bank account

A security right in a right to payment of funds credited to a bank account may be made effective against third parties by registration of a notice in a general security rights registry or by control (Recommendation 50).

While registration of a notice provides an objective way of informing third parties, it may not be imposed on depositary banks without delaying or adding costs to normal banking transactions. So an additional method of third-party effectiveness is introduced, namely 'control'. Control relies on the participation of the depositary bank, since it exists only if:

- the depositary bank is the secured creditor;
- the depositary bank concludes a control agreement with the grantor account holder; and
- the secured creditor or the depositary bank opens a new bank account in the name of the secured creditor to which the funds from the account of the grantor-initial account holder are transferred.[11]

There is no obligation on a depositary bank to enter into a control agreement. In addition, a secured creditor's rights are subject to the rights and obligations of the depositary bank under law and practice governing bank accounts. Moreover, a control agreement requires the consent of the grantor (as well as of the depositary bank), and the grantor retains the right to deal with the funds in the bank account until the secured creditor instructs the depositary bank otherwise (although in some control agreements, the funds would be blocked from the time of the conclusion of the control agreement). This covers situations where:

- an existing account is transferred to the secured creditor;
- the secured creditor agrees with the grantor that funds should be deposited to an account to be opened later; and
- the secured creditor is the only account holder (ie, not merely a joint account holder).

Once a security right is effective against third parties, it remains effective against third parties even if there is a change in the method of achieving third-party effectiveness (Recommendation 47). For example, if the depositary bank relinquishes control and registers, third-party effectiveness dates from the time of registration. This means that third-party effectiveness is continuous and does not depend on the particular way in which it is achieved. However, if there is a time lapse, third-party

11 *Id.*

effectiveness may be re-established, but it begins as of the time it is re-established (Recommendation 48).

If a right to payment of funds credited to a bank account is proceeds of another asset, a security right in such proceeds is effective against third parties when the proceeds arise, which means that there is no need to have a separate act of registration or control (Recommendation 40). This rule reflects the normal expectations of parties and avoids overburdening the parties with additional registration or other requirements.

## 5. The registry system

The purpose of the registry system is to provide:

- a method to achieve third-party effectiveness;
- a basis for determining priority; and
- an objective source of information for third parties.

Registration of a notice about the security right in the general security rights registry is the main method to render a non-possessory security right effective as against third parties.

The notice should contain only:

- the names and addresses of the grantor and the secured creditor;
- a description of the encumbered assets; and
- the term of the registration (if the parties choose to select the duration of registration).

If a state enacting the recommendations considers that a reference to the maximum amount for which the security right may be enforced is necessary to facilitate subordinate lending, the notice should also include a statement of that maximum amount (Recommendation 58).

The condition added in this recommendation is due to a difference of opinion on this matter. It is argued that reference to a maximum amount should not be required as it would:

- overburden transactions in which the amount of the secured obligation fluctuates;
- result in parties having to state amounts much higher than the amount of credit actually provided, thus limiting the grantor's ability to obtain more credit; and
- limit the amount of credit available by the primary source of credit for a grantor.

Unlike traditional real estate registries, the legal consequence of registration is not the creation of a security right. Registration does not establish a non-existing right. It mainly provides a system to determine priority among rights that have been effectively created and warns potential new financiers of security rights that other creditors might have.

The reasons for this structure of the registration system are purely practical. Such a registry is sufficient to promote access to secured credit. Debtors can use the full value of their assets to obtain credit by giving a security right in the same assets to more than one creditor. Creditors have an objective way of determining their priority and other third parties are given sufficient warning permitting them to take the necessary action to ensure their rights before offering credit to the debtor.

Title registries requiring registration of documents are suitable for high-value assets and real estate, but would unnecessarily burden financing markets relying on movable assets with additional costs, delays and inflexibility in dealing with fluctuating amounts of secured obligations, changing pools of encumbered assets (eg, inventory) and assets that are acquired by the grantor after the conclusion of the security agreement (ie, future or after-acquired assets). In fact, the whole registration system recommended in the draft guide is based on a flexible registry, which would allow interested parties to register or to search the record in a simple, quick and inexpensive way (for a description of the key characteristics of the registry, see Recommendations 55 and 56).

## 6. The priority of a security right in a right to payment of funds credited to a bank account as against the rights of competing claimants

'Priority' means the right of a person to obtain the economic benefit of its security right in preference to a competing claimant.[12]

'Competing claimant' means:

- another secured creditor with a security right in the same encumbered asset (whether as an original encumbered asset or proceeds);
- the seller, financial lessor or purchase-money lender of the same encumbered asset which has retained title to it;
- another creditor of the grantor which has a right in the same encumbered asset (eg, by operation of law, attachment or seizure or similar process);
- the insolvency representative in the insolvency of the grantor; or
- any buyer or other transferee (including a lessee or licensee) of the encumbered asset.[13]

The priority of a security right extends to all obligations secured by a security agreement. However, if the registered notice mentions a maximum amount, priority is limited to that amount (Recommendation 74). Whether a competing claimant has knowledge of the existence of a competing security right is irrelevant for the priority position of that competing claimant's right (Recommendation 75). However, knowledge that a transfer of funds out of bank account violates the rights of a creditor under a security agreement results in the transferee taking the funds subject to the security right (Recommendation 103).

The priority of a security right does not depend on the time when a secured obligation was incurred (Recommendation 76). This means that priority dates as of the time third-party effectiveness was achieved (provided, of course, that credit is extended). It also means that all advances made in the context of a security

12 *Id.*
13 *Id.*

agreement have the same priority.

Recognising the need for flexibility in the regulation of priority to meet the needs of financing practices, the draft guide provides that a secured creditor may subordinate its priority unilaterally or by agreement in favour of an existing or future competing claimant (Recommendation 77).

A security right in a right to payment of funds credited to a bank account made effective against third parties by control has priority over a security right made effective against third parties by registration of a notice in the general security rights registry (Recommendation 101). This rule reflects normal banking law and practice, recognising the privileged position of the depositary bank as compared to creditors with a security right in a right to payment of funds credited to a bank account.

The depositary bank has priority even over a secured creditor with which it has concluded a control agreement, other than a secured creditor which has acquired control by becoming the account holder (Recommendation 101). This approach is based on the following reasoning:

- A security right of a depositary bank should be treated no less favourably than a right of set-off which would also have priority;
- A depositary bank would not enter into a control agreement without knowing that it would have priority and that could have a negative impact on the availability of credit; and
- Secured creditors could always seek to obtain a subordination agreement with the depositary bank changing the order of priority provided by the law.

If the depositary bank agrees to open a new account in favour of the secured creditor and transfer to that account the funds in the account of the grantor initial account holder, this in effect would operate as a subordination agreement.

To avoid interfering with the law of set-off, the draft guide provides that any rights of set-off that the depositary bank might have under law other than the secured transactions law have priority over any security right. This rule applies to all secured creditors except a secured creditor which acquired control by becoming the account holder (Recommendation 102). In such case the depositary bank will have agreed to open a new account in the name of the secured creditor and will have already settled any rights of set-off it might have against the grantor initial account holder.

If the depositary bank has concluded control agreements with more than one creditor, priority among those creditors is determined by the order in which the control agreements were concluded. This rule reflects a policy underlying the draft guide that grantors should be allowed to use the full value of their assets to obtain credit. As long as there are sufficient funds in a bank account, there is no reason to limit the account holder's ability to obtain credit from the same or other sources.

## 7. Pre-default rights and obligations of the parties

The draft guide confirms the freedom of the parties to structure their security agreement in any way they wish so as to address their needs. At the same time, the draft guide recognises that party autonomy may have to be limited to avoid affecting rights of third parties.

The draft guide also provides a set of non-mandatory rules that are applicable prior to default in the absence of agreement of the parties (Recommendation 108). Those rules advance a number of policy objectives, such as the reasonable allocation of responsibility for the care of the encumbered assets and the promotion of access to credit at affordable costs.

In addition, the draft guide includes a set of mandatory rules that deal with issues such as:

- the duty of care of the person in possession of the encumbered assets; and
- the duty to return the assets or terminate any notice on the record of the registry upon full payment and termination of all credit commitments (Recommendation 109).

## 8. Rights and obligations of the depositary bank

To ensure that secured transactions law does not change the position of the depositary bank under the account agreement and the law applicable to it and banking activities in general, the draft guide provides that the creation of a security right in a right to payment of funds credited to a bank account does not affect the rights and obligations of the depositary bank. At the same time, recognising the need for flexibility, the draft guide permits a bank to negotiate and agree to such a change (Recommendation 122(a)).

The secured transactions law recommended in the draft guide gives rise to no rights of set-off on the part of the depositary bank. However, if such a right exists under law other than secured transactions law, it is not impaired by any security right that the depositary bank might have (Recommendation 122(b)). This means that the depositary bank is free to decide whether to exercise a right of set-off or a security right.

The rights and obligations of the bank and its relationship to its client are subject to banking and other law. The draft guide does nothing to change that. However, the draft guide does permit the creation of a security right in a right to payment of funds credited to a bank account and notions such as 'control' and 'priority'.

To avoid any misunderstanding as to the effect of those provisions, the draft guide provides that nothing in the secured transactions law obliges a depositary bank to pay any person other than a person that has control with respect to a right to payment of funds credited, and control requires the consent of the depositary bank (Recommendation 123(a)).

Further, the draft guide provides that the depositary bank has no obligation to respond to any requests for information on issues such as whether a control agreement has been concluded or whether an account holder has the right to dispose of funds credited in the account (Recommendation 123(b)).

## 9. Post-default rights

The draft guide does not define what 'default' means. It leaves this to the security agreement and the law governing that agreement. However, to enhance certainty with respect to the enforcement of a security right which may affect the availability and the cost of credit, the draft guide sets out in detail the remedies available to the secured creditor and those available to the grantor of the security right.

Generally, in the case of default, the secured creditor may:

- obtain possession of a tangible encumbered asset;
- sell or otherwise dispose of, lease or license an encumbered asset;
- propose to the grantor that the secured creditor accept an encumbered asset in total or partial satisfaction of the secured obligation; or
- exercise any other remedy provided in the security agreement, except to the extent inconsistent with the secured transactions or other relevant law (Recommendation 134).

Similarly, the grantor may:

- pay in full the secured obligation, including interests and costs, until disposition, collection or acceptance of encumbered assets, and obtain a release of the encumbered assets from the security right;
- apply to the court or other authority for relief if the secured creditor is not complying with its obligations;
- propose to the secured creditor or reject the proposal of the secured creditor to accept the encumbered assets in total or partial satisfaction of the secured obligation; or
- exercise any other right or remedy provided in the security agreement except to the extent inconsistent with the secured transactions or other relevant law (Recommendation 135).

In order to avoid abuse of rights by any party, the draft guide sets a general standard of conduct that refers to good faith and reasonable commercial standards. Failure of a party to comply with these standards may make this party liable for damages (Recommendations 128 and 133).

In recognising the security agreement as a source of remedies, the draft guide gives appropriate recognition to party autonomy, which is essential for parties in structuring their transactions so as to address their particular needs. At the same time, the draft guide sets the appropriate limits of the principle of party autonomy. The general standard of conduct cannot be waived or varied. To avoid abuse of the secured creditor's dominant position in the negotiations, no right or remedy may be waived or varied prior to the debtor's default. Such a waiver is permitted after default as long as it does not affect the rights of third parties. Any person challenging such an agreement has the burden of proving that it is inconsistent with the general standard of conduct or exceeds the limits of party autonomy set out in the draft guide (Recommendations 129 to 132).

The draft guide discusses judicial versus extrajudicial enforcement and their relative advantages and disadvantages. Where extrajudicial enforcement is permitted, the draft guide refers to safeguards to avoid abuse of power by the secured creditor and to the right of the debtor or other grantor to challenge the actions of the secured creditor before a court or other authority (Recommendation 136). Where use is made of the judicial system, the draft guide highlights the need for expeditious court proceedings and enforcement mechanisms (Recommendation 137).

Once the encumbered assets are disposed of out of court and the secured obligation has been satisfied, any surplus must be returned to subordinate claimants which gave prior written notice to the enforcing secured creditor and any balance remaining to the grantor. In any case, the secured creditor may pay any surplus to a judicial or other authority. In the case of a judicial disposition, distribution of proceeds takes place in accordance with the relevant law applicable to execution proceedings. The debtor is liable for any shortfall still owing after application of the proceeds to the secured obligation (Recommendations 152 to 155).

Specifically with respect to a security right in a right to payment of funds credited to a bank account, the draft guide provides that the secured creditor may collect or otherwise enforce (eg, retain or assign) its security right. However, such enforcement may not change the position of the depositary bank under its account agreement and the applicable law (Recommendation 167).

In the case of judicial enforcement, a transferee of rights in encumbered assets acquires the rights prescribed in the relevant law (Recommendation 157). In the case of extrajudicial enforcement, a transferee acquires the assets free of any security right of the enforcing secured creditor and any subordinate rights (Recommendation 158).

If a secured creditor has control, it may enforce its security right without applying to a court or other authority (Recommendation 168). This rule reflects practical reality. If the secured creditor is the account holder or the depositary bank, or has concluded a control agreement with the grantor and the depositary bank, there is no need to require a court judgment for the secured creditor to exercise its rights. Of course, the grantor may always go to court to prevent out-of-court enforcement or seek other relief (Recommendation 141).

If, on the other hand, the secured creditor does not have control, it can enforce its security right only by applying to a court or other competent authority, unless the depositary bank agrees otherwise (Recommendation 169). This rule recognises that a security right may be enforced out of court, as long as the rights of the depositary bank are not affected. Of course, the grantor may have recourse to a court and prevent out-of-court enforcement or seek other relief (Recommendation 141).

## 10. Insolvency

The treatment of security rights in the case of insolvency of the grantor[14] in the draft guide reflects the principles of the UNCITRAL Legislative Guide on Insolvency Law.[15] Where necessary, a few additional recommendations have been added to clarify matters of interest to secured creditors that are not specifically addressed in the Insolvency Guide.

In principle, encumbered assets, including a right to payment of funds credited to a bank account, are part of the estate (Recommendation 35 of the Insolvency Guide) and individual actions, even by secured creditors, to perfect or enforce security rights are stayed (Recommendations 39(a) and 46(b) of the Insolvency Guide). If, however, a security right was already effective against third parties at the time of commencement of an insolvency proceeding, the secured creditor may take

14 Reference is made to the insolvency of the grantor because if the debtor is a different person and becomes insolvent, the creditor is an unsecured creditor in this insolvency proceeding.

15 See www.uncitral.org/uncitral/en/uncitral_texts/insolvency/2004Guide.html.

action to preserve the third-party effectiveness of the security right to the extent and in the manner permitted by secured transactions law (Recommendation 179).

The stay of individual actions remains effective throughout the insolvency proceedings until:

- the court grants relief from the stay;
- a reorganisation plan becomes effective; or
- in liquidation proceedings, a fixed time period expires, unless it is extended by a court (Recommendation 49 of the Insolvency Guide).

A secured creditor may apply to a court to provide protection of the value of the encumbered assets through, for example, cash payments by the estate, provision of additional security rights or other means determined by the court (Recommendation 50 of the Insolvency Guide). A secured creditor may also seek from a court the lifting of the stay if, for example:

- the encumbered assets are not necessary for the reorganisation of the grantor's business;
- the value of the encumbered assets is diminishing, while the secured creditor is not protected against diminution of value; or
- in reorganisation, a plan is not approved within the prescribed time limits (Recommendation 51 of the Insolvency Guide).

The insolvency administrator may use or dispose of the encumbered assets free of any security rights in the ordinary course of business, except cash proceeds. Cash proceeds may be used or disposed of if:

- the secured creditor consents;
- the secured creditor was given notice and an opportunity to be heard by a court; and
- the interests of the secured creditor will be protected against diminution in the value of the cash proceeds (Recommendations 52 and 59 of the Insolvency Guide).

The insolvency administrator may also use and dispose of encumbered assets even outside the ordinary course of business, subject to certain conditions, including:

- adequate notice to creditors;
- an opportunity for them to be heard by a court; and
- the preservation of the priority of the security rights in the proceeds of the sale of the encumbered assets (Recommendations 52, 55 and 58 of the Insolvency Guide).

The insolvency administrator may also give further security rights in already encumbered assets to secure post-commencement finance. Such further security rights do not have priority over existing security rights unless:

- the existing secured creditors agree to subordinate their rights to the rights of the post-commencement financiers; or
- the court authorises the creation of post-commencements security rights

with priority over pre-commencement security rights (Recommendations 53, 65, 66 and 67 of the Insolvency Guide).

Further, the insolvency administrator may relinquish assets provided that notice is given to creditors and they have an opportunity to object. Such notice is not necessary where:

- a secured claim exceeds the value of the encumbered assets; and
- the assets are not required for the reorganisation or the sale of the business as a going concern (Recommendation 62 of the Insolvency Guide).

While the Insolvency Guide recognises that the effective creation of a security right is subject to law other than insolvency law, a security agreement may, under the applicable insolvency law, be subject to avoidance on the same grounds as any other transaction (eg, it is a preferential or fraudulent transfer taking place in the suspect period) (Recommendation (88) of the Insolvency Guide).

As encumbered assets are part of the estate, subject to stay and other limitations, secured creditors should have a right to participate in the insolvency proceedings and be heard on any issue that affects their rights and obligations. For example, a secured creditor may:

- object to any act that requires court approval;
- request review by a court of any act for which court approval was not required or not requested; and
- request any relief available to the secured creditor in the insolvency proceedings (Recommendation 137 of the Insolvency Guide).

If voting on approval of a reorganisation plan is conducted by reference to classes, the Insolvency Guide leaves it to each insolvency law to determine how the vote would be treated. However, at least one class of creditors whose rights are modified or affected by the plan must approve it. In addition, if the insolvency law requires court confirmation of an approved plan, the court can confirm the plan, provided that:

- the necessary approvals have been obtained and the approval process was properly conducted;
- creditors will receive under the plan at least as much as they would have received in liquidation, unless they have specifically agreed to receive less;
- the plan does not contain provisions contrary to law;
- administrative expenses will be paid in full, unless otherwise agreed by the holder of such a claim; and
- unless otherwise agreed, the ranking of a class of creditors that has voted against the plan will not be changed and distribution to that class under the plan will be in line with that ranking (see Recommendation 152 of the Insolvency Guide).

In determining the liquidation value of encumbered assets in a reorganisation proceeding, consideration should be given to the use of the assets and the purpose of the valuation (Recommendation 181).

The draft guide provides that the priority of a security right under law other than insolvency law continues unimpaired in the case of insolvency except if, under insolvency law, another claim is given priority (Recommendation 178). The draft guide also provides that such exceptions should be limited and clearly stated in the insolvency law (Recommendation 188 of the Insolvency Guide).

With respect to applicable law issues, the Insolvency Guide provides that the validity and effectiveness of rights and claims existing at the time of commencement of an insolvency proceeding should be determined by the conflict of laws rules of the state in which the insolvency proceeding is commenced. It also provides that the law of the state in which the insolvency proceeding is commenced (*lex fori concursus*) should govern, among other things, the treatment of security rights (Recommendations 30 and 31 of the Insolvency Guide).

The draft guide includes an additional rule, under which the law applicable to the creation, third-party effectiveness and priority of a security right is the same law that would be applicable in the absence of insolvency proceedings. However, this rule should not affect the application of insolvency rules, such as rules relating to the avoidance, priority or enforcement of security rights (Recommendation 171).

## 11. Conflict of laws

The conflict of laws chapter of the draft guide – which discusses the rules determining the law applicable to the creation, third-party effectiveness, priority and enforcement of a security right – is one of the most important parts of the draft guide. It clarifies where a secured creditor must register and determines the territorial scope of application of the substantive law rules recommended

With respect to security rights in tangible assets, the draft guide recommends the law of the country where the assets are located (*lex rei sitae*) (Recommendation 202). Special rules are provided for security rights in:

- mobile goods (ie, the law of the grantor's location);
- goods that are subject to a title registration system (ie, the law of the state under whose authority the registry is organised);
- goods in transit; and
- export goods (Recommendation 203).

With respect to security right in intangible assets, the draft guide recommends the law of the grantor's location (Recommendation 204). This recommendation is consistent with the principles in Articles 22 and 30 of the United Nations Assignment Convention.[16]

However, the draft guide has a special rule for the law applicable to a security right in a right to payment of funds credited in a bank account. First, the scope of that rule is very broad and covers the creation, third-party effectiveness, priority and enforcement

16 For a discussion of the convention, see Spiros V Bazinas, "UNCITRAL's Contribution to the Unification of Receivables Financing Law: The United Nations Convention on the Assignment of Receivables in International Trade", *Revue de Droit Uniforme* 2003- 1/2, 49; and "Multi-jurisdictional receivables financing: UNCITRAL'S impact on securitization and cross-border perfection", 12 Duke J of Comp & Int'l L 365.

of a security right. It also covers the rights and duties of the depositary bank.

Second, the law applicable is not the law applicable to other intangibles. Two alternatives are offered. The first alternative refers to the law of the state in which the depositary bank has its place of business. In the case of places of business in more than one state, reference is made to the law of the state in which the branch that maintains the relevant account is located. This alternative is based on the premise that a bank account can be located and the law applicable to security rights in bank accounts should be the law that would be generally applicable to that bank.

The second alternative refers to the law of the state expressly stated in the account agreement, provided that the depositary bank has a branch in that state. This alternative is based on the assumption that, like cash in a securities account, cash in a bank account cannot be linked to a certain location and thus the law applicable to security rights in securities under the Hague Convention on the Law Applicable to Certain Rights in Respect of Securities Held with an Intermediary should apply.

The mutual rights and obligations of the grantor and the secured creditor with respect to a security right, whether arising from the security agreement or by law, are governed by the law governing the security agreement (Recommendation 212). This approach is intended to align the law governing the security agreement with the law applicable to the purely contractual rights and obligations of the parties, and thus be in line with the expectations of the parties.

The creation of a security right in proceeds is governed by the law governing the creation of the security right in the assets from which the proceeds arose (Recommendation 211(a)). So, for example, if the original encumbered assets are goods and the proceeds are a right to payment of funds in a bank account, the creation of a security right in the right to payment of funds credited to a bank account is governed by the law of the location of the goods. In this way, creditors obtaining a security right in goods will know that their right will extend to proceeds of goods subject to the law of the same state where the goods are located.

However, the third-party effectiveness and priority of a security right in proceeds are governed by the same law as the law governing those issues with respect to assets of the same kind as the proceeds (Recommendation 211(b)). So if the proceeds of goods are a right to payment of funds credited to a bank account, these issues will be subject to the law of the state in which the relevant branch is located or the law specified in the account agreement, depending on which alternative of Recommendation 206 a state adopts. This approach ensures that the rights of third parties in the proceeds as original encumbered assets will be subject to the same law, at least with respect to the issues of third-party effectiveness and priority.

## 12. Conclusions

The draft guide discusses in a comprehensive and systematic way most key issues to be addressed in legislation on security rights in tangible and intangible assets, with the exception of securities. The draft guide applies to all transactions that serve security purposes irrespective of their name.

In particular with respect to security rights in rights to payment of funds credited to bank accounts, the draft guide codifies current law with respect to the creation of a security right and introduces novel provisions with respect to the third-party effectiveness of such a right by registration or control. While the priority rules of the draft guide are structured around third-party effectiveness methods that will be new in many jurisdictions, their application will lead to results that are consistent with current law governing bank accounts. The main premise of this law is that the rights of the depositary bank under the account agreement and the law governing the agreement and banking activities in general should not be interfered with. The draft guide also includes comprehensive rules dealing with the enforcement of a security right in a right to payment of funds credited to a bank account, in and outside insolvency proceedings. The rules dealing with insolvency reflect the consensus achieved in UNCITRAL between the insolvency and the secured lender groups.

The only issue relating to security rights in rights to funds credited to a bank account with respect to which the draft guide does not have a single rule is the law applicable to such a security right. It is important for UNCITRAL to reach agreement on this issue. Otherwise, depending on where an issue arises, a different law may be applicable – a result that can be hardly described as being conducive to the harmonisation of the law of secured credit, which is one of the key objectives of the draft guide.

*The views expressed in chapter are the personal views of the author and do not reflect the views of the United Nations or UNCITRAL. This chapter is based on an article first published in* Insolvency and Restructuring International*, Volume 1, No 1, May 2007, and is published by kind permission of the International Bar Association, London.*

# Private equity

**Christopher Lawrence**
Macfarlanes

Structuring a debt finance package to fund any corporate acquisition or investment and negotiating its terms are a fundamental part of many corporate transactions, and the use of debt finance is a key tool to allow sufficient funds to be available to fund acquisitions and investments and to enhance the potential returns from them. The majority of this type of debt finance has historically been provided by the major commercial and investment banks; however, the debt finance industry has developed and matured during the past decade to offer increased liquidity levels, and funding on a secured and on an unsecured basis is now available from a wider class of banks, investment funds and, more recently, hedge funds – many of which operate solely in the secondary market.

The development of the debt finance industry, coupled with a period of low borrowing costs, has been one of the drivers of the buoyant private equity market of recent years. The private equity industry has pioneered the use of secured debt to enable it to benefit from maximised leverage ratios from even the lower-credit borrowers. During 2006 €302 billion of leverage loans were made to US and European borrowers owned by private equity sponsors,[1] predominately on a secured and highly structured basis. As the industry has evolved, the providers of debt finance have developed and expanded the variety of debt instruments they offer, resulting in a variety of complex and innovative debt finance structures being available to corporate and private equity investors, particularly in respect of subordinated and secured finance.

This chapter looks at typical debt finance structures used in the European debt markets to fund private equity sponsored leveraged acquisitions of private companies. However, many of the instruments and debt structures employed, and the terms of the debt, are similar to those employed by corporate borrowers raising debt funds.

## 1. A typical newco structure

A newco, or more commonly a series of newcos, will be incorporated to provide a tax-efficient holding company structure, and these newcos will be funded with a combination of equity, quasi-equity and debt finance to allow one or more of them to acquire the target group. Tax considerations may mean that these holding companies are incorporated and tax resident in jurisdictions which are not

1 Market data provided by Standard & Poor's Leveraged Commentary & Data (S&P LCD). The total figure of €302.8 billion comprised €186.9 billion for the US market and €115.9 billion for the European market.

associated with either the private equity sponsor or the target to be acquired. Consideration will also be made as to the laws of these jurisdictions relating to the granting of security and the ranking of debts – stable and creditor-friendly jurisdictions such as England and Wales, Luxembourg and the Netherlands are commonly chosen to ensure that the required debt structure can be created.

Either the lawyers or the accountants acting for the sponsor will develop this structure, which will be specifically tailored to the transaction and the tax sensitivities of the funds advised or managed by the sponsor which are investing in the acquisition. These advisers will prepare a detailed tax structure memorandum for the sponsor, which will provide an in-depth analysis of the relevant laws of the tax regimes applicable to the acquisition. Central to this structure will be the ability to achieve an optimum level of deductibility of the interest costs which will be incurred in respect of the various debt instruments which will be introduced into the structure to finance the acquisition.

Key features of the structure which will be covered by this structure memorandum may include:

- the choice of the jurisdiction of incorporation and tax residence of the newcos and the type of corporate entities incorporated;
- the method of transferring funds through the structure, ultimately to fund the acquisition (eg, by way of intercompany loan, equity subscription or capital contribution);
- the taxes which will be incurred in creating the structure and completing the acquisition (eg, stamp or other transfer taxes, capital taxes, registration duties, notarial costs and the costs of incorporation of the newcos);
- strategies to maximise the corporation tax relief for transaction costs and the recovery of value added tax on those costs;
- the required notifications, elections and rulings which will be required to be made to, or sought from, the relevant tax authorities;
- the taxes which may be incurred in extracting surplus cash to the investors or on an exit; and
- the tax status of the funds' and the management team's investment.

A simplified example of a typical newco structure is shown in the following diagram.

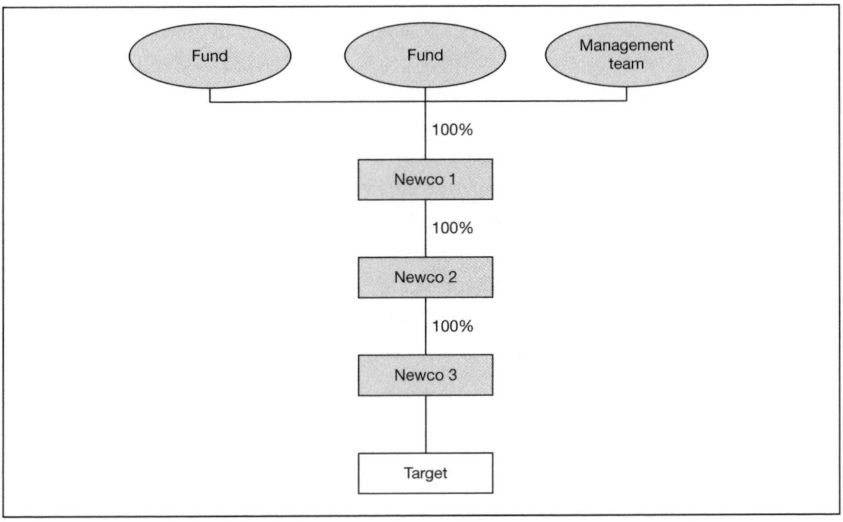


## 2. The total funding package

The total funding package which will be required to fund the cost of the acquisition of the target (the "Sources" column of the table set out below). for a leveraged acquisition will comprise:

| Sources | (£000s) | Uses | (£000s) |
|---|---|---|---|
| Equity contribution, comprising:<br>Institutional equity<br><br>Management equity<br>Institutional and management loan notes | <br>[•]<br><br>[•]<br>[•] | Cash consideration<br>Refinancing existing target debt<br>Transaction costs<br>Transaction taxes | [•]<br>[•]<br><br>[•]<br>[•] |
| Senior debt, comprising:<br>Facility A<br><br>Facility B<br>Facility C<br>Revolving credit facility | <br>[•]<br><br>[•]<br>[•]<br>[•] | Cash over-funding (at completion)<br>Working capital | [•]<br><br>[•] |
| Second lien debt | [•] | | |
| Mezzanine debt[•] | | | |
| Total | [•]* | Total | [•]* |

* These should equal one another.

- one or more layers of debt finance lent into the newco structure, commonly known as senior and junior (or subordinated) debt. This debt finance will usually constitute the largest part of the total funding package, generally at least 50% of the total transaction value, and for most mid-market transactions and above will itself comprise more than one type of debt instrument, with equal or differently ranked priorities; and
- the equity investment made by the management team and the funds managed or advised by the sponsor. This funding will usually comprise true equity, in the form of share equity, and 'quasi-equity', in the form of redeemable preference shares, loan notes, discounted bonds or deeply subordinated debt.

The total funding requirement (the "Uses" column of the table set out on the previous page). will be required to fund:
- the cash consideration payable to the sellers of the target;
- the refinancing of existing bank debt in the target group; and
- the fees, costs, expenses and taxes incurred in connection with the acquisition, the refinancing of the target group and the preparation and execution of the sale and purchase, equity and finance documents relating to the acquisition.

In addition, the senior debt may include additional facilities to be made available to the target group on an ongoing basis (after completion of the acquisition) to:
- fund the target group's capital expenditure;
- fund future strategic and bolt-on acquisitions by the target group;
- fund working capital of the target group; and
- provide ancillary facilities, such as overdrafts, letters of credit, bank guarantees and corporate credit lines.

A simplified example of a typical funding structure is shown in the diagram below.

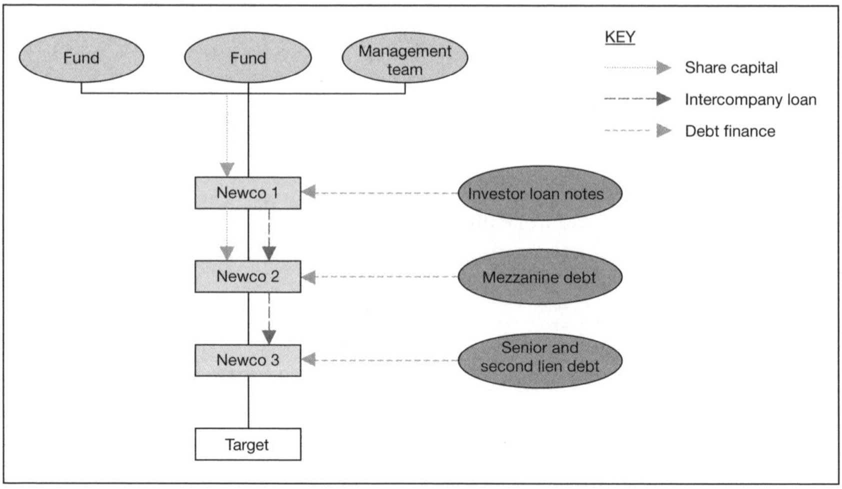

## 3. The debt finance package

The debt finance package for many mid-market and larger acquisition finance transactions will comprise two or more layers of debt, typically comprising senior debt and mezzanine debt, and increasingly in the European lending markets, second lien debt (which is described later in this chapter).

Larger or more complex acquisitions may also source debt funds from the issuance of high yield bonds or payment in kind (PIK) notes, and the mezzanine debt may be sub-divided into senior mezzanine and junior mezzanine layers of debt.

The use of a multi-layered debt finance package offers private equity sponsors a flexible and relatively cheap source of finance. The key benefits of the use of debt finance are as follows:

- Compared to implementing a securitisation finance structure or issuing high yield bonds or equity instruments, debt finance can be put in place relatively quickly, with a minimal number of advisers and with few public disclosure requirements – these features are essential to meeting the demanding timetables on which most private equity transactions are run.
- Depending on the tax regimes applicable, most – if not all – of the interest costs which accrue on and the deal fees associated with the raising of the debt finance can be deducted against the taxable profits generated by the target group.
- The structure, quantum, pricing and terms of a debt finance package can be negotiated to suit the transaction in hand, from 'jumbo' facilities totalling billions of pounds to more moderate facilities offering millions, tens of millions or hundreds of millions of pounds of finance. The wide range of liquidity offered by debt finance caters for a range of risk profiles, allowing the use of multiple layers of debt instruments with different risk profiles. All but the more subordinated layers of debt allow the debts to be repaid early to allow exit opportunities to be taken.
- The ability to grant fixed and floating security over the shares in, and the assets of, the borrowers and other members of the borrowers' group of companies allows lenders to take priority over other creditors and over other lenders comprising the same debt finance package.

## 4. Syndication

The amount of funding available for leveraged finance debt packages would not be achievable without the ability to syndicate the debt, since for all but the smaller deals, one lender would not wish to fund the entire debt required because of capital adequacy and risk management concerns. A loan syndicate is a group of lenders that each fund a portion of the debt being made available. These lenders each become a party to the loan documents, assume a separate and independent participation in the loans comprising the financing package, take a share of the security package granted to support these loan and together make these loans available to the borrowers. The fundamental concept is that in forming a syndicate, the lenders do not enter into any form of partnership and do not assume any liability or responsibility for the actions or omissions of their fellow syndicate members. Each of their participations forms a separate loan from each of them to the relevant borrower (although in practice, the lenders advance their loans to a single bank – the agent bank – which then advances the funds to each of the borrowers as a single loan; and a single financial institution (often the agent bank) will hold the benefit of the security package on trust (or where relevant laws do not recognise trust, as an agent) for the lenders).

Generally, a finance package will be structured, arranged and underwritten by a single bank (commonly called the 'arranger') or, at most, by one bank doing so for the senior layer of debt and another specialised finance provider doing so for the second lien or mezzanine layers of debt.

The commitment by the arranger will usually be made on a 'fully underwritten' or a 'best efforts' basis. Sponsors are generally keen to secure the debt funding required for the transaction on a fully underwritten basis, but if the arranger is unwilling or unable to underwrite the entire balance of the loan, it may be sufficient for the arranger to commit to use its 'best efforts' to form a syndicate to provide the funding. The banks which fulfil the roles of arranger and underwriter receive a fee for their services – commonly referred to as an arrangement and underwriting fee. If offering a fully underwritten commitment, these banks are willing to commit themselves to lend the full amount of the debt on the basis that they are confident, based on prevailing market conditions and the experience of their syndication teams, that they will be able to syndicate the debt, thus reducing their exposure to (potentially) zero, or more commonly to a targeted hold level.

The sponsor will appoint the chosen arranging and underwriting bank(s) at an early stage of the transaction, usually after a short, competitive tender process involving two or three competing banks which will offer term sheets setting out the key terms on which they are willing to arrange and underwrite the debt finance package. More aggressive sponsors might run two or more competing arranging and underwriting bank(s) for a longer period – sometimes until the day of signing the loan documents – before deciding which of them is offering the best terms. This strategy can result in two or more sets of bankers being run all the way to the point of having agreed full-form, final loan documents, with full credit committee approval.

In either strategy, sponsors will take advantage of the competitive tension between the competing banks which will exist at this time to strengthen their negotiating power, and will aim to ensure that terms offered to them (in terms of pricing, structure, covenants and the amount of debt) are as favourable to the sponsor as possible.

These appointments will be documented by written mandate letters, which will set out:

- the terms of appointment;
- the conditions on which the underwriting commitment is being offered;
- the exclusivity of the appointed banks;
- the underwriter's right to syndicate the debt;
- the fees payable for the arrangement and underwriting commitments;
- costs indemnities; and
- confidentiality undertakings.

If the timetable for completing a transaction is particularly short, the underwriting bank may be willing to lend the debt finance on the back of a funded term sheet. In these circumstances, the debt finance is made available pursuant to a short-form loan agreement based on the terms set out in an agreed term sheet. In the weeks or months after completion, the full-form loan and security documents will be negotiated (based on the agreed term sheet), drafted and signed, and will replace the interim arrangements.

Most debt finance structures for private equity transactions are syndicated after completion of the acquisition being financed (rather than before signing of the loan documents, as is more common for corporate lending). This will involve the arranging bank organising a primary syndication of the facilities (save for the amount which it intends to retain) to a number of financial institutions. The number and make-up of the financial institutions approached during primary syndication will depend on the amount of debt to be syndicated and the composition of the debt – the more sophisticated the financing structure, particularly the subordinated layers of debt, the more specialised the financial institutions which will be targeted.

## 5. Senior debt

The key features of senior debt are as follows:

- The first ranking layer of debt is unsubordinated and secured on a first ranking basis.
- It usually comprises several term loan and revolving credit facilities, offering cash and non-cash facilities (eg, letters of credit and bank guarantee facilities), with a mix of amortising and bullet repayment profiles.
- The margin range is generally of 225 bps to 325 bps.
- The tenor range is six to nine years.
- There is no call protection, with some exceptions applying to early refinancing.

The senior debt will form the core, and invariably the largest, part of the debt finance structure and will usually consist of the following:

- Acquisition finance – this is the finance required to purchase the target and is usually provided by way of secured term loans. The total amount of this type of debt is usually split into several tranches of debt, each with its own pricing, repayment profile and ranking in respect of certain types of prepayment – often denoted Facility A (usually the lowest price tranche with an amortising repayment profile),[2] Facility B (usually with increased pricing and a bullet or semi-bullet repayment),[3] Facility C and so on.
- Working capital and ancillary finance – this is the finance that will be required by the target group after the acquisition has completed for its day-to-day operational, working capital and general corporate needs. It is

2 See section 13 for an explanation of this term.
3 See section 13 for an explanation of this term.

provided under a revolving credit facility which is made available during the life of the senior facilities or by way of a separate overdraft facility, often on the bank's standard terms, alongside any other ancillary facilities which are required by the target group's business.

- Capital expenditure and acquisition finance – this may be provided to support the target group's capital expenditure requirements and sometimes also to finance bolt-on acquisitions, each of which will normally be projected in the business plan supporting the acquisition. If required, it is usually provided by way of secured term loans.

These sources of debt finance will be made available under separate facilities contained in a single senior facilities agreement, which will contain many of the standard provisions found in a conventional loan facility agreement. The Loan Market Association[4] has produced a standard form senior facilities agreement for leveraged acquisition finance, and this is invariably used in the London market as the basis for this agreement (although smaller transactions may be based on the lending bank's standard, short-form documents).

## 6. Second lien debt

The key features of second lien debt are as follows:

- It forms part of the senior, first ranking layer of debt, but is subject to a degree of subordination to the rest of the senior debt and is secured on a second ranking basis.
- It generally comprises only a single term loan, drawn in cash at closing, repaid in a bullet instalment at maturity.
- The margin range is generally of 400 bps to 650 bps.
- The tenor generally ends six months after the longest-dated tranche of the 'priority' senior debt.
- Call protection applies during the opening one or two years, but usually at a lower level than that which applies to mezzanine debt.

Second lien debt is now widely employed in mid-market and high-value transactions, both as an alternative to mezzanine finance and in conjunction with it to form a third distinct layer of finance, sandwiched between the senior and the mezzanine debt.

Second lien finance has brought a new investor base into the acquisition finance market. Second lien lending was originally dominated by hedge funds but the investor base now includes all kinds of institutional investors such as insurance companies, pension funds, mutual funds and investment vehicles known as

---

4 The Loan Market Association was created in 1996 to foster the development of a secondary market in Euromarket syndicated loans. One of its accomplishments has been the creation of investment grade loan document templates and, most recently, a leveraged acquisition debt finance facilities agreement template. Its goal is to improve the efficiency of the lending market through the development of standard document templates which have been scrutinised by groups representing borrowers and lenders. It is in the process of rolling out its standard form documents for use in jurisdictions outside the United Kingdom.

collateralised debt obligations and collateralised loan obligations[5]. Traditional lending banks and (more recently) mezzanine funds also participate in second lien debt, attracted by its enhanced margin and unique position in the debt funding structure.

Over time, the documentation of second lien debt has become more standard, being most commonly structured in the London market as a 'Tranche D' in the senior facilities agreement (particularly where there is a layer of mezzanine debt ranking after the second lien debt), thus forming part of the senior debt for many decision-making procedures, but being subject to a degree of contractual subordination to the rest of the senior debt. However, it can be documented separately, as is more common in the United States. In any event, the second lien debt is subordinated to the 'priority' senior debt and benefits from the same guarantees and security which are granted to the senior lenders, but on a second ranking basis and with restricted rights of enforcement. It is usual for the second lien debt to be borrowed by the borrowers of the senior debt – it is not common for it to be structurally subordinated[6] – and it will generally have a maturity falling six months after the longest-dated priority senior debt.

## 7. Mezzanine debt

The key features of mezzanine debt are as follows:

- It ranks after the senior and second lien debt, subordinated and secured on a second/third ranking basis.
- It generally comprises only a single term loan, drawn in cash at closing, repaid in a bullet instalment at maturity.
- The document terms (representations, covenant terms, events of default) mirror those in the senior facilities agreement, modified to reflect the subordinate position of mezzanine debt.
- The margin range is generally of 800 bps to 1100 bps; or 400 bps to 500 bps plus warrants to acquire shares in the target group's holding company.
- The margin comprises part cash pay and part capitalising/PIK interest.
- It is possible to share in the potential equity upside via warrants.
- The tenor ends six months to a year after the longest-dated tranche of senior/second lien debt.
- Call protection applies for up to three years.

Mezzanine debt is popular with private equity sponsors as:

- it offers huge liquidity;
- it is relatively easy to implement (as described above, being substantially

---

5 CLOs and CDOs are funds which issue asset-backed securities, which are backed by a repackaged pool of bonds, loans and related assets.

6 In the Euromarket, it has been customary for certain debt which is to be subordinate to senior debt (eg, high yield bonds) to be borrowed by a holding company of the senior debt borrower(s), such that the senior debt is lent at (or nearer to) the operating company level, whereas the subordinated debt is lent at a higher, holding company level, one step removed from (or 'structurally subordinated' to) the assets of the operating companies. This structuring technique is called structural subordination. Contractual subordination may be used as an alternative, whereby the parties agree that the senior and subordinated debts are borrowed at the same level and the subordination is created by contract, such as pursuant to an intercreditor agreement.

based on the senior covenant and security package);
- its impact on cash flows is softened by the non-cash pay (capitalising or PIK) element of the interest charge;
- it accommodates early exits and recapitalisations, subject to any prepayment fees which may apply during the early years; and
- it does not require a public credit rating.

Mezzanine debt is subordinated to the senior and second lien debt, but ranks ahead of the equity, including any equity investor loan notes and vendor loan notes. The subordination of the mezzanine debt is usually achieved by contractual subordination, pursuant to an inter-creditor agreement, but the mezzanine may also be structurally subordinated by being borrowed by a holding company of the senior and second lien borrowers.

The mezzanine debt will generally consist of a single term loan (or, for some cross-border acquisitions, one loan in each currency required to fund the acquisition) and will usually share (to the extent legally possible in the relevant jurisdictions) the same guarantee and security package with the senior and second lien debt, but its interest in and rights to it will rank behind the senior and second lien debt. As a result of its second/third ranking status, mezzanine debt has a greater risk profile, and as a result the mezzanine lenders receive a higher interest margin to compensate them for this risk, usually around 800 to 1,100 bps over funding costs for mezzanine with no warrants, or a margin of 400 to 500 bps over funding costs when warrants are also given, resulting in each case in an overall internal rate of return over the life of the facility of 1,300 to 1,500 bps (although competition has been driving this range downward over the past few years).

In addition to receiving interest, the mezzanine lenders have historically received some kind of performance-related reward, often in the form of warrants to subscribe for shares in the target group's holding company at the time of, for example, a sale or listing (this is often called an 'equity kicker'). These warrants could typically allow the mezzanine lenders to subscribe for up to 5% of the holding company's equity share capital. The increased liquidity in the debt markets, coupled with the increased competition between debt finance providers and the willingness of some CDOs to lend mezzanine debt without receiving warrants (as their constitution is often not set up for the uncertainty of investing in warrants), has allowed sponsors to retain the potential rewards of holding equity for themselves and to negotiate mezzanine debt without warrants being granted.

If of sufficient size, the mezzanine debt will be syndicated in a similar manner to the senior debt.

The mezzanine debt will be documented in a mezzanine loan agreement, which will be based on, and will contain substantially all the same terms (particularly the prepayment terms, representations, covenants and events of default) as, the senior facilities agreement. In practice, the first draft of the mezzanine loan agreement is produced at a relatively advanced stage of the negotiations, when the senior facilities agreement is in a near-final form. Amendments will be made to the senior facilities agreement to tailor it to the structure of the mezzanine loan and its financial terms.

These amendments are likely to include:

- adding additional conditions precedent to provide for the granting of the mezzanine lenders' warrants (if any) and to confirm that the senior and second lien debt have become unconditional, save for any condition relating to the funding of the mezzanine loan;
- deleting any margin ratchet;[7]
- changing the repayment profile to a single 'bullet' repayment of the full amount of the mezzanine loan at the end of its term (which is usually six months to one year after the final repayment of the senior and second lien debt);
- providing that prepayments of the mezzanine debt will be subject to the prior repayment in full of the senior and second lien debt;
- adding the right to appoint a board director or observer to the board of one of the holding companies of the target group, to represent the interests of the mezzanine lenders; and for this person to receive notice of, and any papers for, these board meetings;
- notching down (ie, relaxing) the financial covenants (other than any cash-flow covenant and capital expenditure covenant) to a level 10% to 15% below those applicable to the senior and second lien debt; and
- amending the cross-default terms so that they are not automatically triggered by a default under the senior facilities agreement.

## 8. The structure of the senior facilities agreement and the mezzanine loan agreement

Given that the newcos are off-the-shelf, shell companies with no assets of their own other than the target shares which they acquire, the terms of the senior facilities agreement are relatively restrictive (compared to those which could be expected to be offered to a corporate or investment-grade borrower). The sponsor will not offer any form of credit support from itself, from the funds which it advises or manages or from its other investments, so the lenders will only have credit support from, and recourse to, the value in the target group. As a result, the lenders are particularly concerned to ensure that:

- the profits generated by the target group and the cash held by it are protected, to ensure that they are available to service the fees, interest and principal payable on the debt finance;
- the target group does nothing which might harm its financial position, or change its nature and therefore its credit profile (judged by reference to the status of the target group at the time of its acquisition, as set out in the financial model and the business plan);
- they receive an agreed package of regular financial information to allow them to monitor the performance of the target group against the business plan and

7 A margin ratchet (or 'pricing grid') is a provision which provides that as the borrowers hit certain financial targets, the margin (the portion of the total interest cost to the borrower represented by an amount of basis points over funding costs, which is usually represented by LIBOR or EURIBOR) decreases.

to identify, as early as possible, any potential difficulties; and

- they receive the benefit of a comprehensive guarantee and security package so that, should the target group run into difficulties after its acquisition, their position will be protected from the claims of other creditors and they will be able to 'control' any restructuring.

**9. Parties**

The original parties to the senior facilities agreement and the mezzanine loan agreement will typically be the lead arranging bank – which often fulfils the roles of arranger, facility agent, security trustee, issuing bank (if letters of credit are available under the senior facilities) and original lender – and the newcos as guarantors and, where appropriate, borrowers. As these agreements will usually be entered into before the acquisition is completed, the members of the target group will not be original parties, but will (to the extent required) become parties (as guarantors and, for those companies which need direct access to the funds either to refinance existing debts or to finance working capital and capital expenditure, as borrowers) by way of an accession mechanism. Each of the syndicate of lenders will become a party to these agreements by way of an individual or a global transfer certificate during syndication of the facilities.

**10. The facilities and the stated purposes**

The loan agreements will set out a description of the facilities being made available and a detailed description of the purpose to which they are to be applied, in order to ensure that the funds lent are applied in the manner envisaged by the lenders. The stated purposes for a leveraged acquisition financing will include:

- funding the cash consideration due to the seller;
- paying related transaction costs; and
- usually, refinancing existing bank debt in the target group.

**11. Conditions precedent**

Conditions precedent are intended to confirm the legal, financial and commercial condition of the borrowers and guarantors before any of the debt is lent, and they must be satisfied (or waived by the facility agent) before the facilities become available to be drawn down. The extent and type of conditions precedent will largely depend on the type of transaction being financed. As a result of the complexity of private equity financing structures, the conditions precedent are invariably extensive.

The conditions precedent will be divided into two main types:

- Initial conditions precedent – these must be satisfied before the first drawdown of funds can be made, and will be satisfied by delivery of appropriate documents and evidence for matters falling under the following categories:
  - legal conditions precedent, including the constitutional documents of the borrowers and each company giving guarantees or security, all necessary corporate and shareholder authorities for each of these

companies, the documents for any English law financial assistance whitewash procedure[8] (or the equivalent overseas in respect of any non-English incorporated companies) and legal opinions from each relevant jurisdiction (usually provided by the lenders' counsel);
    - transactional conditions precedent, including the senior, second lien and mezzanine debt documents, mandate, fee and certain other side-letters, intercreditor and priority documents, security documents, equity and quasi-equity documents and acquisition or, as the case may be, offer documents;
    - financial conditions precedent, including the target group's recent financial statements, the financial model, budget and business plan, and a completion funds flow statement; and
    - information conditions precedent, including certificates of title for real property, documents of title, share certificates, 'know your customer'[9] information and due diligence reports, which may include an accountants' report, a legal report (often incorporating a review of tax and pensions issues), a market analysis, an insurance review, an environmental report and property valuations.
- Additional conditions precedent – these require the continued accuracy of a selected number of the representations and warranties and the absence of any potential or actual event of default. They must be satisfied at the time of, and immediately following, the drawings made at closing, at selected periods during the life of the facilities and before any subsequent drawing can be made after completion.

## 12. Interest

The total interest charge on each facility is invariably a fluctuating rate, which is the aggregate of:

- the margin applicable to that facility;
- the lenders' cost of funds, usually calculated by reference to the London interbank offered rate (LIBOR) or, for loans denominated in euros, the euro interbank offered rate (EURIBOR); and
- mandatory costs, which are the costs of complying with the requirements of the Bank of England and the Financial Services Authority (in respect of loans funded in the London market) and the European Central Bank (in respect of loans funded in the euro zone).

The margin is the amount of basis points above funding costs of funds which the borrowers must pay on any loan and it represents a lender's profit on the loans, on

8 Many jurisdictions prohibit a company from giving financial assistance (which may include any guarantees and security granted by the English companies which are members of the target group) for the purchase of its own shares or those of any of its holding companies. Under English law, a private company may give financial assistance in certain circumstances if it undertakes a statutory 'whitewash' procedure.

9 Lenders are under increased regulatory pressure to undertake extensive due diligence on borrowers in an effort to combat money laundering.

the assumption that it has match funded its participation in these loans in the relevant interbank market and that it is subject to average mandatory costs – for any one lender these assumptions may or may not apply in practice, but the principle that debts of this nature bear interest at a fluctuating rate represented by 'cost of funds plus a fixed margin' is the market standard approach to loan pricing.[10]

Interest will be paid in arrears at the end of sequential periods selected by the borrowers as interest periods (which are usually of one, two, three or six months' duration).

LIBOR and EURIBOR will be set by reference to a screen rate. LIBOR is often set by reference to the British Bankers Association Interest Settlement Rate and EURIBOR by the rate determined as such by the European Central Bank. Alternatively, and if these rates are not available for any reason (eg, due to the suspension of the service or where a rate is needed for a non-standard interest period), two or three banks, called 'reference banks', which are generally members of the lending syndicate located, for LIBOR, in London or, for EURIBOR, in the eurozone, will be selected to provide an average rate.

It is fairly common for the margin applicable to one or more of the senior facilities to be subject to a margin ratchet. A margin ratchet provides for stepped reductions in the margin (usually three or four steps) if the target group meets agreed financial performance objectives. These targets are often set by reference to the leverage ratio[11] of the target group – the understanding being that as the leverage of the target group falls (as a result of a combination of the repayment of part of the debt and increased earnings, as would be projected by the original business plan and financial model) and the creditworthiness of the target group improves, the lenders should receive a reduced margin reflecting the reduced credit risk to which they are exposed. If performance worsens, the margin increases accordingly, up to its maximum (ie, day one) level.

## 13. Repayment and prepayment

The senior debt facilities will be repayable by way of regular, fixed instalments (often called an 'amortising' repayment profile), on a semi-amortising basis (where the instalments are weighted towards the end of the debt's maturity), in a single lump at maturity (often called a 'bullet' repayment) or, for revolving credit facilities, on a revolving basis, all falling over a six to nine-year period.

Second lien and mezzanine debt is invariably repayable in a single bullet instalment, falling after the repayment in full of the prior ranking debts.

Once repaid, term loans cannot be re-borrowed. Advances drawn under revolving credit facilities are usually repayable at the end of a short term (usually one, two, three or six months), but once repaid, they may be re-borrowed – and this cycle may continue until the final maturity date. Revolving credit facilities are therefore more flexible for the borrowers and allow them to meet their fluctuating working capital requirements.

---

10 Lenders do not fund every loan from deposits, but typically access the interbank market for loans for short-term periods coincidental with the applicable interest periods chosen by the borrowers.

11 The ratio of debt to earnings before interest, tax, depreciation and amortisation.

Generally, no repayments of the senior term debt will be scheduled for a period of six to 12 months following completion, to allow the target group's cash flow some breathing space before it is required to service the repayment of these debts.

The loan documents will allow the borrowers to prepay the debts (in their order of priority) before their respective scheduled repayment dates. This is an essential feature of private equity financing structures, allowing all the debts to be repaid if an opportunity to exit arises and allowing the borrowers to repay part of the debts to reduce the target group's leverage if cash becomes available to do so – perhaps as a result of outperforming the business plan or as a result of disposals being made. A prepayment fee is generally payable to the relevant lending group (so-called 'call protection') if the second lien or mezzanine debt is prepaid during the first few years following completion. This fee may be negotiated to apply only to prepayments funded by the proceeds of a third-party bank refinancing, so that it would not fall due on an exit.

In addition to scheduled repayments, certain events will trigger an obligation to prepay part or all of the debts. These are referred to as 'mandatory prepayments' and may include the prepayment of:

- all debts on the occurrence of a change of control, listing or flotation of any of the holding companies of the target group or the sale of the target group. These heads aim to cover the commonest exit routes pursued by private equity sponsors;
- part of the debts from the cash proceeds received from the disposal of assets (over and above an agreed threshold and net of costs and taxes incurred). Cash proceeds which are used for re-investment in the target group's business are usually excluded from this obligation;
- part of the debts from the cash proceeds received from warranty claims, such as claims against the seller(s) for a breach of warranty or under an indemnity in the acquisition agreement or from insurance claims (in each case, often above an agreed figure and net of costs and taxes incurred). Cash proceeds which are used for re-investment in the target group's business or which are applied in meeting any loss or liability relating to the claim are usually excluded from this obligation; and
- part of the debts from the excess cash flow generated by the target group's business (this prepayment obligation is called the 'cash sweep'). After an initial grace period, a proportion (often 50%, or a ratcheting percentage set by reference to the leverage ratio which can reduce the proportion down to zero) of the cash flow generated by the target group's business over and above amounts applied to service the debts are required to be applied in prepayment of the debts.

## 14. Representations

A principal reason to include representations is that under English law there is no general duty to disclose to the other contracting party when entering into a contract – for example, a borrower is under no obligation to tell the lenders that it knows of a potential liability, claim or lawsuit which it expects to be incurred by or made against it.

Representations concentrate the borrowers' minds on ensuring that certain factual matters are as the lenders believe them to be – and they fulfil a useful 'fishing exercise' to ensure that they tell the lenders everything that the lenders need to know before committing to lend. The representations will be made at the time the loan documents are entered into, and a selected number of them will be repeated (the 'repeating representations') on the date of each drawdown and at the start of each interest period. The occurrence of a misrepresentation which is not remedied within any available grace period (often 10 to 20 business days' grace is given for remedial misrepresentations) will lead to an event of default being triggered.

Examples of standard representations are:

- the corporate status of the borrowers;
- the due corporate authority and legality, validity and binding nature of the loan documents;
- the borrowers' tax position;
- that no default exists;
- that all information provided to the lenders is true and accurate;
- *pari passu* ranking of the debts;
- compliance with all laws and regulations (including environmental laws);
- that good title is owned for all assets (including shareholdings and intellectual property); and
- the absence of material litigation.

## 15. General covenants

Loan covenants are intended to protect the lenders' loan investment, and they will be binding on the borrowers (and, by way of procurement obligations under which the borrowers will covenant to ensure that their subsidiaries also comply with the covenants, effectively all the other members of the target group) throughout the life of the facilities. The wording of these covenants – usually split into positive covenants (setting out what the borrowers (and their subsidiaries) must do) and negative covenants (setting out what the borrowers (and their subsidiaries) must not do) – is where the views of the lenders will be most at odds with those of the borrowers. The sponsor and the borrowers will want to be free to run the business of the target group in the manner which they see as best serving their interests; and the lenders will want to maximise their control over the target group in order to protect their investment in it. Counsel for each of these sides will spend considerable time negotiating the wording of the covenants to balance these opposing demands while meeting the needs of the underlying business and the business plan.

The borrowers will undertake to provide the lenders with a regular package of information, typically comprising financial and operational information useful to the lenders in overseeing covenant compliance, with the overall objective of giving the lenders advance warning of possible debt service or repayment problems.

The occurrence of a breach of covenant which is not remedied within any available grace period (as with remedial misrepresentations, often 10 to 20 business days' grace is given for remedial breaches) will lead to an event of default being triggered.

Examples of common covenants are:

- maintenance of the borrowers' and the guarantors' corporate status;

- compliance with laws (including environmental laws);
- a restriction on the creation of security (the 'negative pledge');
- restrictions on disposals, acquisitions, mergers, joint ventures and the incurrence of further debt;
- a prohibition or restriction on dividends and other payments to the equity investors and the subordinated lenders;
- maintenance of a minimum level of guarantor coverage;
- a restriction on changing the target group's business; and
- maintenance of at least a *pari passu* ranking of the debts

## 16. Financial covenants

In addition to the general covenants, a suite of financial covenants will be set. These apply for defined periods, usually rolling periods of 12 months, throughout the life of the facilities. The financial covenants are tied to selected balance sheet and income statement levels and ratios, and are designed to monitor the target group's performance against the business plan and the borrowers' ability to meet their payment obligations under the debt finance package.

On highly leveraged transactions, the level of the covenants will change over time, in line with the business plan underlying the transaction – for example, the leverage ratio would be expected to improve over time (as earnings become enhanced and the debt is reduced by repayments and prepayments) and the restrictions on capital expenditure may relax.

The definitions of each element of these covenants are thoroughly negotiated, often with the guidance of the reporting accountants advising the sponsor. The lenders will be seeking to ensure that the financial covenant ratios give a true reflection of the borrowers' financial performance and creditworthiness. The sponsor and the borrowers will be seeking to ensure that the definitions give maximum flexibility to allow them to meet the test levels and to absorb one-off hits which they expect will or could arise and which could affect the covenant ratios.

Examples of common financial covenants are:

- the ratio of total debt to earnings before interest, taxes, depreciation and amortisation (EBITDA) (the leverage test);[12]
- the ratio of EBITDA to total debt costs (the interest cover test);[13]
- the ratio of cash flow to total funding costs (the cash-flow cover test); and[14]
- a maximum level of capital expenditure.[15]

---

12 This tests the aggregate amount of debt to the target group's earnings. Leverage covenants are key indicators of the viability of the target group's debt structure and its ability to service and repay the debt finance.

13 Interest cover tests show whether earnings are sufficient to service the debt and are often an early warning of cash-flow problems.

14 Cash cover ratios (sometimes called fixed charge ratios) measure operating cash flow against financial costs. Cash-flow calculations usually take the accounting measure of profit (EBITDA) and convert it to a 'cash' measure of profit. The lender is thus able to calculate the number of times that a company's cash flow covers total funding costs, though in most leveraged deals this is usually set at 1:1.

15 Capital expenditure covenants restrict the amount that can be spent on long-term assets such as equipment or machinery. These are often limited in highly leveraged financing structures to ensure there is enough cash to service debt, though these levels will be set at industry standards and based on the company's business plan.

Generally, the better the creditworthiness of the target group, the more relaxed the financial covenants. Most private equity transactions involve an initially high leverage and as a result have relatively restrictive financial covenant controls. The leverage test, interest cover test and cash-flow cover test are employed almost universally in the loan documents for leverage finance debts.

Failure to meet a financial covenant will lead to an event of default being triggered. Although no grace period is given, as such a failure is not remediable, it has become common for an 'equity cure' right to be included which allows the sponsor to inject further equity into the target group, which is applied notionally to increase one or more of the variables constituting the relevant financial covenant which is not met – for example, by inflating EBITDA or cash flow by the amount of the cash injection. The use of any equity cure right is intended to be used as a quick fix for any blip in financial covenant compliance and, as such, its availability is usually limited to ensure that the lenders' rights to take action in respect of systematic underperformance are not curtailed (eg, it may be permitted only once or twice during the life of the facilities).

## 17. Events of default

These are an essential part of the lenders' protection, giving the lenders the right, upon the occurrence of the events specified as being an event of default, to cancel the commitments and to demand (or have the right immediately to demand) immediate repayment of the outstanding loans (this is called 'accelerating' the loans).

The right to place the debts on demand or to accelerate is a powerful remedy for the lenders relying on the uncertainties inherent in exercising their rights at law, such as the right to:

- obtain an injunction or specific performance;
- terminate the loan documents on the basis of a repudiatory breach of contract;
- sue for damages arising from a non-repudiatory breach of contract; or
- sue for damages or rescinding the loan documents on the basis of misrepresentation.

The events which may trigger an event of default may relate to some act or omission by the borrowers or any other member of the target group, or they may relate to external circumstances such as a deterioration in trading conditions that materially and adversely affects the creditworthiness of the target group.

If repayment is not made following acceleration of the loans, the lenders will have an action against the borrowers for non-payment of a debt.

Examples of standard events of default are:

- non-payment of amounts due under the loan documents;
- breach of the terms of the loan documents (often subject to a remedy period for remediable breaches);
- misrepresentation (often subject to a remedy period for remediable misrepresentations);

- cross-default and cross-acceleration;
- the occurrence of insolvency events affecting any member of, or any material member of, the target group;
- auditors' qualification to audited financial statements;
- departure of key members of the management team; and
- the occurrence of a material adverse change.

## 18. The security package

The senior, second lien and mezzanine debt is invariably supported by a guarantee and security package granted by the newcos and (subject to legal restrictions applicable in the relevant jurisdictions, such as restrictions and prohibitions on granting financial assistance) the target group over all, or substantially all, of their respective assets and shareholdings. This security from the target group is required as the newcos are shell companies without any assets (other than, in the case of the newco which bids for and purchases the target, the shares it acquires in the target) against which the lenders could have recourse in the event of insolvency or receivership. Further, the security provides the lenders with a degree of protection in circumstances where any company becomes insolvent and ensures that the lenders' claims for repayment of the debts owed to them rank ahead of other unsecured (or second ranking, secured) claims, such as trade creditors.

Typically, those of the newcos and the members of the target group which are English companies grant a guarantee and a debenture in support of their own borrowings and those of the other borrowers. In addition, any members of the target group which receive funds (eg, under intercompany loans, rather than as direct borrowers) or which are material in the context of the target group's business or overall value will do likewise.

The debenture is a standalone document encompassing fixed and floating charges and the guarantee is (usually) contained in the loan documents. The debenture would commonly include fixed charges over the following assets owned by the charging company (including those owned at, and those acquired after, the date of the debenture):

- freehold and leasehold property – fixed, perfected and registered security is commonly taken, given the tangible value that property offers to the lenders in the event of enforcement of the security, even in circumstances where the business itself has stopped trading. Any leasehold property which is leased on short-term, market-rate terms or where charging is prohibited without the landlord's consent might be excluded from the fixed charge, particularly if the company's occupation of that property is not essential for its operations (eg, office space, leased for a few years with a current rent payable);
- fixed plant and machinery – fixed security is commonly taken over these assets as a class, with any specific examples of any valuable assets identified;
- investments, including the company's shareholding in any subsidiaries. This security may be perfected by registering the beneficiary of the security in each subsidiary company's shareholders' register. However, common practice is that the beneficiary of the security is not registered unless and until there

is a default under the banking documents. The debenture will contain terms governing the exercise of voting rights and the payment of dividends in circumstances both before and after any such default;
- book debts, including both intra-group and trading receivables;
- bank accounts and deposits, including cash in current and deposit accounts and any cash equivalent investments held by the charging company;
- intellectual property, including both registered and unregistered patents, trademarks, service marks, designs, business names, copyrights, design rights, moral rights, inventions, confidential information, know-how and other intellectual property rights interests;
- goodwill and uncalled share capital of the charging company;
- material contracts – fixed security is commonly taken over these assets as a class, with any specific examples identified and, where the value and commercial practicalities allow, counterparties notified of the security created. Some material contracts may be assigned by way of security instead of being subject to a fixed charge – for example, the security package for an acquisition finance transaction will include the assignment of the purchaser's rights under the sale and purchase agreement; and
- proceeds from certain insurance policies, including policies against the loss, damage or destruction of assets and for business interruption and policies protecting against the death or illness of key members of the management team. Policies taken out to protect third parties' losses or liabilities should be excluded, such as directors' and officers' insurance and employers' liability insurance.

In addition, the debenture will create a floating charge over the balance of the charging company's assets. Some assets may be excluded from this floating charge if it would otherwise breach negative pledges or other agreements against creating security pertaining to those assets (eg, prohibitions on creating security without the landlord's consent contained in leases).

The lenders' legal advisers will advise on the perfection requirements applicable to each type of security interest created under the debenture. Common perfection requirements include:
- registering the debenture under Section 395 of the Companies Act 1985, where the company is incorporated (or has a place of business) in England and Wales;
- registering the debenture at the Land Registry against any registered freehold or leasehold titles;
- registering the debenture with relevant intellectual property registers;
- transferring shares into the name of the beneficiary of the security;
- giving notice of the security to banks which hold the company's bank accounts, contract counterparties and debtors; and
- other asset-specific registration and perfection requirements – such as those applicable to security created over ships and aircraft.

The debenture will include 'further assurance' terms, which oblige the charging company to enter into any further documents or undertake any further acts required to protect, perfect or create the security intended to be created by the debenture, including over assets acquired after the date the debenture is entered into.

The security will be structured to allow enforcement against particular assets or to allow the sale of the company as a going concern, giving the beneficiaries of the security the option to choose the route which gives them the best recovery rate.

In cross-border transactions, the nature of the security package granted by companies incorporated in an overseas jurisdiction will be dictated by:

- the type of assets located in that jurisdiction;
- the type and extent of security interests available under the laws of that jurisdiction; and
- the costs and taxes which will be incurred in connection with granting that security.

This structure gives the lenders an unsecured claim (under the guarantee) and a secured claim (pursuant to the debenture or other security instrument) against each of these companies. The security and guarantee package should help ensure that any material assets on which the target group's forecast performance is based are retained and that the lenders' charges take priority over any interests of other creditors (eg, trade creditors) in an insolvency, except for the prescribed part of any insolvent borrower's floating charge assets required to be made available to unsecured creditors (under Section 176A of the Insolvency Act 1986, as amended by Section 252 of the Enterprise Act 2002).

It will also give the lenders an element of control over any restructuring, as they will be able to appoint an administrator if they hold a floating charge over all, or substantially all, of the assets of a company (a 'qualifying floating charge') (under paragraphs 14-21, Schedule B1 of the Insolvency Act 1986, as amended by paragraphs 14-21, Schedule 16 of the Enterprise Act 2002). Although the insolvent company can also appoint an administrator, it must notify the secured creditors holding the qualifying floating charge, which may in turn nominate an administrator of their choice. Since the Enterprise Act 2002 came into force, it is now possible to appoint an administrative receiver only in very limited prescribed circumstances.

Notwithstanding these changes, the Enterprise Act 2002 has had little effect on the drafting of lenders' standard debentures, comprising only relatively minor amendments directly required as a consequence of the legislation. A concurrent change introduced by the Enterprise Act 2002, which enables either a lender or the company itself to appoint an administrator simply by filing certain papers with a court office rather than by a hearing before a judge, has also meant that the process of entry into administration is now only marginally more complex than – and with adequate preparation, probably as quick and as certain as – entry into administrative receivership was prior to the new legislation coming into force.

In practice, it has proved comparatively rare for lenders to enforce directly or to need to substitute their own choice of administrator for that of the company. A troubled company will often appoint the lenders' choice of administrator itself, having already liaised with the lenders. However, this is perhaps not greatly different from the pre-Enterprise Act 2002 position, where it would be the company which would invite the lenders to appoint an administrative receiver in similar circumstances. This is mainly a result of the onus which English insolvency law places on company directors to protect creditor interests.

Where the debts are syndicated, a security trustee will be appointed to hold the security on trust on behalf of all the syndicate lenders. Where there are secured senior and junior debts, the security trustee (usually being the senior lender which arranged the senior debt package) will hold the security on trust for all those lenders, and this arrangement will be governed by an intercreditor agreement entered into between the borrowers, the guarantors and security providers, the security trustee, the senior and junior lenders and certain other creditors of the newcos and the target group (eg, the sponsor and members of the management team where their investment takes the form of shareholder debt or loan notes).

If the security trustee has to enforce the security, the proceeds of enforcement (net of the security trustee's costs) will be held by the security trustee on trust and applied in accordance with the provisions of the intercreditor agreement. The terms of the intercreditor agreement are an essential component of ensuring the proper ranking of senior and subordinated debts. Its contractual terms allow the order of priorities or order of payments which would otherwise be applied by applicable law to be modified to suit the debt finance structure – for example, the proceeds of enforcement of security granted by a subsidiary can be applied to pay the debts owed by its holding company, notwithstanding that the lenders' claims against that holding company are structurally subordinated to other creditors of that subsidiary.

As a consequence of the way public acquisitions are structured and for a variety of reasons in private acquisitions (eg, the need to obtain competition clearances), there can be a gap between the time that the lenders commit to lend the debt finance and the date the acquisition completes and the debt finance is borrowed and paid to the seller(s). This means that the guarantee and security package is often put in place in a number of phases, as follows:

- The newcos will enter into the relevant guarantee and security documents at the time the lenders commit to lend the debt finance (ie, at the time of signing the loan documents).
- The target group will enter into the relevant guarantee and security documents immediately after completion of the acquisition.

The second of these phases may, depending on the laws applicable to the guarantee and security package being put in place, be further split as follows:

- The target group will enter into the relevant guarantee and security documents in respect of that part of the debt finance which is not affected by applicable legal restrictions relating to financial assistance (eg, the prohibition against giving financial assistance under Section 151 of the Companies Act 1985). This debt could comprise debts which have not been used to acquire shares in the target, such as debts arising under refinancing or working capital facilities.

- Once any necessary procedures (eg, the whitewash procedure available pursuant to Sections 155 to 158 of the Companies Act 1985) have been completed to allow guarantees and security to be granted in respect of affected acquisition debt, the target group will enter into further guarantee and security documents, or will amend the terms of the documents entered into in the phase above, in respect of the balance of the debt finance.

## 19. Syndication and transferability of loan participations

Part of the reason that the commercial and investment banks have been able to increase the levels of debt which they are willing to underwrite and take onto their balance sheet is the increased breadth and depth of the capital markets which allows them to sell their loans in primary syndication and, if required thereafter, in the secondary market.

Although sponsors generally prefer their relationship banks to retain a meaningful participation in the debt package, the loan documentation usually allows for the transfer of the loans by the lenders, often subject to no conditions (including no requirement to obtain the borrower's consent to the transfer) or to minimal borrower protection conditions (eg, a minimum transfer amount or minimum commitment). Loans for which no conditions apply to the ability to transfer are called 'freely transferable'.

Lenders are keen to ensure that they have freedom to manage their balance sheets and credit exposures, as well as comply with regulatory capital risk management requirements. As a result lenders have, over the past five or so years, sought to ensure that the transfer provisions of the loan documents allow the loan to be freely transferable, or at worst, subject to minimal conditions to protect the borrowers' interests. Borrowers may try to insist that they have the right to approve the potential transfer and transferee. If allowing borrowers a complete veto right over a loan transfer is not acceptable to the lenders, the lenders may still agree to retain a minimum amount of their loan commitment or that they will transfer only an agreed minimum amount. A minimum credit rating of the transferee may also be set.

# Aircraft

**Jeremy Edwards**
Norton Rose LLP

## 1. Introduction

In this chapter we consider the particular types of security involved in the context of aircraft financing and any special considerations that arise.

There are many good and lengthy books dedicated solely to aircraft financing and related matters: it is not the purpose of this chapter to explain the principles underlying aircraft financing generally, but rather to focus on the specific security issues that arise in the context of this particularly high-value and uniquely moveable asset.

## 2. What is an aircraft?

In order to understand what types of security interest need to be taken into consideration, it is important to have a closer look at the asset itself and what gives it its value.

### 2.1 The physical asset

An aircraft itself is not a single asset, but a series of valuable components whose marketability and value at any given time will depend upon their age and maintenance status. Most of us would feel much more confident purchasing a car which had recently undergone a major service by a registered dealer than one which had not been serviced for many years and which was clearly in need of a trip to the garage. In the same way, the value of the major aircraft components (eg, airframe, engines, landing gear) will fluctuate as these components are overhauled and replaced. For an older aircraft, the engines may be worth more than the rest of the aircraft. From a security perspective, the financier will therefore want to make sure that it has taken security to the fullest extent over the major components and any manufacturer's warranties that relate to them. Such warranties typically cover the minimum useful life of major components, guaranteed maximum repair costs and availability of spare parts. The financier will also want to have a certain degree of control over those matters which may adversely impact upon the value of the secured asset, such as subleasing and change in the state of registration. But this desire for the financier to control the asset must always be balanced against the airline's need to operate it in as flexible a manner as possible in order to generate sufficient income to repay the financing.

### 2.2 Maintenance records

The technical manuals and aircraft maintenance records which certify the maintenance history of an aircraft and its components have a significant impact on its value. It is therefore important for a financier to be able to obtain these records if an aircraft is being repossessed or returned at the end of a lease.

### 2.3 Registration

Similarly to ships, all commercial aircraft must be registered pursuant to the Chicago Convention with an aviation authority which is responsible for supervising the operating and maintenance regimes relating to all aircraft on its register. An aircraft cannot be recorded on more than one register at any time and it is therefore important for a financier to be able to ensure the de-registration of an aircraft in the event of repossession or on lease expiry. The state of registration is of fundamental importance to the creation and registration of security interests in the aircraft and to the preservation of the aircraft's value.

### 2.4 Insurance

As with any other asset, the financier will wish to be satisfied that there is suitable insurance in place in respect of the financed aircraft, covering the value of the aircraft itself and any liabilities which may attach to it. The financier will then need to make sure that it has a suitable interest in these insurances so that proceeds are paid to it in appropriate circumstances.

### 2.5 Leases

In addition to taking security over the asset itself, a financier will often wish to take security over any lease of the aircraft so that the income generated by that asset can be paid direct to the financiers. If rent continues to be paid to the lessor pending a default, the assignment may amount only to a floating charge.

## 3. Aircraft financing structures

In addition to briefly considering the nature of the underlying asset, it is important to have a basic understanding of the types of legal structure utilised in aircraft financing. At its most fundamental level, almost all aircraft financing is structured as a secured loan, a lease or a combination of the two.

### 3.1 Secured lending

In a typical secured loan transaction for the financing of an aircraft, one or more banks or other financial institutions (lenders) will advance a loan to an airline or aircraft lessor and the repayment of the loan will be secured by a first priority mortgage over the aircraft. As discussed below, a valid aircraft mortgage may not be available in all circumstances.

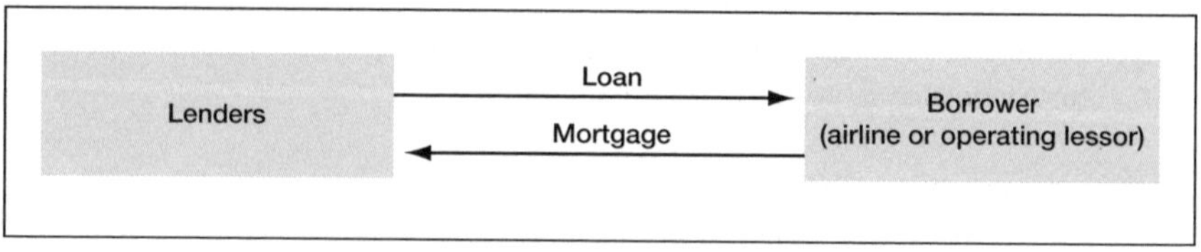

In addition to the aircraft mortgage, the lenders are likely to require an assignment of insurances, an interest in the main warranties relating to the airframe and engines and, possibly, security over maintenance reserves. We will look at the considerations relating to each of these types of security in more detail later in this chapter.

### 3.2 Aircraft leasing

In a simple aircraft leasing transaction, the airline will identify a third party (the lessor) which agrees to purchase the aircraft and lease it to the airline.

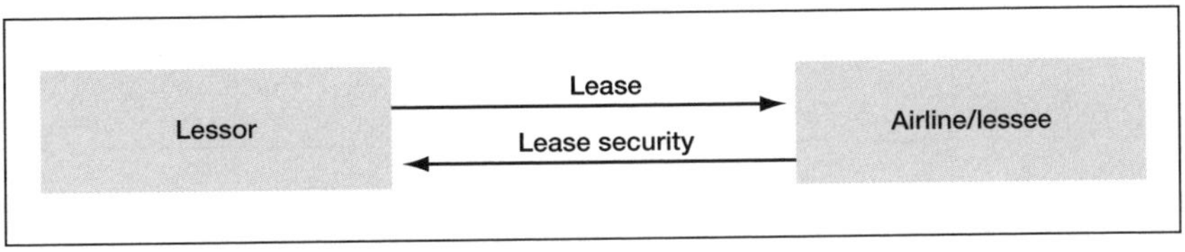


Leases can generally be categorised as either operating leases or finance leases.

In an operating lease, the owner/lessor will retain the interest in the residual value of the aircraft at the end of the lease term, whereas in a finance lease, it is the operator/lessee which will retain this interest. The type of lease which the parties decide to document will largely be driven by the commercial requirements of the airline, in particular the tax treatment they are intending to achieve, the implications on the balance sheet of each party and whether they wish to retain the residual value risk/reward at the end of the lease term.

A finance lease is quasi security and, in some countries (eg, the United States) would be re-characterised as real security. It is a particularly useful tool in situations where a mortgage may not be available.

Because the lessor in a leasing transaction will have retained the ownership of the aircraft, it will not require any mortgage but may seek additional security from the airline by requiring a security deposit (either in cash or by way of a letter of credit), a parent company guarantee, maintenance reserves, an assignment of insurances, some form of asset value support, repossession insurance, a remarketing agreement and an ability to procure the de-registration of the aircraft when the lease expires or is terminated. Again, we examine the main reasons behind each of these elsewhere in this chapter.

### 3.3 Combined loan/lease structure

In order to improve the security position of the financing parties, it is quite common to see a combination of the loan and lease structures whereby the lenders will advance their loan to a special purpose vehicle (SPV) established in a tax-friendly jurisdiction which will purchase the aircraft and lease it to the airline/lessee under a hire purchase agreement.

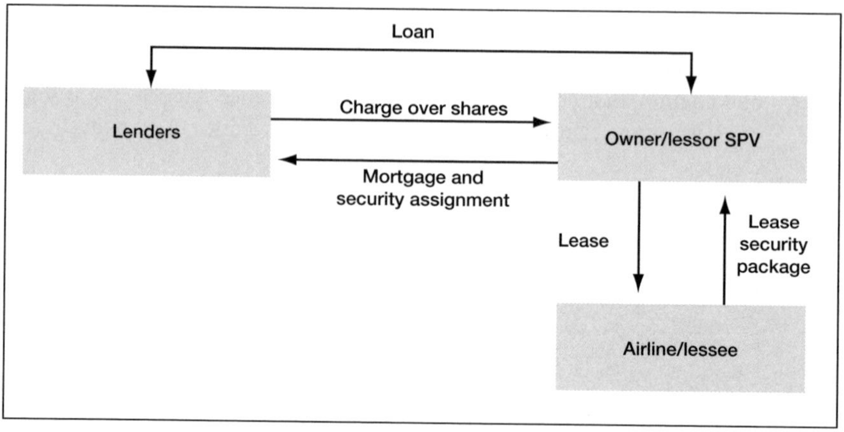


The reason for this combined structure is to give the financier the ability either to terminate the lease in the event of an airline default or to enforce the mortgage. By using an SPV as the owner/lessor, financiers will also hope that any potential liability they may incur relating to the ownership of the asset will be removed.

In a combined loan/lease structure, the same security instruments will be found as apply for both a secured loan financing and a lease structure, in addition to which there will usually be an assignment of lease rights (and the related security package) by the owner/lessor in favour of the lenders and, if the owner/lessor is an SPV set up and used for the specific transaction, a charge over the shares in the owner/lessor.

## 4. Specific security interests

This section looks first at the types of security interest found in most transactions, whether they are secured lending or leases, followed by those which are more usually found only in lease or secured loan financings, and finally those which would be found in the combined structures.

### 4.1 Assignment of insurances

Assignment of insurances (and occasionally reinsurances) is frequently found in both lease and secured loan financing transactions for aircraft. Whether it is strictly speaking necessary is a matter of some debate.

In any aircraft financing transaction, the lessor or lender will require, as a condition precedent to the commencement of the transaction, that it receive a certificate of insurance from acceptable insurance brokers which includes it as an additional insured party under the hull and liability insurance policies. As a named additional insured party, the lessor or lender should be able to make its own claim under the insurance policy in the event of damage to, or total loss of, the aircraft or if there is a claim covered by the liability policy. That right of the lessor or lender to make a claim leads some practitioners to question the necessity for an assignment of insurances by the airline. However, it remains customary for most lessors and financiers to require the airline to assign their right to receive any payments due under the insurance contract in excess of an agreed threshold and also to instigate claims on behalf of the airline should the airline fail to do so.

In certain jurisdictions there is a legal requirement for the airline to place its primary insurances with an insurance company established in the same jurisdiction. In these situations, and where the creditworthiness of the primary insurance company may be questionable, it is usual for the lessor/lender to require at the very least that the primary insurer take out reinsurance in the principal aviation insurance markets and that these reinsurances include a 'cut-through' clause requiring the reinsurers to pay direct in accordance with the primary insurance certificate, thereby effectively bypassing the primary insurers altogether. Because the lessor/lender is not a party to the reinsurance contract, they would be unable, as a matter of English law, to enforce the cut-through clause because contracts of insurance are excluded from the Contracts (Rights of Third Parties) Act 1999. In any event, a cut-through clause may not be enforceable in the event of the primary insurer's insolvency if it constitutes a preference. Some lessors will therefore require an assignment of the proceeds of the reinsurances to be entered into. In such circumstances, it is important to remember that the party which can assign its rights to receive payments under the reinsurance contract is the primary insurer and not the airline. It is also important to make sure that the reinsurance contract itself permits the primary insurer to assign its right to receive payments under the contract (otherwise the assignment will not be enforceable against the reinsurers), and to limit the assignment to the right to receive payments under the reinsurance contract rather than to an assignment of the reinsurance contract itself, it being a condition of reinsurance contracts that the insured party is itself an insurance company.

## 4.2 Airframe and engine warranty assignments or agreements

Most aircraft lease or loan transactions will also include some form of airframe and engine warranty assignment or agreement. The purpose of these documents is to ensure that the lessor/lender will be able to benefit from any remaining warranty rights in the event of repossession or on expiry of a lease while permitting the airline to enjoy the warranties during the term of the lease or loan financing.

In an airframe or engine warranty assignment, the original owner of the warranties (which will often be the airline that initially purchased the aircraft from the manufacturer) will assign all of its rights in respect of the relevant warranties relating to the aircraft in question to the lessor or lender. The lessor or lender will then need to grant a licence to the airline permitting it to benefit from the warranties during the term of the lease or loan and, in the context of a secured financing or finance lease (as opposed to an operating lease, where the aircraft will eventually be returned to the lessor), to reassign the warranties to the airline absolutely once the secured obligations have been fulfilled.

Notice of the assignment and granting of a licence will be given to the relevant manufacturer, which will normally be content to consent to the assignment provided that the assignee agrees to comply with any contractual requirements relating to the exercise of the warranties which would have had to be complied with by the airline.

In an airframe/engine warranty agreement, the same end result is achieved through a different mechanism. Rather than transferring ownership to the warranties to the lessor/lender at the outset of the transaction, the airline will retain the warranty rights but the manufacturer will agree to grant to the lessor/lender a package of warranties equal to any remaining warranties at the time that the operating lease ends or on early repossession of the aircraft. In recent years, the use of warranty agreements has increasingly replaced the use of warranty assignments.

### 4.3 Security deposits

It is common to find a requirement for less creditworthy airlines to provide a cash security deposit to the lessor in an operating lease. This deposit will be held by the lessor as security for the lessee's obligations and returned following expiry of the lease and redelivery of the aircraft.

There is no special treatment of security deposits in aircraft finance transactions as compared with any other type of financing, although it is common for these to be outright payments with an obligation to repay rather than the placing by the airline of an amount of cash on a charged deposit account.

Many leases will permit the replacement of any cash security by a letter of credit issued by a first class bank. The same considerations will apply in an aircraft financing as for any other transaction where a letter of credit is provided – namely, that:

- the letter of credit issuer is suitably creditworthy;
- the letter of credit can be called on first demand; and
- there is a suitable opportunity in all circumstances for the letter of credit to be called if it has not been renewed sufficiently in advance of its expiry date.

### 4.4 Corporate guarantees

Many aircraft lease and loan financings are secured by the provision of a parent company guarantee, especially where the airline is part of a larger group. However, there is no difference between these guarantees and those provided in respect of any other corporate borrowing.

### 4.5 Maintenance reserves

As mentioned earlier in this chapter, the value of an aircraft is affected significantly by the maintenance status of the principal aircraft components and the cost of maintenance can be considerable. It is therefore not uncommon, especially in operating lease transactions, to find a requirement for the airline to make regular monthly payments to the lessor by reference to each flight hour or cycle operated by each of the major components. These maintenance reserves will then be accumulated by the lessor and released to the airline against production of suitable invoices and evidence that the relevant maintenance event has been performed. Unused accruals will be retained by an operating lessor at the end of the lease term because they will be needed by the next airline operator to pay for maintenance becoming due at a later stage, but which relates to the previous operation of the aircraft. In the absence of such reserves, a lessor might find itself having to repossess an aircraft from an insolvent airline at a time when major maintenance was shortly required to be performed in order to keep the aircraft airworthy and remarketable.

It is occasionally the case that letters of credit are provided to cover the potential exposure to undertake periodic maintenance, but the operation of such provisions can become cumbersome if the letters of credit need to be frequently renewed or increased in value.

A complication can arise where the airline wishes to enter into a 'power by the hour' maintenance contract with its maintenance provider, under which regular payments are due by the airline to the maintenance provider as opposed to larger sums based on the actual work undertaken each time a shop visit is required. In such situation the airline will not wish to pay monthly reserves to the lessor as well as making monthly 'power by the hour' payments to its maintenance provider. This conundrum can be solved where a pragmatic approach is taken by both the lessor and the maintenance provider, but invariably neither will be in such a good position as it would have been without the involvement of a third party.

### 4.6 Asset value support

In certain aircraft lease and secured loan financings, additional security is provided to the lessor/lender as the result of some kind of asset value support.

Asset value support comes in many shapes and sizes, from fully enforceable first loss deficiency guarantees in the event that an aircraft is sold for less than a pre-agreed amount, to more conditional residual value guarantees which depend on the operational history and maintenance condition of the aircraft at the time the guarantee is invoked.

Asset value support is normally provided either by a manufacturer seeking to underpin the residual value of its aircraft or by a third-party financier or insurance company which is prepared to take the future residual value risk of an aircraft in return for a fee at the outset of a transaction.

### 4.7 Repossession insurance

Another less common type of security occasionally required by lessors and lenders in aircraft lease and finance transactions is repossession insurance, sometimes referred to as political risk insurance.

The purpose of a repossession insurance policy is to provide cover for the lessor or lender in the event that the aviation authority in the state of registration of the aircraft fails to permit the deregistration and export of the aircraft on termination or expiry of the lease, consequently depriving the lessor/lender of its asset/security.

Repossession insurance policies can be expensive and frequently contain a number of exclusions and conditions which mean that the extent of cover is limited. They remain useful, however, in certain jurisdictions and under certain political conditions where aircraft financing would not otherwise be possible.

### 4.8 Remarketing agreements

Although not strictly speaking security, there is no value for a finance lessor or secured lender in being entitled to enforce a mortgage or terminate a lease and repossess an aircraft unless the lessor/lender has the ability and market knowledge to remarket the asset successfully. For this reason, many financiers enter into remarketing and lease management agreements with experienced third parties which are more readily able to monitor the value preservation of an asset during the term of a lease or loan financing and, if necessary, to remarket the aircraft at short notice in the event of a default and forced repossession.

## 4.9 Aircraft mortgages

For a secured lender in an aircraft finance transaction, the aircraft mortgage has historically been the primary source of security. That remains the case for most financial institutions, although some lenders are now prepared to consider their effective control of ownership through a combined loan and lease structure as equivalent security to, or even better than, an aircraft mortgage.

It is a common misconception that the parties to an aircraft finance transaction are free to choose the governing law of the mortgage over the aircraft. This is not the case.

As a matter of English law, the relevant law governing the creation of a security interest in property should be the law of the country in which that property is situated at the time the mortgage is created (or the *lex situs*). Many other countries have different rules. In particular, those countries which have ratified the Geneva Convention on the International Recognition of Rights in Aircraft, 1948 (eg, the United States, France and Germany, but not including, for example, the United Kingdom, Japan and Russia) require security over aircraft to be constituted in accordance with the laws of the state of registration. What really matters is that the security should be enforceable wherever the aircraft happens to be at the time of enforcement. Since an aircraft is constantly changing jurisdiction, this can be difficult to predict.

The first step in taking an aircraft mortgage is therefore to determine the actual and deemed location of the aircraft at the time the mortgage will be created and to verify what the requirements are of the local law in that jurisdiction for creating a mortgage over an aircraft.

In many jurisdictions, there is no specific law relating to the creation of mortgages over aircraft. In others, there are prohibitively expensive stamp duties related to the creation or registration of aircraft mortgages. For this reason, a practice has developed of purporting to create English law mortgages over aircraft which are located or registered in various jurisdictions but, as mentioned above, the validity of these mortgages is sometimes questionable.

In the United Kingdom, aircraft mortgages are specifically contemplated by the Mortgaging of Aircraft Order 1972 (as amended). An aircraft mortgage created by an English company over any aircraft needs to be registered against the company itself in Companies House to perfect the validity of the mortgage. In addition, for UK registered aircraft, the mortgage will need to be registered with the Civil Aviation Authority to ensure its priority.

It is essential to take informed local legal advice on both the form and registration requirements for an aircraft mortgage in the relevant jurisdiction.

## 4.10 Lease assignment

Where a combined loan/lease financing structure is used, and also where a valuable sublease is in place, it is customary for the lenders to require the lessor to assign all of their rights under the lease as security for the loan obligations.

Any lease assignment will also need to include whatever security may have been provided by the airline to the lessor, such as rights under the assignment of insurances and any security deposit, maintenance reserves or airframe/engine warranty agreements.

As with any legal assignment, notice of the assignment will be given to the lessee, which will normally be required to enter into a direct acknowledgement with the lender confirming, in particular, that the airline will enter into a new lease with the lender on the same terms as the existing lease if the existing lease is terminated as a result of the lessor's default or insolvency.

There will usually be certain rights under the lease which should not be assigned to the lenders because they relate to property which should rightfully remain with the lessor. Such rights will normally include any indemnity payments in respect of the lessor's liability to third parties and any part of the rental income stream which is required to enable the lessor to satisfy its tax or ongoing administration costs. In more complex structured financings, there may well be streams of rental income which are intended to remain with the lessor and it would also be normal to exclude these from the assignment.

A practice has developed over recent years in certain transactions of including in the assignment a description of certain obligations of the airline under the lease as 'co-extensive rights'. The intention is that certain rights, such as the right to inspect the aircraft or to terminate the lease following an airline default, should be exercisable by either the lessor or the lender as assignee. Careful consideration needs to be given as to whether it is in fact reasonable for the airline to owe an obligation to two parties instead of the original one.

In certain jurisdictions it will be necessary for the notification of the assignment to be given to the airline in a formal manner, for example under Section 1690 of the Civil Code in France, and local advice should be sought in this respect.

## 4.11 Charge over shares

As a final layer of security in combined loan/lease financing structures, the lenders will often ask for a charge or pledge over the shares in the lessor SPV. This may be considered by some as a 'belt, suspenders and braces' approach to security because the lender will then have three separate enforcement routes in the event of lessor default:

- enforcement of the mortgage;
- enforcement of lease assignment; and
- enforcement of the charge over shares, effectively becoming the lessor itself.

The intention behind this three-pronged security is to ensure that the lessor is genuinely bankruptcy remote and will not be incurring liability to any third parties.

## 5. Preferential liens

The financier of an aircraft, whether an owner/lessor or a mortgagee, needs to be aware of certain rights over the aircraft which may take preference over its ownership or mortgage.

Such preferential rights and liens vary from jurisdiction to jurisdiction.

In the United Kingdom, the following rights will take priority over the rights of an aircraft owner or mortgagee:

- statutory detention rights, including the rights of airports and air navigation authorities to detain and sell an aircraft for payment of their charges, similar rights for customs and unpaid tax and, most significantly, the ability of the Civil Aviation Authority to detain and sell an aircraft in respect of all charges owing to Eurocontrol by the operator of that aircraft, not just in respect of the aircraft itself;
- contractual liens, most commonly found in maintenance and repair agreements and which authorise the maintenance shop to detain and sell an aircraft in the event that the maintenance charges are not paid when due; and
- possessory liens arising under common law as a result of labour performed on an aircraft which enhances that aircraft's value.

Pursuant to the Cape Town Convention, it will be possible for a contracting state to make a declaration that certain rights (eg, those of Eurocontrol and other air navigation service providers) will obtain priority without a requirement for registration. The availability of such a published list will be of some assistance to aircraft financiers in better understanding potential preferred liens.

## 6. The Cape Town Convention

The Convention on International Interests in Mobile Equipment and the related Protocol on Matters Specific to Aircraft Equipment (more commonly known as the Cape Town Convention) came into force on March 1 2006.

The primary purpose of the convention and protocol is to provide a method for the creation, registration, recognition, priority and enforcement of certain ownership, security and leasing interests in aircraft and aircraft engines.

The Cape Town Convention is interesting because it contemplates the creation of an entirely new security interest known as an 'international interest'. An international interest will be created where a security agreement, conditional sale agreement, leasing agreement or contract for sale of an aircraft object is entered into in writing by a debtor/seller located in a contracting state at the time of conclusion of the agreement or where the aircraft is registered (or agreed to be registered) in a contracting state at that time.

In order for an international interest to obtain priority, it must be registered in the International Registry, which is located in Ireland. Registration is electronic, simple, relatively inexpensive and does not require the documents evidencing the relevant international interest being registered to be lodged. Each registration will require the consent of both the applicable debtor and creditor, and the registration will not be effective until consent is given to the International Registry.

Priority is generally based on the order of registration, which is strictly time based, and a registered international interest will also have priority over one that is not registered.

It is therefore now important to consider in all new secured aircraft financing transactions, or where novating or otherwise amending existing transactions, whether the provisions of the Cape Town Convention are applicable and, if so, to arrange for the relevant parties to register themselves with the International Registry so that the necessary international interests can be recorded and the additional security contemplated by the Cape Town Convention properly established.

## 7. Conclusion

In summary, when considering what security interests will be relevant in the context of a secured aircraft financing, very much the same analysis will be required as for any other asset or project. Who owns the asset? Where is it located and registered? What income does it generate? What factors impact on its value? How is it possible to repossess and remarket it? What interests may take priority?

# Ships

**John Forrester**
Holman Fenwick & Willan

## 1. Introduction

Shipping is a fascinating and complex industry, and this complexity must be understood by anyone seeking to take security over a ship. As an asset class, ships are (obviously) moveable. Ships engaged in international trades travel from jurisdiction to jurisdiction and, as they pass from one jurisdiction to another, certain laws relating to that ship (eg, as to arrest procedures and the rights of creditors of that ship) will change. Ships can attract claims *in rem* which attach to the ship and stay with her notwithstanding any subsequent change of ownership. Moreover, these claims can arise by virtue of the acts of third parties (eg, charterers) and may rank in priority ahead of the rights of a mortgagee of the ship, even if the mortgage came first in time. Ships are technically chattels but, unlike most types of chattel (the other obvious exception being aircraft), ships are subject to a system of registration similar to land registration. Registration systems vary from jurisdiction to jurisdiction, but in essence, every maritime nation maintains a national register (or system of local registers based in its main ports)[1] in which are recorded the ownership and mortgage details of each ship registered in that jurisdiction. This gives ship (and aircraft) finance an advantage over other areas of chattel finance because it generally allows the lender to take a fixed security over a registered asset and perfect that security simply by recording the relevant mortgage instrument in a public register without having to take physical possession of the asset.

The purpose of this chapter is to provide an overview of the securities customarily taken by a lender in a standard ship mortgage-based financing (including also, in the case of ships under construction, the securities typically taken during the construction period). These asset-based financings are to be distinguished from lease-based financings in which the lender takes title to the ship (usually through a special purpose subsidiary) and then lets the ship on charter to the borrower, which will pay charter hire at a rate which covers the underlying funding costs (plus the lender's margin). Such leasing deals fall outside the scope of this chapter.

## 2. Meaning of 'ship'

What constitutes a 'ship'? This is rarely an issue (like the proverbial elephant, one

1 As is the case, for example, in Russia and Italy. Before the United Kingdom centralised its ship registry in Cardiff in 1994, individual ship registers were maintained in 114 different ports around the United Kingdom.

can usually tell when one is dealing with a ship even if it is hard to come up with an exact definition),[2] but it is worth pointing out that assets such as offshore oil rigs will usually be treated as 'ships' for the purposes of ship registration legislation even though one might not naturally think of them as such. Ultimately, it is a matter for the national legislation of each jurisdiction to define what it will accept as a ship. This means, for example, that a structure known as a 'linkspan' (a fixed but floating loading ramp used for certain types of ferry) is classified as a ship under both Dutch and Swedish law, but not under English law, where it is treated as a mere chattel.

It is also worth pointing out that some registries maintain separate registers for different vessel types and that the status of the vessel's registration may differ depending on the particular register used. For example, the UK ship register is split into different parts so that fishing vessels and small ships (being ships of less than 24 metres in length overall) will be recorded on separate parts of the register to merchant ships and other large (non-fishing) vessels. In the case of small ships, there is no obligation to register these ships on the register and registration principally acts as a means of evidencing the owner's title. Importantly, there is no means of recording mortgages on the small ships register. With this in mind, the remainder of this chapter will use the expression 'ship' to include only those ships which are registered on a full public register in which details of any mortgages on that ship may be recorded.

## 3. Ship registration and the importance of flag

Systems of ship registration vary from jurisdiction to jurisdiction (eg, as to nationality requirements for the owner, what constitutes a ship and the formalities of registration), but leaving aside small ships of the type discussed above, the key fundamental is that title to the ship and the details of any registered mortgages over the ship will be recorded on a public register. Normally, the ship will derive her nationality from the jurisdiction in which her title is registered (the title registry state) and will be required to display this nationality by flying the flag of that jurisdiction. The one exception to this is where the ship is let on bareboat charter to a charterer that temporarily registers the ship in its own jurisdiction (the bareboat registry state) for the duration of the bareboat charter.[3] In such cases, the ship's registration in the title registry state is suspended and the ship will instead take her nationality from, and be required to fly the flag of, the bareboat registry state. Crucially, however, the ship's ownership title and any mortgages remain registered in the title registry state during this period.[4] As we will see later, this is important because the governing law of a ship mortgage will be the law of the title registry state.

Registration in a bareboat registry state is possible only if the laws of both the title registry state and the bareboat registry state permit it. Moreover, such

---

2 The statutory definition under the UK Merchant Shipping Act, 1995 simply defines a 'ship' as including "every description of vessel used in navigation". One then has to fall back on a large body of case law to determine whether something is a 'vessel' or is 'used in navigation'.

3 A bareboat charter is a charter (or lease) under which the charterer takes over full possession and control of the ship.

4 It may, however, be necessary to record details of the mortgage in the register maintained by the bareboat registry state (as is the case in, for example, Australia and Venezuela).

arrangements will almost invariably require the formal consent of any registered mortgagee (and indeed, as a matter of contract between the owner and the mortgagee, there will usually be a prohibition on the owner entering into bareboat charters at all without the mortgagee's consent).

The jurisdiction whose flag a ship flies (be it the title registry state or a bareboat registry state) is known as the 'flag state' and has the responsibility for ensuring that the ship maintains certain standards relating to matters such as crewing, seaworthiness, pollution prevention and ship safety (flag state control). The identity of the flag state is important to a lender because some registries have a reputation for failing to enforce these standards rigorously. This is of concern to lenders for several reasons. First, there is the reputational risk: if a lender agrees to finance a ship whose flag state has a poor reputation and the ship has a major accident or causes a pollution spill, the lender risks adverse publicity by reason of its association with that flag state. Second, lenders take comfort from the inspections and monitoring that the flag state should be carrying out. Third, ships registered in jurisdictions with a poor reputation for flag state control face a higher likelihood of being detained for inspection by port state authorities[5] (with the consequent delays and loss of earnings that may ensue). Finally, ships registered under a flag with a poor reputation are likely to be less attractive to major charterers (eg, the oil majors), meaning that their earning capacity may be reduced

## 4. Standard ship finance security documents

No two deals are the same, but leaving aside construction financing, which is discussed in section 12, any secured shipping loan will inevitably involve a mortgage on the ship (and, if appropriate, a collateral deed of covenants). The lender will also want a secured interest in the ship's insurances and, unless this is conferred by other means,[6] will require an assignment of the ship's insurances. Similarly, the lender should obtain an assignment of the ship's requisition compensation. Unless the borrower is a particularly strong credit, the deal will almost invariably involve an assignment of the ship's earnings (and possibly also a specific assignment of any charter or other employment contract relating to the ship).[7] The earnings assignment is often supplemented by a charge over one or more accounts into which the earnings are to be collected and/or retained. The lender may also take a charge or pledge over the shares in the owner of the ship. Other security documents may include parent company guarantees and undertakings from third parties such as the ship's charterer or manager whereby they agree to subordinate their claims against the ship to the rights of the mortgagee. These different securities (apart from guarantees) are discussed in further detail below.

---

5 This refers to the regime for inspecting ships when they call into port and are inspected by the maritime authorities of the jurisdiction in which that port is located (the port state).

6 For example, with regard to ships insured under the Norwegian Marine Insurance Plan, the mortgagee is automatically granted an interest in the insurances without the need for an assignment.

7 The assignments of insurances, requisition compensation and earnings are sometimes combined in a single document known as a 'general assignment' or may even be incorporated in any deed of covenants.

## 5. Ship mortgages and deeds of covenant

### 5.1 Introduction

A ship mortgage creates a fixed security which attaches to the ship *in rem* (ie, it will survive a change of ownership of the ship and does not confer just personal rights against the owner), and entitles the lender to sell the ship and use the sale proceeds to pay off the amount owing to it if the owner is in default. Jurisdictions vary as to the way in which the mortgagee's right of sale may be exercised. Some jurisdictions require the ship to be sold by a court sale (via a public auction), whereas others permit private sales as well as court sales. In England and certain other common law jurisdictions, it is even possible to negotiate a sale privately but effect that sale through the court. The significance of this is that a court sale has the effect of clearing the ship's title of all claims against the ship and transferring them instead to the sale proceeds, which will be held by the court for distribution to the ship's creditors once the merits of their claims, and the rankings of those claims, have been determined. This feature of court sales is important because it allows the ship to be sold before the claims of her various creditors have been considered (this can be a lengthy process) and enables the buyer to take title free of any claims against the ship. Contrast this with the position under a private sale, where the buyer will take title subject to all claims then attaching to the ship, even if neither the owner nor the mortgagee is aware of them. In such cases, the mortgagee will often have to give a warranty as to clean title in order to achieve a sale (which usually makes a court sale preferable).

In most jurisdictions, in addition to the power of sale, the mortgagee will be entitled to take possession of the ship in the event of a default by the owner. This allows the mortgagee to direct the ship to a port of the mortgagee's choice and can be important in achieving a successful mortgage enforcement because the laws of the place of arrest will govern the enforcement procedure and determine the ranking of all competing claims on the ship (of which there are likely to be several).[8] However, the disadvantage of taking possession as a mortgagee is that this renders the mortgagee responsible for paying the operating costs of the ship and may also expose the mortgagee to liability to the owner for any imprudent use of the ship.

### 5.2 Is the mortgage bankable?

As mentioned above, the governing law of a ship mortgage will be the law of the ship's title registry state. The lender therefore needs to be satisfied that the rights of a mortgagee under that law, and the integrity of the ship registration regime itself, are sufficiently wide and robust to give it a reliable and enforceable fixed security over the ship (one usually speaks of such mortgages as being 'bankable'). This means that the lender may need to carry out due diligence on the laws of the proposed title registry state, although most shipping banks and ship finance lawyers will already know from experience which registries are acceptable.

If a ship owner wishes to register its ship under a flag which is not considered

---

8 See below at section 5.7.

bankable because it fails to give sufficient protection to mortgagees, but the lender has no objections to that flag on the grounds of reputation, one solution may be for the ship to be registered in a title registry state acceptable to the lender but then be registered simultaneously in the owner's preferred jurisdiction on the basis of a bareboat charter made between the owner and one of its subsidiaries or a sister company. This satisfies both the lender and the owner because the lender has a bankable mortgage and the owner is able to operate the ship under its preferred flag. This may be important to the owner for commercial reasons. For example, in some jurisdictions locally flagged ships enjoy financial privileges such as reduced port charges or subsidised fuel costs.

## 5.3 Form and content

The form and content of a ship mortgage will vary from jurisdiction to jurisdiction depending on the title registry state.

### *(a) Statutory mortgages*

In the United Kingdom and other common law jurisdictions such as the Bahamas, Cyprus, Gibraltar, the Isle of Man and Malta whose maritime laws derive from the British Merchant Shipping Acts, the mortgage is in a form set out by statute (and hence is known as a 'statutory mortgage'). These statutory mortgages are single-page forms which are broadly similar but which differ slightly from jurisdiction to jurisdiction (rather charmingly, the Bahamian statutory mortgage retains the nineteenth century language stating that the mortgage is granted over the ship and "her boats, guns, ammunition, small arms and appurtenances", whereas the United Kingdom one now refers simply to the ship and "its appurtenances").

Statutory mortgages come in two basic forms: one to secure an 'account current' and one to secure 'principal sum and interest'. As its name implies, the latter of these secures only a fixed sum and interest on it. Accordingly, the account current form is almost invariably used as this allows the mortgagee to secure other amounts such as sums expended by it to protect its security (eg, insurance premiums if the owner fails to keep up the insurance cover). A feature of account current mortgages is that they do not need to state the amount or maturity date of the indebtedness being secured. Instead, all that is required is that they identify the underlying documents by reference to which the amount secured can be ascertained.

### *(b) Deeds of covenant*

It is universal practice (though, with at least one exception,[9] not strictly necessary) for a statutory mortgage to be supplemented by a separate deed of covenants made between the owner and the mortgagee.

The purpose of the deed of covenants is to supplement the statutory mortgage with a contract setting out the owner's specific obligations for insuring, maintaining

9 Cyprus requires the owner to enter into a deed of covenants. In other jurisdictions, in the absence of a separate set of agreed mortgage covenants, the owner will have certain general duties at law such as to preserve the ship from deterioration (fair wear and tear excepted) and not to do anything to impair the lender's security.

and operating the ship during the period of the mortgage. These obligations are imposed for the purpose of maintaining the value of the mortgagee's security by ensuring, for example, that:

- the ship is properly insured, repaired and maintained;
- she maintains class with an approved classification society;[10]
- she is not encumbered with liens which rank (or may rank) ahead of the mortgage;
- no material modifications are made to the ship;
- she is not sold or bareboat chartered without the mortgagee's consent;
- the mortgagee is given rights to inspect the ship; and
- the owner is required to notify the mortgagee of any accident, arrest or other material incident affecting the ship.

The deed of covenant also contains detailed provisions setting out the mortgagee's rights in the event of a default by the owner, including the right to appoint a receiver. Additionally – and perhaps rather strangely, given that the mortgagee already has a registered mortgage on the ship – the deed of covenants will usually also contain a provision mortgaging the ship to the mortgagee. This takes effect as an equitable mortgage only and its principal purpose is to create a security interest over any items which relate to the ship, such as onshore spare parts and future additions, which may not be caught by the statutory mortgage (the deed of covenants will often make its definition of 'ship' as wide as possible so as to include all types of present and future items belonging to the ship, whether onboard or onshore).

The deed of covenants is usually a private document between the owner and the mortgagee and need not be registered at the relevant ship registry along with the statutory mortgage. One exception to this is Cyprus, which requires that both the mortgage and the deed of covenants are registered together. Note also that if the deed of covenant creates a charge over the ship (as is usually the case), it will need to be filed with any relevant companies registry.[11]

### *(c)* ***Preferred mortgages***

The most common alternative to the statutory mortgage is a long form of mortgage (often referred to as a 'preferred mortgage') which combines in one single document the charging clause creating the mortgage security and the various mortgage covenants in respect of the ship given by the owner (ie, the same types of covenant as are found in a deed of covenants). There is no prescribed form for preferred

10 Classification societies perform an important role in the shipping industry by inspecting ships and keeping records on their design and condition which can be made available to interested parties such as ship registries, insurers, charterers, purchasers and financiers to demonstrate that the ship is seaworthy and in general good condition. There is no strict legal requirement for a ship to be entered with a classification society, but in practice no ship can be registered, insured, operated or financed without adequate class records. The owner can choose from several classification societies such as Lloyd's Register of Shipping, Det Norske Veritas and American Bureau of Shipping, and a ship is said to be 'in class' if her condition complies with the relevant requirements of that classification society.

11 See section 5.5(c).

mortgages although the title registry state may impose some conditions as to its form and content (eg, as to the language in which the mortgage is written, the basic types of covenant to be given and whether a maximum mortgage amount or maturity date must be stated). This type of mortgage is used in jurisdictions such as the Marshall Islands, Liberia, Panama and Greece.

*(d)* ***Other mortgages***

While statutory mortgages and preferred mortgages are the most common types of mortgage, there are other forms. For example, Norway and Denmark have a printed form which is longer than a statutory mortgage but which need not be supplemented by a deed of covenants. Sweden has a system under which the owner registers a mortgage instrument in abstract against the ship for a specified priority and amount, and then pledges that document to the lender (the lender's security being perfected by the physical delivery to it of the mortgage instrument).[12]

**5.4 Loan to value covenants**

The maximum amount that a mortgagee can hope to recover under a ship mortgage (before associated costs of enforcement and the claims of any preferred creditors) is obviously the amount that the highest bidder is prepared to pay for the ship. This means that the value of the mortgage is directly linked to the value of the ship and the mortgagee will want to ensure that the market value of the ship never falls below a certain threshold (say, 130% of the outstanding loan amount). This is addressed by obtaining a covenant from the owner (usually in the credit agreement) providing for regular valuations of the ship and requiring the owner to make good any shortfall in the required loan to value ratio by prepaying part of the loan or putting up additional security.

**5.5 Formalities for perfecting the mortgage**

The formalities for perfecting a ship mortgage depend upon the laws of the title registry state and these need to be checked and observed carefully (the author was once asked to help enforce a mortgage on a Bahamian ship where the mortgagee had registered the mortgage without taking Bahamian legal advice and was alarmed to discover that the mortgage was not fully valid, despite having been recorded in the ship register, because a small red seal had not been affixed to the mortgage by the owner's signatory).

Some key points to bear in mind are as follows:

- The mortgage may need to be executed as a deed or observe other formalities regarding the manner in which it is executed (particularly as to notarisation and/or legalisation).
- Without exception, in order to be fully effective, a ship mortgage will need to be registered against the ship's name in the title registry state. Failure to do so will not necessarily invalidate the mortgage which, from the point of view

12 This leads to the situation where a junior lender can end up with a second priority pledge over a first priority mortgage instrument and/or a first priority pledge over a second priority mortgage instrument.

of English law at least, would take effect as an equitable mortgage and be binding as between the owner and the mortgagee. However, an unregistered mortgage would almost certainly rank behind any registered mortgage (this is the case in the United Kingdom) and may also fail to create rights *in rem* against the ship.

- In addition to registering the mortgage in the relevant ship registry, it may be necessary to file the mortgage (or particulars of it) with a companies registry in the jurisdiction in which the owner is incorporated or has a place of business. For example, if the owner is incorporated in England and Wales, the mortgage will need to be filed against the owner at Companies House within 21 days of the date on which the mortgage is created; otherwise, it will be void against any liquidator, administrator or creditor of the owner. The mortgage must also be registered at Companies House if it is created by an overseas company with a place of business in England and Wales (whether it has registered that place of business or not) and the mortgaged property is situated in England and Wales (whether at the time and date of creation of the mortgage or at any later date – an obvious possibility with ships). It is therefore advisable in shipping transactions where the mortgage is governed by English law or secures an English law debt to present the ship mortgage and all other relevant security documents to Companies House even if the owner is incorporated overseas and has no registered place of business in England and Wales (regardless of the nationality of the ship). In such cases the mortgage will be refused registration in the register of charges (because the owner does not have a registered place of business in England and Wales), but the registrar will issue a letter confirming that the mortgage has been presented for registration and that details have been entered in the so-called Slavenburg register.[13] This will protect the lender in the event that the owner subsequently registers, or is found to have, a place of business in England and Wales.

## 5.6 Priority of claims

### *(a) Maritime liens*

A registered ship mortgage can never give the lender a superior position to all creditors because claims known as 'maritime liens' which attach to the ship *in rem* will rank ahead of a registered mortgage, even if created after the mortgage. Despite international attempts to harmonise maritime liens, what constitutes a maritime lien will vary from jurisdiction to jurisdiction.

In England, the claims that constitute maritime liens are as follows:

- claims for salvage remuneration;
- claims for collision damage;
- claims for wages of the master and crew;
- claims for disbursements incurred by the master in the course of a voyage;

13 Named after the case which established these principles: *NV Slavenburg's Bank v Inter-Continental Natural Resources Ltd* [1980] 1 All ER 955.

and
- claims for bottomry and respondentia.[14]

This contrasts with the position in, say, the United States, where claims for unpaid repair costs are included in the list of maritime liens recognised by US law.

As noted in section 5.7, the maritime liens that will be recognised upon an arrest of the ship will depend upon the place of arrest.

***(b) Possessory liens***

Another class of lien which ranks ahead of a registered mortgage is a possessory lien. Such a lien will arise, for example, where a shipyard is in possession of a ship to carry out repair work on her. In such cases, the shipyard is entitled to retain possession of the ship until its bill for the repair works has been paid. This right is based entirely on the actual physical possession of the ship so that if possession is handed over while the repair bill still remains unpaid, the shipyard's possessory lien lapses.

***(c) Statutory liens***

Under English law, in addition to claims which fall within the scope of maritime liens, there are a number of other claims which by statute give the claimant a right of action *in rem* against a ship.[15] These claims are listed in the Supreme Court Act 1981 and may be summarised as follows:

- claims in respect of the possession or ownership of a ship;
- claims arising between co-owners as to the possession, employment or earnings of a ship;
- claims in respect of a mortgage or charge on a ship;
- claims for damage received by or done to a ship;
- claims for loss of life or personal injury arising from any defect in a ship or her equipment or arising from the use or management of that ship;
- claims for loss of or damage to cargo carried in a ship;
- claims arising out of any charterparty or contract of carriage in respect of a ship;
- claims in respect of salvage, towage or pilotage of a ship;
- claims in respect of goods or materials supplied to a ship;
- claims in respect of the construction or repair of a ship and dock charges in respect of a ship;
- claims for wages of the master and crew of a ship;
- claims for disbursements incurred on a ship's account;
- claims for general average in respect of a ship;
- claims for bottomry in respect of a ship; and

---

14 These are two (now obsolete) types of lien which survive from the days before modern communications. If the master of the ship found himself in need of money to effect repairs or buy supplies in order to return home but could not contact the owner to obtain funds, he could borrow this amount against the security of the ship's hull (bottomry) or her cargo (respondentia).

15 The same claims as give rise to maritime liens are also included in the list of claims giving rise to a statutory right of action *in rem*.

- claims for forfeiture or condemnation of a ship.

Any of these claims may be brought against a ship provided that there has been no change in the beneficial ownership of the ship between the date on which the claim arose and the date on which the proceedings are commenced. This differs from the case with maritime liens, which will survive any change in ownership. Another difference from maritime liens is that the claim attaches to the ship *in rem* only when the claimant brings an action *in rem* against the ship. Until that time the claim is inchoate and will not have any preferential status. Accordingly, a mortgage will as a general rule have priority over any such claim unless prior to the date of the mortgage a writ *in rem* has been issued against the ship.

***(d) Prior registered mortgages***

A registered mortgage ranks in priority behind any mortgage which has already been registered against the ship. It is the date and (usually) time of registration which determines the priority, not the date of the mortgage.[16]

## 5.7 Mortgage enforcement

If a ship is arrested by the mortgagee (or indeed any other creditor), the law of the place of arrest will determine both the procedure for arresting and selling the ship and the order of priority of the various claims on the ship. The place of arrest can therefore be important for achieving a successful mortgage enforcement and, as far as possible, mortgagees will want to arrange for any ship arrest to take place in a jurisdiction whose laws are favourable to it.

When a ship is arrested in a particular jurisdiction, there are generally three possibilities as to how that jurisdiction will determine which claims are to be treated as maritime liens on that ship. First, the place of arrest may apply its own law to decide what is a maritime lien (as is the case in England).[17] Alternatively, it may apply the law of the flag (as is the case in South Korea). Finally, it may apply the law of the jurisdiction in which the claim arose (as is the case in Canada).[18] Thus, a repairer's lien arising in the United States, and which is recognised under US law as a maritime lien, will not be recognised as a maritime lien if the ship is arrested in England (because the English courts will apply English law, which does not recognise repairer's liens as maritime liens), but will be recognised as a maritime lien if the ship is arrested in Canada because the Canadian courts will look to US law as the law of the claim to determine whether it is a maritime lien (this despite the fact that Canadian law does not recognise repairer's liens as maritime liens). If the same ship were arrested in South Korea the claim would be recognised as a maritime lien if the law of the ship's flag recognised it as such.

One final point to make about ship arrests is that often it will be creditors of the ship with claims ranking behind the mortgage that will arrest the ship. There is a

16 In a few jurisdictions, such as Greece, if two or more mortgages are registered on the same day, they will enjoy equal ranking rather than be ranked according to the time of registration.

17 See *The Halcyon Isle* [1981] AC 221 (PC).

18 See *The Ioannis Daskalelis* (Canada) [1974] 1 LR 174.

significant nuisance value attached to these arrests (since they prevent the ship from trading) and such arrests are often a tactical attempt by the creditor to force the mortgagee into paying off the claim in order to allow the ship to continue trading (or, if things are getting dire for the owner, to enable the mortgagee to arrange for the ship to be taken to a more favourable jurisdiction for its own enforcement proceedings).

## 6. Assignment of insurances

### 6.1 Purpose

If a mortgaged ship becomes an actual or constructive total loss (ie, she is lost or damaged beyond economic repair), the ship mortgage effectively becomes worthless and the mortgagee will then want to have recourse to the proceeds of the ship's insurances. Moreover, if the ship suffers damage falling short of a total loss, the mortgagee will be concerned to ensure that the insurance proceeds are properly applied to make good the damage (an unrepaired ship has a reduced value and this in turn reduces the value of the lender's mortgage). This assumes that no event of default has occurred under the credit agreement. If it has, the mortgagee may want to apply the insurance proceeds directly against the outstanding mortgage debt rather than towards the repair of the ship. For each of these reasons, unless the mortgagee is automatically granted an interest in the insurances by other means (eg, under the Norwegian Marine Insurance Plan), the mortgagee will want to take an assignment of the ship's insurances.

### 6.2 Brief summary of marine insurances

The three principal categories of marine insurance taken out by a ship owner are:

- hull and machinery insurance (including increased value cover);
- war risks insurance; and
- protection and indemnity (P&I) insurance.

In basic terms, hull and machinery insurance (including increased value cover) covers the ship for physical loss or damage arising from certain maritime perils, but not from war risks, which are covered by a separate war risks policy. P&I insurance is a third-party liability insurance (covering, for example, liabilities to crew and cargo and liabilities for pollution) which operates on a 'pay to be paid' rule.[19] A mortgagee will want an assignment of each of these insurances.

Hull and machinery insurance (including increased value cover) is usually taken out in the commercial insurance markets through specialist insurance brokers, whereas P&I cover is usually obtained by means of an entry in a mutual insurance association of ship owners (known as a 'P&I club'). War risks cover falls somewhere between the two, in the sense that it is common for it to be taken out either in the commercial markets or through a mutual war risks association.

A further category of insurance which is sometimes taken out by a ship owner

---

19 Meaning that the ship owner has to pay the third-party claim itself before being able to claim reimbursement under its insurance cover.

(and which a lender will sometimes insist on the owner taking out) is loss of hire insurance. This is a type of business interruption insurance which compensates the owner for any loss of earnings following a claim under its hull and machinery cover (eg, if the ship goes off-hire while repairs are carried out).

A lender will need to conduct a careful review of the insurances on any ship that it finances and will often enlist the assistance of specialist insurance advisers to issue a formal insurance report as a condition precedent to advancing funds. The ship mortgage or deed of covenant will contain various detailed provisions as to the scope, terms and quality of the insurance cover. These provisions will normally require that the ship is insured for at least, say, 130% of the outstanding mortgage debt and in any case for not less than her market value. They will also require that the insurances must be placed and renewed on terms approved by the mortgagee with brokers and insurers acceptable to them (the creditworthiness of the underwriters being a key factor to check). The mortgagee will also impose various information covenants on the owner requiring it to keep the mortgagee advised of various material matters such as any cancellation of cover or failure to renew the insurances when due.

A specific point to note in respect of P&I insurance is that the P&I club's rules will usually prohibit an assignment of those insurances (and, in most cases, will also say that the owner's cover will be terminated if the ship is mortgaged without the club's consent). This means that it is essential to obtain a letter of undertaking from the P&I club confirming its consent to the mortgage and insurance assignment.[20] In such cases, the consent to the insurance assignment is usually stated to be on terms that it is given only to give efficacy to a loss payable clause stating that any amounts otherwise payable to the owner will be paid to the mortgagee following receipt by the P&I club of notice that the owner is in default under its mortgage.

### 6.3 Invalidation of insurances; mortgagee's interest insurance

An important point to note about an assignment of insurances is that the insurance proceeds will be payable to the mortgagee only if, but for the assignment, they would have been payable to the owner. Put another way, the mortgagee will be unable to recover any insurance proceeds if the owner has done something to invalidate its claim under the insurance policy. Circumstances in which the owner's claim would be invalidated include:

- misrepresentation or non-disclosure of any material circumstances;
- breach of any express or implied warranty or condition, including those relating to seaworthiness, breach of trading warranties and failure to keep the ship in class;
- failure to exercise due diligence in respect of loss or damage to the ship; and
- deliberate or fraudulent damage to the ship.

A lender can protect itself against non-payment in these circumstances by taking out an insurance policy known as mortgagee's interest insurance. This policy should

20 See section 6.6.

be taken out in the lender's name, but the lender will ordinarily require the owner to reimburse its costs in doing so.

**6.4 Mortgagee's additional perils (pollution) insurance**

Another form of insurance policy sometimes taken out by lenders is a mortgagee's additional perils (pollution) insurance policy. This type of policy indemnifies the lender to the extent of any loss under a credit agreement caused by the mortgaged ship being held responsible for a pollution incident where the owner's liability exceeds the liability limit for which it has taken out insurance. In such a case, under US law, plaintiffs can acquire a maritime lien on a ship that is held responsible for damages where any consequential legal liabilities have not been paid or are unrecoverable. This lien will rank ahead of the lender's mortgage and could well exceed the market value of the ship, thereby wiping out the value of the lender's mortgage entirely. Mortgagee's additional perils policies are therefore relevant for ships trading to the United States (particularly tankers).

**6.5 Formalities for perfecting the assignment**

Various formalities need to be observed in order to perfect an assignment of insurances; these will depend upon the governing law of that assignment and, if different, the governing law of the insurance policies themselves. In the case of an English law assignment, the following steps need to be taken:

- A written notice of the assignment must be served on the relevant insurers (usually via the broker or, as the case may be, manager of any P&I club or war risks association), which will endorse it on the insurance policies together with a statement known as a loss payable clause which stipulates to whom, and in what circumstances, the insurance proceeds are to be paid. In the case of insurances covering the ship's hull and machinery (whether under her ordinary hull and machinery cover or her war risks cover), this will usually specify that all amounts above a certain threshold amount are to be paid to the mortgagee but that, in the absence of a notice from the mortgagee advising the insurers that the owner is in default under the credit agreement, amounts below such threshold amount are to be paid direct to the owner.
- As noted at section 6.2, it will usually be necessary to obtain the P&I club's consent to the mortgage and insurance assignment. The relevant insurer's consent will also have to be obtained if this is a condition of any other insurance policy.
- If any of the insurance policies covered by the assignment is governed by a law other than English law, it is important to observe any relevant formalities in that jurisdiction. For example, in the case of French law insurances, the notice should be formally served on the insurers or their broker by a court bailiff.
- The assignment should be presented for registration at any relevant companies registry.[21]

---

21 See section 5.5(c).

6.6 **Letters of undertaking**

It is customary in the London marine insurance market (and various other markets, particularly in Europe) for insurance brokers and the managers of any relevant P&I club or war risks association to issue a letter of undertaking to the mortgagee confirming various matters, such as that copies of the notice of assignment and loss payable clause will be endorsed on the ship's insurance policies and that the mortgagee will be given notice of certain material matters such as non-renewal or cancellation of the policy. Additionally, in the case of P&I clubs, the letter of undertaking is required in order to confirm the club's consent to the insurance assignment and mortgage relating to the ship.[22] The mortgage or deed of covenants should therefore impose an obligation on the owner to procure that letters of undertaking are issued to the mortgagee in the appropriate form.

6.7 **Reinsurances**

If a ship owner places all or part of its insurance cover with a state-owned or captive insurance company,[23] the assignment of insurances will give the mortgagee recourse only to that insurer. This means that the mortgagee will be taking a credit risk on that company's ability to meet any claim under the insurances in full. In such cases, the mortgagee will usually consent to such arrangements only if the insurance company has taken out adequate reinsurances and the mortgagee has recourse to those reinsurances (preferably by means of an assignment from the insurer but sometimes simply by means of a special loss payable clause, known as a 'cut-through clause', which is endorsed on the reinsurance policy and stipulates that payments are to be made direct to the mortgagee). Such security can be taken in practice only if the reinsurances are placed on a facultative basis (ie, where the reinsurances relate just to the relevant ship or ships concerned) and not on a treaty basis (ie, where the insurer reinsures the whole of its overall insurance risk under a single policy).

Reinsurance assignments should be perfected in the same manner as assignments of primary insurances and letters of undertaking should also be required in the ordinary way.

7. **Assignment of requisition compensation**

Requisition compensation is the compensation paid by the title registry state in the event that it requisitions for title (ie, compulsorily acquires) a ship registered with it. This is an extremely rare event but it is a possibility, in theory at least, and should be covered by taking an assignment of the requisition compensation. This assignment is usually contained in the same document as the assignment of insurances, but is not perfected by giving notice to the requisitioning authority. Instead, the assignment will contain an undertaking on the owner's part to give a notice of assignment in the event that the ship is ever requisitioned for title (and the lender will normally be given a power of attorney under the assignment to execute such a notice on behalf of the

---

22 See section 6.2.

23 A 'captive insurance company' is a company which is owned by the ship owner or another company under common ownership with it.

owner, and undertake any other appropriate remedial actions, in the event that the owner fails to comply with its obligation to give the notice itself).

Requisition for title should not be confused with requisition for hire, which occurs when the flag state compulsorily takes on hire a ship registered with it.[24] In such cases the requisitioning authority will pay hire to the owner and this will be captured by the assignment of earnings made by the owner.

## 8. Assignment of earnings/charters and account charges

The purpose of the assignment of earnings is to give the mortgagee a secured interest in the income of the ship which may be the only means of servicing the mortgage debt. Where the ship is subject to a medium or long-term charter, the assignment of earnings will often be expanded to contain an assignment of the charter itself and, if relevant, any charter guarantee (although it is important to check that there are no prohibitions on assignment in the charter documents – if there are, the assignment will be invalid in the absence of consent from the charterer and/or charter guarantor, as appropriate).

In order to perfect an English law assignment, notice of the assignment should be served on the charterer and any relevant charter guarantor. However, in the case of short-term charters it is often agreed that no notice needs to be given unless a default occurs under the credit agreement (with the lender having the same remedial powers as mentioned in section 7).

The assignment will almost invariably contain a requirement that the ship's earnings be paid into a specified collection account (known as an 'earnings account' or 'operating account') which is usually held with the mortgagee and over which the mortgagee will often take a charge. In many cases the owner will be required to establish a second account with the mortgagee (known as a 'retention account'), which will also be charged to the mortgagee. The purpose of this account is to build up a sufficient sum in advance of each repayment date under the credit agreement so that there will always be sufficient funds to cover each payment of principal and interest. Thus, where charter hire is received on a monthly basis but repayments under the credit agreement fall every six months, the idea is that one-sixth of the next payment of principal and interest is taken out of the earnings account each month and placed in the retention account. Any surplus on the earnings account after paying this retention amount (and after also meeting the ship's monthly operating expenses) will often be released to the owner as long as it is not in default under the credit agreement.

Any charge over an earnings account and/or retention account should, as a general rule, be governed by the law of the jurisdiction in which the account is situated and will need to be perfected in accordance with those laws.

## 9. Charge or pledge over shares

Another form of security which is sometimes used in ship finance transactions is the shares charge or shares pledge. These are well suited to shipping transactions because

---

24 As occurred during the Falklands war between the United Kingdom and Argentina in 1982 when several British flagged ships were requisitioned for hire by the UK government.

the registered owner of a ship will often be a limited liability company with no assets other than the ship itself.[25] Under this document all of the shares in the owner are charged or pledged to the lender which, in the event of a default under the credit agreement, will be able to step in and take over ownership of the owner or, alternatively, sell the shares to a third party. An advantage of this is that the ship may at that time be subject to a valuable charter which would be terminated if the lender were to enforce its mortgage but which would survive a change of ownership in the owner.[26] The downside is that the purchase of a company (as opposed to its ship) is riskier for the purchaser because it is more difficult to identify with absolute certainty the liabilities attaching to the company. This contrasts with the sale of a ship through a court sale, which will wash the ship clean of all existing claims.

The form that the shares charge or shares pledge will take (and its governing law) depends upon various factors such as the place of incorporation of the owner, the provisions of its constitutional documents and whether the shares are registered or bearer shares. In simple terms, one takes a pledge when the shares are bearer shares but a charge when the shares are registered. This is because a pledge depends upon having physical possession of the relevant asset (in this case the bearer share certificates), whereas a charge takes effect without physical possession being required.

In the case of a shares charge the lender has two options:

- It can take a full legal charge (where it or its nominee becomes the registered shareholder for the duration of the security period); or
- More commonly, it can take an equitable charge under which the shareholder executes a blank stock transfer form which the lender can complete in favour of itself or its nominee in the event of a default under the credit agreement.

The lender should also require undated letters of resignation from each of the directors and officers of the company so that it can replace them with its own nominated management team in the event of a default.

The shares charge or pledge should be presented for registration against the shareholder at any relevant companies registry.[27]

## 10. Charterer's subordination undertakings (and quiet enjoyment undertakings)

Under English law, the charterer of a ship may be entitled in tort to obtain an injunction preventing the lender from enforcing its mortgage. Additionally, the lender may be liable in damages to a charterer for any losses arising from the lender's enforcement action. This is a complicated area of law and the case law is not settled. However, it is prudent for a mortgagee to proceed on the basis that if the owner

25 It is common in the shipping industry for the registered owner of a ship to be a limited liability company with no assets other than the ship itself. Ship owners often arrange their affairs so that all of their ships are owned indirectly through a series of such single-purpose owning companies. The purpose of this is to avoid the risk of sister-ship arrests whereby a person with a claim against a ship can pursue its claim by arresting any other ship owned by the same (registered) owner.

26 Though the charter may prohibit changes of ownership in the owner.

27 See section 5.5(c).

enters into a charter which does not impair the mortgagee's security, and if the owner is both willing and able to continue performing the charter, the mortgagee will not be entitled to interfere with the charter and will be restrained from enforcing its mortgage by the English courts.

The risk of a charterer seeking to prevent the lender from enforcing its mortgage can be dealt with by way of a contractual undertaking from the charterer whereby it agrees to subordinate its rights under the charter to those of the lender under the mortgage. In practice, third-party charterers will not be willing to give such undertakings (other than in exceptional cases), but the lender should insist that any in-house charterer be required to provide such an undertaking.

Depending upon the commercial circumstances of the case, the charterer may in fact demand that the lender give it a quiet enjoyment undertaking, whereby the lender agrees to subordinate the mortgage to the charter. This is written in terms whereby the lender agrees not to enforce the mortgage as long as the charterer is performing the charter. The theory here is that if the charterer is performing, then by definition it must be paying the charter hire which is being used to service the mortgage debt. Accordingly, it is argued, the lender's position is not materially prejudiced by giving the quiet enjoyment undertaking. This is true in the sense that the lender is receiving the income from the ship. However, it does leave the lender exposed to a fall in the market value of the ship. If the market value were to decline below the outstanding credit amount, the lender would be exposed to a shortfall in its security value at the end of the charter period.

## 11. Manager's subordination undertakings

It is common for ship owners to appoint a manager to handle the technical and/or commercial management of their ships and the manager is likely to have claims from time to time against the owner for payments under the management agreement. The lender will want these claims to be subordinated to its rights under the mortgage and insurance assignment so that it receives payment ahead of the manager. It will also want the manager to agree not to arrest the ship in support of its claims.

As with charterers, genuine third-party managers are unlikely to give subordination undertakings but the lender should insist on such undertakings from any in-house managers.

## 12. Construction financing

Ships are expensive assets to construct and are usually only ever constructed to order. The expense is such that the buyer is almost invariably required to pay instalments of the purchase price at various milestones during the construction period (eg, contract signing, first steel cutting, keel-laying and launching), with the balance being payable on delivery. Usually the title to the ship will remain with the shipbuilder until delivery and the buyer will be given a refund guarantee by the shipbuilder's bank to secure the shipbuilder's obligation to refund the pre-delivery instalments (with interest) if the ship is not delivered in accordance with the shipbuilding contract. Alternatively, although this is far less common, title to the ship will pass to the buyer during construction so that the buyer can take the ship away and complete her at another yard if the shipbuilder defaults.

Where a lender provides finance to a ship owner to help it pay the pre-delivery instalments under a shipbuilding contract, and where in such cases title to the ship remains vested in the shipbuilder until delivery, the lender will usually require the owner to assign to it by way of security all of its rights under the shipbuilding contract and any associated refund guarantees. One of the main purposes of this assignment is to protect the lender so that if a default by the shipbuilder occurs requiring it to refund the pre-delivery instalments to the buyer, the refund amount will instead be payable to the lender. If, as may well be the case, the shipbuilder is incapable of making that payment, the lender will then be able to call under the refund guarantees. The lender is more exposed, however, in the event of a default by the buyer. In such case the builder will be able to retain the pre-delivery instalments and recover the balance of its losses by selling the ship. Although any surplus above this amount will normally be payable to the buyer (and hence to the lender under the assignment), this may leave the lender with a shortfall. In such case the lender will want to have prior notice of the buyer's default from the shipbuilder so that the lender has an opportunity to remedy the default and step into the contract so that the builder completes the ship's construction and delivers it to the lender or the lender's nominee. The lender can then arrange for the ship to be sold and apply the sale proceeds against the outstanding amount owing to it.

Where pre-delivery finance is provided in respect of a ship whose title passes to the buyer during construction, the lender will normally still require an assignment of the shipbuilding contract (so that it can step in and have the ship completed if the buyer defaults), but will supplement this with a mortgage on the ship under construction.

A shipbuilding contract (like any other contract) cannot be assigned if the contract contains a prohibition on assignment. This may mean that the builder's consent will have to be obtained for the assignment.

In order to perfect an English law assignment of a shipbuilding contract and any associated refund guarantees, notice of the assignment must be served on the shipbuilder and refund guarantor. In addition, the assignment should be presented for registration against the buyer at any relevant companies registry.[28]

As noted above, it may be necessary to obtain the builder's consent for any assignment (and, for commercial reasons, this is not always forthcoming). Another problem faced by lenders is that in some jurisdictions an export licence must be obtained from the local authorities for the ship to be delivered to the buyer. If the lender subsequently steps into the building contract under its assignment it may find that it cannot take effective delivery (either itself or through a nominee) because it does not have an export licence. Both of these problems can be addressed by taking a charge or pledge over the shares in the buying company since, as we have seen before, this will leave the buyer's contractual arrangements unaffected. The one proviso to this is that the shares cannot be pledged or charged without the builder's consent if the shipbuilding contract contains a prohibition on a change in the ownership of the buyer (but such provisions are rare).

---

28 See section 5.5(c).

# Eastern Europe

**Grzegorz Dyczkowski**
Norton Rose Piotr Strawa and Partners, LP
**Tomas Gärdfors**
Norton Rose LLP
**Dmitry Gravin**
Norton Rose (Central Europe) LLP
**Pavel Kvícala**
Norton Rose vos

## 1. Introduction

Lending carries an inherent risk. As a result, lenders will always seek security from which they can realise value should the borrower fail to comply with the loan agreement or other principal finance documents. In order to reduce the lender's risk in real terms, the security provided must be readily realisable upon acceleration of the loan. Further, the security provided must be enforceable and, ideally, the enforcement procedure must be transparent and swift.

As is the case with other emerging markets, the legal infrastructure in many Eastern European countries remains underdeveloped. In the principal finance documents, an underdeveloped legal infrastructure can be mitigated by simply choosing a governing law with which the parties are familiar and which provides a higher level of certainty and predictability. For the security documents, however, this approach is not necessarily possible, as security will normally be granted under the law of the jurisdiction where the assets in question are located or, where they are intangible assets, under the law of the jurisdiction which governs the intangible asset concerned.

This chapter gives a brief overview of taking and enforcing security in Eastern Europe, with a focus on the Czech Republic, Poland and Russia. As we will see, there are ways to address and mitigate some of the issues that arise when taking and enforcing security in Eastern Europe.

## 2. Security

The ability to realise the real value of a secured asset in cases where a borrower's non-compliance leads to acceleration is vital when providing financing in any market. As one would expect, secured transactions play a key role in emerging and transitional market economies. A commercial investor is interested in making a profit from its investment, but in many cases its primary concern will be to obtain protection against the loss of its investment. Security is therefore required to:

- mitigate the risk of giving credit;
- enhance creditors' confidence in recovering real value from mortgaged or charged assets;
- increase the availability of credit;
- improve the terms (often the loan amount, the term and the interest rate) on which finance is available; and

- facilitate foreign investment.

A lender unfamiliar with the relevant jurisdiction will seek comfort that the security is what it expects it to be. Will the creditor really get what it thinks it is going to receive? The security may walk and talk like a pledge, but it may not necessarily behave like one. It is important to try to understand what level of protection a creditor will really receive from its security interest rather than blindly concentrate on the name of the security interest, which, at the end of the day, could well be the product of an incorrect translation.

Ordinarily, a lender would rely on a legal opinion from a firm of lawyers suitably qualified to advise on the laws of the relevant jurisdiction. Such a legal opinion will, subject to certain assumptions and qualifications, state that the documents to which it relates are enforceable in accordance with their terms, and confirm that the security documents create the security they purport to and that the party which has entered into the documents had the requisite power to do so. However, this practice is still not as straightforward in many Eastern European jurisdictions as it is in Western Europe. Legal opinions, although now standard practice, as little as 10 years ago were not widely used in many Western European jurisdictions. In Eastern Europe, experience shows that it can prove quite difficult not only to obtain a 'proper' legal opinion, but also to determine what the market standard for such a legal opinion actually is.

## 3. Which law is relevant?

It is common for finance documents to contain choice of law clauses, by which the parties agree that the document will be governed by a particular law. Many jurisdictions allow the parties to choose whichever law they wish to govern the document. These clauses can also provide how a dispute will be dealt with, either by specifying which courts will have jurisdiction or by providing for arbitration in a particular form.

The position with regard to security documents is more complicated. It is common for security documents also to have choice of law clauses, but the effectiveness of the security will not generally be determined by the law which governs the security document.

Where the asset which is the subject of the security is a tangible asset, such as land or goods, the effectiveness of the security will largely be a matter for the law of the country where the asset concerned is located. In the case of land, this is straightforward because its location does not change. In the case of movable assets, however, whose location can change over time, the effectiveness of the security is likely to be governed by the law of the place where the asset was located at the time the security was created.

The position in relation to intangibles is more complicated still. Intangibles do not have locations, but some jurisdictions may attempt to invent a location for the intangible asset concerned and then apply the same rule as in relation to tangible assets – that the effectiveness of the security depends on the law of the location of the asset. Other jurisdictions look instead to the law which governs the intangible concerned. In this case, if security is being taken over a contract, the effectiveness of the security will be a matter for the law which governs that contract.

As a result, establishing whether the security is effective is not simply a question of looking at the law which is expressed to govern the security document concerned. In many cases, the effectiveness of the security will be a matter for the law of the place where the asset is located at the time the security is taken or, in the case of an intangible asset, the law which governs the intangible asset itself (which may not necessarily be the same law as the law which governs the finance documents).

## 4. General issues in Eastern Europe – a brief overview

Having established that one should apply the law of the jurisdiction where the secured asset is located or the law which governs the intangible asset concerned, one needs to consider how effective that law is at protecting the interests of the secured creditor concerned.

The key issue for a creditor whose claim is not satisfied is how easily and quickly it can recover its funding by realising its charged assets. Any analysis of taking and enforcing security should concentrate on these core areas.

There has been relatively little research into the development and effectiveness of taking and enforcing security in Eastern Europe to date. A survey[1] as well as an empirical study[2] carried out by the European Bank for Reconstruction and Development (EBRD) provide some interesting and useful insights. Before going into any detail on the surveys' main findings, it is important to note that while they have statistical value, they may in some respects be too general and not provide sufficient detail, particularly as security and enforcement legislation form only parts of complex systems of law. The surveys also date back to 2003 and 2004 and some of the issues raised by EBRD may already have been rectified.

EBRD has extensive hands-on experience on lending into Eastern Europe[3] and its findings provide food for thought. It is not our intention to go into any great detail on how the surveys were carried out or to discuss the results in detail. However, a brief comment on the findings creates an interesting backdrop for understanding issues concerning the taking and enforcement of security in Eastern Europe.

One cannot necessarily group all Eastern European jurisdictions together for the purpose of looking at security and enforcement, as the geographical scope is large and as such the results differ dramatically between jurisdictions such as Hungary and Turkmenistan. However, EBRD carried out its surveys on the back of its involvement in arranging finance in each of its jurisdictions of operation. The surveys were carried out in close cooperation with local counsel in each of the jurisdictions concerned who were presented with a number of questions regarding the key elements of taking and enforcing security. In its analysis EBRD took into account not only the raw

---

1 "The New Legal Indicator Survey", EBRD 2003.

2 "Enforcing secured transactions in central and eastern Europe: an empirical study", EBRD 2004.

3 EBRD's jurisdictions of operations are Albania, Armenia, Azerbaijan, Belarus, Bosnia and Herzegovina, Bulgaria, Croatia, Czech Republic, Estonia, FYR Macedonia, Georgia, Hungary, Kazakhstan, Kyrgyz Republic, Latvia, Lithuania, Moldova, Poland, Romania, Russian Federation, Serbia and Montenegro (at the time of the surveys, Montenegro was still a part of Serbia and Montenegro), Slovak Republic, Slovenia, Tajikistan, Turkmenistan, Ukraine and Uzbekistan.

statistical data, but also a number of qualifying factors. Not unexpectedly, the new EU states are the most developed, followed by those in south Eastern Europe, with the Commonwealth of Independent States[4] (CIS) as the least developed. Following its surveys, EBRD has grouped the jurisdictions on the basis of their level of reform:

| **Advanced reform countries** | **Major reform countries** | **Minor reform countries** | **Deficient reform countries** | **Unreformed reform countries** |
|---|---|---|---|---|
| Hungary | Albania | Armenia | Azerbaijan | Bosnia and Herzegovina |
| Lithuania | Bulgaria | Belarus | Georgia | Serbia and Montenegro |
| Slovak Republic | Czech Republic | Croatia | Tajikistan | |
| | Kazakhstan | Estonia | Turkmenistan | |
| | Kyrgyz Republic | FYR Macedonia | Uzbekistan | |
| | Latvia | Russian Federation | | |
| | Moldova | Slovenia | | |
| | Poland | Romania | | |
| | | Ukraine | | |

'Advanced reform countries' are jurisdictions where not only the legal system has been reformed, but also the institutional framework. Although EBRD notes that there are deficiencies in their insolvency regimes or formalistic requirements, all three countries have modern and efficient regimes for secured transactions.

'Major reform countries' are those where reforms have been undertaken, but where such measures have proved insufficient in practice. Particularly, delay appears to be an issue in that although reforms have been made, complexity and delay remain barriers against attracting secured lending.

'Minor reform countries' have introduced some level of reform, but it has not

4 Armenia, Azerbaijan, Belarus, Georgia, Kazakhstan, Kyrgyzstan, Moldova, Russia, Tajikistan, Turkmenistan (associate member), Ukraine and Uzbekistan.

been implemented as originally intended. An example of this is the Russian Federation's introduction of new laws in 1992 promising reform across the CIS states; the non-implementation of these laws has made it no less problematic to take security in Russia. We will look closely at Russia later in this chapter.

'Deficient reform countries' are countries where the legal framework is seriously lacking and suffers from inconsistencies and contradictory legislation.

Finally, 'unreformed countries' are those jurisdictions where no reform had been undertaken at the time of the surveys. Interestingly, it seems that these jurisdictions are now on their way to introducing significantly revamped laws on security and enforcement which, it is hoped, will propel them into becoming advanced reform countries.

There is reason to believe that in general, creditors are still prejudiced in their attitudes towards Eastern European countries. Clearly, in some cases, creditors' fears concerning the lack of transparent, quick and efficient systems for taking and enforcing security are still justified in certain countries. However, the surveys gave a perhaps surprisingly positive overall picture. It is encouraging to note that certain countries, particularly in Central Europe and the Baltic states, have made significant developments, offering creditors a reasonable degree of comfort in terms of reliable regimes for taking and enforcing security. In nine of the surveyed countries (Croatia, Czech Republic, Estonia, Hungary, Kazakhstan, Latvia, Lithuania, FYR Macedonia and the Slovak Republic), it is possible to recover at least 80% of the market value of the secured asset in six months or less, and in seven further surveyed countries (Albania, Belarus, Bulgaria, Moldova, Romania, Serbia and Montenegro and Slovenia) one can expect to recover up to 60% in nine months or less.

These results benchmarked against a number of Western European jurisdictions would probably show that these Eastern European jurisdictions are today just as reliable and transparent (or perhaps rather that Western European jurisdictions sometimes also suffer from a lack of transparency and efficiency which could categorise some of them as not necessarily advanced reform countries). However, although there are deficiencies in some Western European jurisdictions, creditors are more familiar with those deficiencies and the resulting risks thereof. This is not yet the case in Eastern Europe as the reforms are fairly new (often within the last 10 years), resulting in relatively few examples of outcomes in practice, with a consequent lack of practical experience of the resulting risks. With an ever-increasing number of financing transactions in Eastern European jurisdictions, this is bound to change if Eastern Europe's legislatures are prepared and willing to follow through with the necessary reforms to create transparency and predictability from the creation of security to the effective realisation of charged assets.

One can conclude from the surveys' results that the reforms and changes being implemented in order to create regimes which will meet the expectations of secured lenders are being taken seriously. It appears that there is no generally applicable way to implement the necessary reforms, and that the most successful countries are those which have succeeded in adapting their existing strengths without creating institutions and practices which do not fit their particular markets. In addition, reforming legislation governing secured transactions is not sufficient if the institutional framework is not sufficiently prepared. A lack of implementation in practice and insufficient institutional frameworks will prevent the reformed laws from working effectively. The surveys suggest that where a market economy has been introduced to a larger extent, the regime for secured transactions is more advanced; though which of these two is the driver for such advancement is unclear, perhaps even irrelevant.

Further development of Eastern European legislation will increase the possibility of attracting more sophisticated financial structures such as leveraged finance, mezzanine finance and high yield. The availability of sophisticated finance is, in turn, very likely to spur further developments in other areas of legislation and movement closer towards a market-oriented economy. While certain countries, such as the new EU states, show strong progression, others are falling behind. In particular, the CIS states are worse off than the others. The unwillingness or inability of a jurisdiction's legislature to make the necessary reforms is likely to lead to isolation.

## 5. A closer look at the Czech Republic

As a general rule, security has an accessory nature under Czech law.[5] This means that there must be a debt to be secured by the security interest and that a security interest cannot exist independently. There are exceptions to this rule (eg, bank guarantees).

The most common forms of security interest in the Czech Republic are:

- guarantee (surety);
- pledge or mortgage;
- security transfer of ownership; and
- security assignment of receivables.

There is no concept of a floating charge under Czech law. The closest form of security interest to a floating charge is arguably a pledge of an enterprise or part of an enterprise or other collective assets/collection of assets. It is unclear whether the pledge of an enterprise constitutes a direct pledge over each asset in the enterprise. Given that an enterprise is made up of both assets and liabilities, it can also have a negative value.

In some cases perfection of a security interest requires the entry of the security interest in a register (see table below). There is no one general security register in the Czech Republic; instead, there are various security registers which are each maintained by different bodies. Some of the registers are publicly accessible (eg, the Real Estate Register) and some can be searched upon proving legitimate interest for doing so (eg, the Pledge Register).

The table below provides a general overview of the types of asset that are commonly given as security and the types of security interest generally used to secure these assets in the Czech Republic.

---

5 The terms used to describe security interests are translations from Czech to English and as such these terms may not have the same meaning as under English law.

| Asset | Security |
|---|---|
| Aircraft | Pledge (non-possessory)<br>Perfected by its entry in the Aviation Register |
| Enterprise | Pledge<br>The pledge agreement must be concluded in the form of a notarial record and the pledge is perfected by its entry in the Pledge Register |
| Inventory | Pledge (non-possessory)<br>Perfected by its entry in the Pledge Register |
| Ownership interest (participation in a Czech limited liability company) | Pledge<br>Perfected by its entry in the Commercial Register |
| Real estate | Mortgage or security transfer of ownership<br>Transfer and pledge perfected generally by its entry in the Real Estate Register |
| Receivables | Pledge or security assignment of receivables<br>Pledge and assignment perfected as stipulated in the relevant agreement. Notification to the debtor of the receivable is required<br>A security over bank account receivables is usually taken in the form of a pledge |
| Sea vessel | Pledge (non-possessory)<br>Perfected by its entry in the Sea Register |
| Shares (participation in a Czech joint stock company) | Pledge<br>Perfected by the handing over of share certificates or registration with the Securities Centre (or the Central Depository of Securities, once established) in the case of dematerialised shares. Registered share certificates also need to be endorsed for perfection of the pledge |

### 5.1 Satisfaction in insolvency

Under the Bankruptcy Act, specified secured creditors that benefit from priority treatment in bankruptcy proceedings are entitled to up to 70% of the net sales proceeds of the asset held as security. The remaining portion their claims, if any, will be treated as unsecured. Creditors with security interests created in the two months prior to (or in the period after) the filing of an application for bankruptcy will not have the benefit of such priority treatment.

In practice, this drawback is dealt with by taking security over assets with a value sufficient to ensure that the 70% share will cover the secured claim (ie, by 'oversecuring'). Provided that the value of the asset is not grossly disproportionate to the nominal value of the secured claim, the prevailing view in the Czech market is that this triggers no major legal issues.

On January 1 2008 a new Insolvency Act should come into effect. Under this new act, the 70% limitation will cease to apply and secured creditors should be able to obtain satisfaction from 100% of the net sales proceeds of the asset used as security.

### 5.2 Financial collateral

The EU Financial Collateral Directive (2002/47/EC)[6] has been implemented into Czech legislation.

Compared with other security interests, a financial collateral arrangement will give creditors greater comfort in respect of insolvency, creation of security and enforcement of security.

A financial collateral arrangement can take the form of:

- a pledge of a financial instrument;
- a pledge of a claim for the repayment of deposited money;
- the security transfer of a financial instrument; or
- the security transfer of moneys.

However, a financial collateral arrangement can be created only between certain specified entities. These entities include financial institutions (eg, Czech or foreign banks). With respect to ordinary business enterprises, only a company meeting certain financial criteria can be a party to a financial collateral arrangement. An individual cannot enter into a financial collateral arrangement.

### 5.3 Guarantee (surety)

If a Czech company issues a guarantee securing the liabilities of a party connected to it, the guarantee may require prior appraisal by a court-appointed expert. Although the law is unclear on this point, in practice, if the guaranteed amount is in excess of 10% of the guarantor's registered capital, then the guarantee can be provided only for a fee, the amount of which is determined by the expert. This fee, if any, is payable by the party whose obligations are being secured to the guarantor. In practice, the fee is usually determined by the expert as being zero. The whole process of obtaining the expert's fee recommendation usually takes several weeks.

---

6 The aim of the directive is to create a uniform EU legal framework to limit credit risk in financial transactions through the provision of securities and cash as collateral.

### 5.4 Pledge or mortgage

A pledge (over movables) or a mortgage (over immovables) is in many cases the most practical and efficient way for a creditor to take security over an asset.

A pledge may be possessory or non-possessory. A non-possessory pledge (ie, where the pledgee does not take physical possession of the pledged asset) is created by entering the pledge in the relevant security register. A possessory pledge need not be entered onto a security register as the pledgee takes physical possession of the asset.

Generally, there are no limitations on who can be a pledgee/mortgagee. A pledge/mortgage may secure present and future indebtedness. With respect to future indebtedness, in practice, the pledge/mortgage agreement will specify:

- the maximum amount up to which the pledgee is secured; and
- the timeframe within which the future indebtedness can arise.

Indebtedness secured by a pledge/mortgage may be specified in a foreign currency.

In general, when enforcing a pledge/mortgage, the pledgee/mortgagee must sell the asset in the manner prescribed by Czech law. The manner of sale will depend on the asset being sold.

### 5.5 Security transfer of ownership and security assignment of receivable

Both the security transfer of ownership and security assignment of a receivable are expressly mentioned in the Civil Code as methods of taking security over assets.

A security transfer of ownership will result in the secured creditor becoming a conditional owner of the asset in question. A security assignment of a receivable will result in the secured creditor becoming a conditional creditor of the owner of the assigned asset.

Generally, there are no limitations on who can be a security transferee/assignee. A security transfer of ownership/assignment of a receivable may secure present and future indebtedness. Indebtedness secured by a security transfer of ownership/assignment of a receivable may be specified in a foreign currency.

There are no specific rules on the enforcement of a security transfer of ownership or a security assignment of a receivable. Either may be enforced by way of a sale of the asset in question executed with due care by the secured creditor; alternatively, the secured creditor can elect to recover the assigned debt from the underlying debtor. The general view is that the secured creditor is not entitled to enforce such security by becoming an unrestricted owner of the asset in question.

The advantage of a security transfer of ownership and a security assignment of a receivable over pledge/mortgage is that the secured creditor can effectively prevent transfer of the asset to a third party and does not have to rely on an undertaking by the debtor not to transfer the asset.

### 5.6 Conclusion

Czech security law and practice are developing. Good progress has been made since the Czech Republic became a free market democratic country. Both the Czech legislature and the Czech judiciary are increasingly acknowledging the need to protect the position of secured creditors and to defend secured creditors' legitimate interests.

On the other hand, further improvements must still be made in order to create a legal environment conducive to taking security over assets, and to ensure that the subsequent enforcement of such security is reliable, flexible, quick and free of any unreasonable burdens for secured creditors. To this end, a new Civil Code and Commercial Code are being prepared.

## 6. A closer look at Poland

The table below ranks particular types of security interests available in Poland in order of their general effectiveness in banking, private equity, project and asset finance transactions.[7]

| | Registered pledge (fixed) | Registered pledge (floating) | Financial pledge | Ordinary pledge | Transfer of title by way of security | Security assign-ment | Mortgage |
|---|---|---|---|---|---|---|---|
| Equipment | 3 | 3 | N/A | 1 | 1-2 | N/A | N/A |
| Sea vessels | N/A (3[a]) | N/A | N/A | 1 | 1-2 | N/A | 3[b] |
| Aircraft | 3 | N/A | N/A | 1 | 1-2 | N/A | N/A |
| Inventory | 2 | 2 (3[c]) | N/A | 1 | 1-2 | N/A | N/A |
| Whole business | N/A | 3[d] | N/A | N/A | 2 | N/A | N/A |
| Real estate | N/A | N/A | N/A | N/A | 2 | N/A | 3 |
| Receivables | 2 | 1-2 | 2 | 1 | N/A | 3[g] | N/A |
| Bank account[e] | 2 | N/A | 2 | 1 | N/A | 3[g] | N/A |
| Shares[f] | 3 | N/A | 2 | 2 | 2[g] | N/A | N/A |
| Bonds (notes)[f] | 3 | N/A | 2 | 2 | 2[g] | N/A | N/A |

7 The terms used to describe security interests are translations from Polish to English and as such these terms may not have the same meaning as under English law.

**Key to table**
N/A – legally not possible
0 – not practicable or not recommended
1 – recommended only in specific circumstances
2 – recommended in most cases
3 – highly recommended
a – possible only if the vessel is not registered in the Register of Vessels
b – specific ship mortgage is available; not available if the vessel is not registered in the Ship Register
c – if taken with all other movable assets and rights (ie, in the event of whole business pledge)
d – available over all movable assets and transferable rights, but excludes real estate, among other things
e – also bank account blockade available
f – specific advice with regard to publicly traded securities may be necessary
g – may take a form of a financial collateral

In the following sections we shall look at each of the security interests above in greater detail.

## 6.1 Registered (non-possessory) pledge (fixed and floating)

A registered pledge is in many cases the most practical and efficient way for a creditor to secure a debtor's liabilities. It is established by a written agreement between the parties but it takes effect only upon registration in the Register of Pledges. A registered pledge is a non-possessory security interest – that is, the pledgor may continue to use the pledged assets. In general, a pledge is available over almost all types of asset (except real estate), including physical items, debts due to the pledgor and a floating pool of assets.

The Registered Pledge Law states that a registered pledge will secure only the claims of registered parties (eg, Polish and foreign banks and companies doing business in Poland). A registered pledge established in favour of other (non-registered) creditors will have no legal effect. In certain cases this restriction can be mitigated by appointing a 'pledge administrator' acting for the benefit of all lenders or bondholders, even if some of them are not eligible to be named as pledgees in the Register of Pledges.

A registered pledge may secure present and future or contingent liabilities, provided that their maximum amount is specified in the pledge agreement. The secured liabilities may also be specified in foreign currencies.

The Registered Pledge Law also allows the pledgee or the pledge administrator to use a wide variety of enforcement methods, including out-of-court methods. In particular, the pledge agreement may provide for seizure of the pledged assets.

## 6.2 Financial collateral

The Act on Financial Collateral Arrangements (April 2 2004) introduced three new types of financial collateral arrangement:

- a pledge over title to cash or financial instruments;
- an outright transfer by a collateral provider to a collateral taker of title to cash or financial instruments; and
- a 'blockade' of cash or financial instruments, which is similar to a pledge in that the debtor may not dispose of its cash or financial instruments, or create another security over such cash or financial instruments.

These types of collateral are primarily designed to secure financial transactions involving financial institutions and may not be used where one of the parties is an individual.

### 6.3 Ordinary (possessory) pledge

The usefulness of the so-called 'ordinary pledge' is relatively limited, as it lacks most of the advantages of a registered pledge. It can be used to take security over assets such as a debt due to the pledgor and physical items, but it cannot be used to take security over real property, future assets or a floating pool of assets. An ordinary pledge over a physical item requires physical delivery of a pledged item to the pledgee (or a nominated third party), which in practical terms eliminates the use of this type of security in most corporate transactions.

### 6.4 Transfer of title by way of security and security assignment

The transfer of title by way of security (in relation to physical items) and the security assignment of rights and receivables have been developed by commercial practice, and as a result they are not fully regulated by legislation. In a transfer of title by way of security and security assignment, the debtor transfers or assigns the legal title to certain assets, rights and/or receivables to the creditor on the condition that upon repayment of the debt, the title to such assets, rights or receivables will be re-transferred to the debtor. The debtor will usually retain possession of the transferred assets or may use the rights/receivables (as the case may be), unless, of course, the debt is not repaid. Should the debtor fail to repay the debt, it will normally lose its right to have the title re-transferred to it. Following an event of default, the creditor will have the right immediately to sell the secured item and apply all proceeds from such a sale to satisfy the secured claim.

The transfer of title by way of security and security assignment can generally be enforced directly by the creditor. In many cases, however, a creditor will need to involve the court (or sometimes other state authorities) in order to take physical possession of the assets over which it has taken security.

In order to be recognised in the event of bankruptcy, the agreement for the security transfer should be executed in writing with the date certified by a notary public.

### 6.5 Mortgage

A mortgage may be created over:

- land, and buildings erected on that land;
- flats, apartments or parts of buildings, as long as they constitute real property separate from the building itself;
- perpetual usufruct rights; and
- receivables secured by the mortgage.

In most cases a mortgage must be established in the form of a notarial deed and must always be entered in the Land and Mortgages Register.

A mortgage may be established as an ordinary mortgage in relation to an existing debt of a specified amount, or a ceiling mortgage. A single mortgage to secure one debt may be established over one or several properties (joint mortgage) for the full amount on each property. A ceiling mortgage can be used to secure a debt of an unspecified amount, in particular future or conditional indebtedness arising under an agreement (the agreement must be specified on the ceiling mortgage's entry in the Land and Mortgages Register). A ceiling mortgage can be used to secure amounts relating to one agreement only.

### 6.6 Conclusion

The Polish system of security interests is constantly developing. New legislation expected to be enacted in the near future will include amendments to the Registered Pledge Law aimed at facilitating the registration process and abolishing certain restrictions relating to that type of security. Changes are also planned for the Bankruptcy and Recovery Law which will have an impact on all security arrangements, in particular transfer of title by way of security and security assignment.

## 7. A closer look at Russia

Conceptually, Russian law treats security as a way of encouraging a debtor to comply with its contractual obligations by providing the debtor with negative consequences should it breach its contract.[8] This helps us to understand why, although under Russian law universally recognised security interests do exist (eg, surety and guarantee, pledge and mortgage), unusually, Russian law treats 'penalties' as a type of security interest.

Russian law allows parties to agree among themselves types of security not directly specified in the Civil Code (which is the main piece of legislation governing civil relations, including security). However, in practice, the Russian judiciary is not keen to enforce security not specified in the Civil Code. Therefore, certain legal instruments which are widely used in Western jurisdictions to secure obligations (eg, assignment by way of security) will most probably be unenforceable in Russia.

In general, Russian security (excluding bank guarantees) is treated as a secondary (and not an independent) obligation which is totally dependent on the underlying (secured) obligation. This means that if the underlying obligation is for any reason void, the security will also be invalid.

### 7.1 Surety and guarantee

Russian law distinguishes between corporate guarantees (sureties), which may be issued only by corporate entities or individuals, and bank guarantees, which can be granted only by either banks (ie, entities holding a banking licence issued by the Russian Central Bank) or insurance companies.

Russian law links a surety to the personality of the debtor and the guaranteed amount. Under Russian law, a corporate guarantee will be terminated if the

---

8 The terms used to describe security interests are translations from Russian to English and as such these terms may not have the same meaning as under English law.

underlying obligation is altered to such extent that the guarantor's obligation is increased without the guarantor's prior consent, or the underlying debtor's debt is transferred to a new debtor without the guarantor's prior agreement to guarantee the new debtor's obligations. Therefore, in practice, when amending or assigning a debt secured by a Russian surety, it is very important for a creditor to obtain the relevant surety's prior consent.

The timing of a claim against a Russian guarantor is another important issue to be considered. Under the Civil Code, a corporate guarantee terminates on expiry of the term for which it was given, or, if no such period is specified, if the creditor fails to file suit against the guarantor within one year of the due date for payment under the underlying obligation (or, in the case of a surety of a sum payable on demand, two years after the date of the surety). It is therefore extremely important for a creditor to submit a claim within the relevant time period. Failure to do so will render the corporate guarantee invalid.

A bank guarantee is a relatively popular type of Russian security for use in cross-border transactions since enforcement of bank guarantees is simpler than enforcement of surety. In addition, credit risks of the reputable Russian banks are lower than those of the majority of corporate entities. However, the commercial viability of a bank guarantee will vary with each particular project as it is usual practice for the banks to charge a fee for giving a guarantee, thereby affecting the economics of a project.

## 7.2 Pledge

Russian law recognises a pledge as being security over movable assets (it treats vessels and aircraft as immovable assets). The main difference between a pledge and a mortgage is that a pledge requires no state registration and the parties are free to agree on out-of-court enforcement procedures.

The main advantage of a pledge in Russia is that in the event of the debtor becoming bankrupt, a pledge will give creditors preferential treatment, since the pledged assets do not form part of the insolvency estate under Russian law. A pledge in whatever form and a mortgage are the only types of security that give creditors such preferential treatment.

Under Russian law, a pledgee cannot physically take transfer of the pledged assets, except in very limited circumstances. Instead, the pledgee is paid (in roubles) the proceeds of the sale of the pledged assets at auction, such auction being conducted in accordance with Russian law (ie, the auction must be publicised). Any dispute between the parties (commonly over the starting price of the pledged asset at the auction) must be resolved by a court, which will delay enforcement of the pledge. However, if a pledge must be enforced through the courts, the creditor will have the benefit of avoiding certain practical problems relating to enforcement (eg, arranging the auction), since in such cases the auction of the pledged assets will be performed by court bailiffs.

## 7.3 Pledge of goods in turnover

Russian law is familiar with a pledge of inventory – that is, a 'pledge of goods in turnover' – which is normally used in trade finance. This is a pledge by which the pledged goods are left in the possession of the pledgor and the pledgor has the right to change the composition and form of the pledged goods, provided their value does not drop below their value as set out in the pledge agreement.

In order for this type of security to function in practice, it is necessary at all times to be able to identify and keep separate the goods which form the pledged assets. Under Russian law, the pledgor must maintain comprehensive records monitoring the goods during the various stages of production up to the stage of finished product. The records must identify those goods comprising the pool of goods subject to the pledge.

Russian law gives the lender the right to verify the maintenance of such records. Should the requirement to maintain records of the pledged assets be breached, the lender is entitled to intervene in order to identify the pledged assets and to stop any transactions involving the pledged assets until the breach is rectified. In practice, these rights may be very difficult to enforce.

A pledge of inventory is thus inherently weak as:

- it requires the pledgor's constant cooperation in maintaining the necessary records (unless the lender has a professional warehouse agent, which is undesirable and impractical); and
- it assumes that a lender/pledgee will have unrestricted access to a pledgor's records and the power to 'freeze' transactions with the pledged assets in order to update the records. This is not an entirely realistic scenario, particularly in a default situation. The lender must inevitably resort to the Russian courts, which may be too late if the records have been maintained defectively or if goods have been sold (albeit in breach). For a foreign lender, this may prove virtually impossible.

## 7.4 Pledge of an enterprise

The Civil Code defines an enterprise as a 'property complex'[9] used to carry out entrepreneurial activity. An enterprise in this sense may be sold, pledged, leased or disposed of. The enterprise includes plots of land, buildings, structures, equipment, inventory, materials, products, receivables, claims and liabilities, products, works and services (eg, the firm's name, trademarks and service marks), as well as other rights, unless otherwise provided by law or contract.

Despite the fact that the Civil Code establishes the concept of an enterprise, Russian has no rules on the method of ascertaining or identifying the assets of a company that constitute an enterprise. Russian law does not definitively state whether an enterprise includes the whole business of a company or whether it is possible to allocate only part of a company's assets into an enterprise. It is thought that an enterprise will comprise such property as is necessary to carry out its day-to-day business activities.

9 This roughly translates as 'a set of assets' – for example, a property complex of a factory will consist of everything required to run its day-to-day business, including the infrastructure, materials, computers and machinery.

Under Russian law, an enterprise is considered immovable property. Therefore, before an owner can sell, pledge or otherwise dispose of its enterprise, the enterprise must be state registered as a subject of real estate in the unified state register of rights to immovable property and the relevant legal entity must be registered as the owner of the enterprise.

The serious uncertainties surrounding what constitutes an enterprise, coupled with a distinct lack of clarity over the procedures which must be followed to effect, maintain and enforce a pledge of this kind, mean that pledges of an enterprise are not commonly used and should be approached with extreme caution.

## 7.5 Mortgage of buildings and underlying plots of land

The mortgage of a building is regarded as one of the most reliable Russian security interests, due to Russian law's stringent regulation requirements and its state registration system. From a practical point of view, a creditor is advised to undertake thorough due diligence to ensure that the mortgagor has good title to the building (and the plot of land beneath it) to be mortgaged.

It is not possible to mortgage a building without also mortgaging the plot of land beneath it. A mortgage contract is subject to state registration and enters into force only from the date of registration.

The rules applicable to a Russian pledge apply equally to a mortgage, but the parties cannot avoid court proceedings when enforcing a mortgage.

## 7.6 Security over a bank account of a Russian company

As Russian law does not recognise the concept of a pledge over bank accounts, banking practice has developed a 'withdrawal arrangement' as an alternative mechanism of giving more comfort to a creditor. In simple terms, a withdrawal arrangement is an agreement between the creditor, the debtor and the bank with which the debtor has its bank account. Under the agreement, the debtor allows the creditor to withdraw funds from the debtor's bank account without requiring the debtor's prior approval in each case and the bank agrees to accept the creditor's withdrawal instructions.

Despite the fact that such withdrawal agreements have been recognised under Russian law for a number of years, the legal regulation of such arrangements is underdeveloped; withdrawal agreements are dealt with in only two articles in the Civil Code (which are not entirely consistent with one another). The legal position of withdrawal agreements has not been helped by a lack of judicial attention and jurisprudence on the subject.

Although a withdrawal agreement may be viewed as providing a degree of comfort for a creditor, its reliability in practice is questionable. As it is not recognised as proper security under Russian law, it does not provide any preferential treatment in case of a debtor's bankruptcy. Further, a withdrawal agreement requires a certain level of cooperation from a Russian bank (normally, a Western bank would use its Russian subsidiaries for such purposes). Moreover, under Russian law a client of a Russian bank is entitled to close its bank account at any time and the bank cannot prevent it from doing so, thus rendering withdrawal arrangements unenforceable.

### 7.7 Conclusion

Although there is a clear tendency for the Russian judiciary to favour creditors and enforce security, Russian law is still at a developmental stage. As a result, the enforcement of Russian security may be a time-consuming and uncertain process. Given the recent relaxation of Russian currency legislation, there are now opportunities to strengthen a foreign creditor's security structure by using offshore security, and lenders should carefully consider the full range of available options when structuring their Russian security interests.

## 8. Dealing with issues in practice

How, then, should a creditor deal with these risks and uncertainties in practice?

Clearly, the first option would be to accept that there are issues in certain jurisdictions and deal with those within the scope of the relevant transaction. A higher risk profile requires a higher price, which means that lending into a jurisdiction with an uncertain legal framework and infrastructure will inevitably lead to more expensive financing. This – unfortunately, but by necessity – leads to less funds being available in those jurisdictions than would otherwise be the case, thus slowing down the development not only of the legal infrastructure, but also of the community as a whole.

Another option is to structure a transaction so that the assets to be secured in the relevant jurisdiction are limited. Clearly, certain assets, such as real property and shares, cannot 'move' to another jurisdiction. Other assets, however, can be maintained outside the jurisdiction and thus be subject to security in a foreign jurisdiction where the lenders are more comfortable. By way of example, it is not uncommon in project finance transactions that an intermediate holding company is introduced above the local special purpose vehicle that is the operating entity, for instance holding a concession. This has two benefits to the creditors:

- The creditors can receive a charge over the shares in a jurisdiction familiar to them; and
- It may not be as crucial to obtain step-in rights in respect of the concession agreement (which in many cases in Eastern Europe is not only difficult, but practically impossible).

However, if not structured properly, the introduction of a foreign intermediate holding company may trigger change of control issues, as well as adverse tax consequences.

A further option is to structure the payment streams so that cash in domestic accounts is limited to the amounts required in the relevant currency within a certain period (eg, two weeks), while all other cash is channelled elsewhere (eg, to an account in a foreign jurisdiction more familiar to the creditors). This will require a bank account structure to be put in place, covering both the Eastern European jurisdiction ('onshore' or domestic) and the creditors' preferred jurisdiction ('offshore' or foreign), and security is created over the foreign accounts. However, in many Eastern European jurisdictions, there are still limitations and prohibitions on moving money out of the country and making payments between local entities in currencies other than the local currency. These limitations and prohibitions would need to be assessed on a case-by-case basis.

As long as these challenges and barriers to taking and enforcing security remain in place, creditors will still seek to find ways of gaining comfort for their funding. However, a higher degree of sophistication, transparency and predictability in Eastern Europe's legal infrastructure and institutional systems should be an important factor in creating greater comfort for lenders lending against local security, at a lower price reflecting a lowered risk profile, which in turn should spur further development.

# Mexico

**Carlos de Maria y Campos Segura**
Galicia y Robles, SC

## 1. Introduction

Structuring an adequate security package is one of the most relevant decisions in any financing transaction. Generally, a security package should be designed to achieve the following objectives:

- create a mechanism that allow the lenders to sell the relevant assets in order to receive funds to repay the debt;
- protect the secured assets from rights of other creditors, affording preferential rights to the secured lenders; and
- in some project financings where the secured assets will become the main source of repayment of the loan, establish control over the assets by designating a new entity that will continue to operate the project and ensure a continuous flow of revenue that will be used to repay the loans.

Mexican law offers a wide range of options for structuring a security package, depending on the characteristics of the transaction.

Unlike the United States and other jurisdictions, Mexico has no single body of law governing secured transactions. The regulation of security interest vehicles in Mexico is governed by separate statutes, including:

- the General Law of Negotiable Instruments and Credit Operations;
- the Law of Credit Institutions;
- the civil code of each Mexican state; and
- the special laws regulating liens over specific assets (eg, ships and telecommunications assets).

Depending on the nature and characteristics of the particular transaction, creditors may establish different security structures to secure payment of their claims. Basically, the type of security interest is determined by the nature of the asset over which the security interest will be created and sometimes by the nature of the creditor. Recently, Mexican law was amended to regulate expressly certain security interests which, with certain limitations, may cover various assets and rights of the borrower (floating lien), affording greater certainty and flexibility to creditors.

The security package of a transaction will vary significantly, depending on whether the financing is to be structured as a corporate loan or as a project finance loan. Project finance loans are best suited to large projects – particularly those involving the financing of infrastructure projects, which are in great demand in emerging markets such as Mexico.

This chapter summarises the most common types of security interest available in Mexican credit transactions.

## 2. *In rem* guarantees

*In rem* guarantees create a lien on the secured asset which survives the transfer thereof and protects the beneficiary against the rights of other parties. The holder of an *in rem* guarantee has priority of payment over other parties from the proceeds of sale of the secured asset. If the proceeds of sale are insufficient to satisfy the holder's claim in full, the balance will be treated as an unsecured debt and will rank *pari passu* with all other unsecured claims of the debtor.

### 2.1 Civil mortgages

A civil mortgage creates a right *in rem* over specifically determined real estate, entitling the creditor, in the event of default, to payment from the proceeds of a foreclosure proceeding. Mortgages may be created by agreement between the parties, by voluntary unilateral acts or pursuant to a legal provision. In order to be effective against third parties, the mortgage must be formalised before a notary public and registered with the Public Registry of Property in the state where the property is located.

A mortgage will cover the corresponding asset. It will extend implicitly to:

- natural accessions to the real estate;
- improvements made by the owner;
- movables permanently attached to the real estate which may not be removed without deterioration of the real estate; and
- new buildings constructed by the owner on the real estate and new stories added to a mortgaged building.

It may also extend, if expressly provided, to:

- any goods produced by the mortgaged assets, provided they are produced prior to the date on which the creditor requests payment of the underlying obligation; and
- any unpaid rent outstanding at the time the creditor requests payment of the underlying obligation.

In the event of default, a mortgage entitles the secured creditor to payment from the liquidation value of the mortgaged assets in the order of priority determined by the applicable legal provisions. Pursuant to the Bankruptcy Law, in the event of bankruptcy, labour and often bankruptcy-related claims, such as fees payable to bankruptcy offices, have priority in payment over obligations guaranteed by a mortgage. Likewise, pursuant to the Federal Tax Code, if a mortgage was recorded with the Public Registry of Property before the date on which a tax claim is made, the mortgage will have priority over tax credits.

According to the principle of *lex rei sitae*, the execution, registration and foreclosure of a mortgage are governed by the civil code of the state in which the mortgaged assets are located. Thus, the regime governing mortgages may vary from state to state, causing legal uncertainty and a lack of homogeneity. This notwithstanding, foreclosure procedures have been tested before the courts many times, resulting in numerous court precedents which afford comfort to creditors as to the judicial interpretation of the applicable legal provisions.

### 2.2 Industrial mortgages

This mortgage is specifically regulated under Article 67 of the Law on of Credit Institutions, which provides for the establishment of a floating lien over an entire unit of agricultural, commercial, service or industrial enterprise. An industrial mortgage will also cover any corresponding concession or authorisation, and all material elements – whether real or personal property – considered as a business unit. The industrial unit may also include machinery and equipment, accounts receivable and operational cash.

Industrial mortgages must be formalised before a notary public and registered with the Public Registry of Property in the state in which the mortgaged assets are located. Given the variety of assets that may be subject to an industrial mortgage, creditors commonly request the additional registration of the mortgage with the Public Registry of Commerce in the state where the debtor is domiciled.

Banking institutions that are beneficiaries of industrial mortgages will permit the exploitation of the mortgaged assets. However, the creditor may object to the sale, lease or other disposal of the mortgaged assets, or part thereof, where this represents a risk to the creditor's guaranty.

As the industrial mortgage is governed by the Law of Credit Institutions, which regulates banking activities in Mexico, the general opinion is that this form of security is reserved to banking institutions duly authorised to act as such in Mexico. Some state civil codes provide for the possibility of creating mortgages over an entire industrial unit, similar to the industrial mortgage, thus affording foreign creditors and other non-bank creditors the same security interest protection.

### 2.3 Special mortgages

As a general principle, movable property need not be recorded with any governmental authority in Mexico, as opposed to real estate, which must be registered with the Public Registry of Property in the state where the real property is located. In other words, title to real estate is generally evidenced through a certificate issued by the Public Registry of Property, whereas title to movable property is *prima facie* evidenced through possession of the relevant asset. This notwithstanding, pursuant to public policy and international treaties, Mexican law requires that certain movable property be registered in a similar manner to real estate (eg, vessels, aircraft and certain telecommunications equipment such as satellites). This registration system creates certainty for creditors and potential buyers, as certificates issued by the public registry are evidence that the registered party is acknowledged as the legitimate owner, and that the asset has no liens or attachments thereon other than those disclosed in the certificate. Mexican law allows for the creation of security interests over some of these assets, including the following mortgages.

### (a) *Aircraft mortgages*

Mortgages over Mexican aircraft[1] are not specifically regulated under Mexican aviation law. They must therefore comply with the general legal framework of the civil mortgage regulated under the Federal Civil Code, pursuant to which a mortgage is an *in rem* security over specifically determined assets which are not delivered to the creditor, and which empowers the creditor to foreclose on the collateral should the debtor default on the secured obligation. The lien created thereunder is valid and binding on the parties from the moment of execution of the relevant agreement or unilateral declaration of the debtor. However, as in this case the asset remains in the borrower's possession, in order to be enforceable against third parties the lien must be recorded with the Aeronautical Registry.

To perfect a security interest in an aircraft, the mortgage must be formalised before a notary public and registered with the Aeronautical Registry. The mortgage must clearly identify the collateral (eg, registration number of the aircraft, manufacturer, weight, span, number of fuselage, manufacturer and model of the engines). Further, Mexico is a signatory to the Geneva Convention on the International Recognition of Rights in Aircraft 1948. As a result, mortgages created and recorded as provided above should be recognised and enforced by other signatories to the convention.

Mexican law does not allow creditors to foreclose on security interests without prior due process before a court. Foreclosure requires the filing of a petition before a court of competent jurisdiction, which will issue an order for commencement of the foreclosure procedure. In the case of a mortgage on an aircraft, the procedure is a summary procedure commonly known as a *'juicio hipotecario'* or mortgage trial. The mortgagee is also entitled to foreclose pursuant to an executive or ordinary procedure.[2]

### (b) *Maritime mortgages*

Mortgages over vessels[3] are regulated under the Maritime Navigation and Commerce Law and the Federal Civil Code.

A maritime mortgage is an *in rem* security over a specifically determined vessel, whether built or in the process of being built, which is not delivered to the creditor and which empowers the latter to foreclose on the collateral should the debtor default on the secured obligation. The lien created thereunder is valid and binding on the parties from the moment of execution of the relevant agreement or unilateral declaration of the debtor. However, because in this case the borrower retains possession of the asset, in order to be enforceable against third parties, the lien must be recorded with the National Public Maritime Registry. The order in which maritime mortgages are registered determines their priority.

---

1 Pursuant to the Civil Aviation Law, an 'aircraft' is any vehicle capable of transiting airspace independently with people, cargo or mail.

2 The ordinary procedure, unlike the mortgage trial and the executive procedure, does not begin with a precautionary attachment on the collateral.

3 Under the Maritime Navigation and Commerce Law, a vessel is any type of construction designed to navigate over or under navigable ways.

The lien created under the mortgage may secure the principal amount of the secured debt, interest accruing[4] and any other outstanding obligations thereunder (ie, fees and expenses payable to the lender). It can also secure future and conditional obligations, and may be created by the debtor or by a third party to secure the obligations of the former.

Maritime mortgages must be formalised in a public deed executed before a notary public. The mortgagor may not grant any security over the vessel, lease it, enter into a charter agreement or agree to anticipated rent or charter payment for a period exceeding the duration of the maritime mortgage without the mortgagee's consent.

The maritime mortgage grants the mortgagee priority over other creditors to be paid from the proceeds of sale of the mortgaged vessel. However, the Maritime Navigation and Commerce Law establishes that the following creditors have preference over creditors secured with a maritime mortgage:

- salary and other sums owed to the crew of the mortgaged vessel, including repatriation expenses and social security quotas owed to crew members;
- claims due to indemnities deriving from death or injury, whether caused on land or sea, regarding direct exploitation of the vessel;
- claims deriving from salvage of the vessel;
- claims deriving from the use of port infrastructure, maritime routes and maritime signalling; and
- claims deriving from extra-contractual indemnities resulting from loss or material damage caused by exploitation of the vessel, other than loss or damage caused to cargo, containers and passengers' property on board the ship.

The aforementioned maritime privileges over vessels shall cease on the first anniversary after they became enforceable, unless an action to establish an attachment over the vessel has been initiated. If the vessel has caused environmental damage, only the preferred creditors mentioned above will have priority over indemnities resulting from such damage.

Further, a party that is building or repairing the vessel has the right to retain it until it has received payment for its services. The same right is enjoyed by a party which salvages the vessel. This retention right has priority over the maritime mortgage and creates a lien on the vessel until it is physically delivered to the owner. This right terminates upon delivery of the vessel, even if the relevant debt remains outstanding.

In case of material damage to the vessel, the mortgagee may exercise its rights over what remains of the vessel and over:

- indemnification payments due as a result of material damage caused to the vessel;
- amounts owed to the vessel due to ordinary damage;

4 Pursuant to the Maritime Navigation and Commerce Law, maritime mortgages secure outstanding interest only for a one-year period, unless the parties expressly agree to extend such term and register such agreement in the National Public Maritime Registry.

- indemnities resulting from damage caused to the vessel due to services rendered; and
- insurance proceeds.

Upon the occurrence of an event of default, the creditor may initiate a foreclosure procedure before a court of competent jurisdiction in order to foreclose on the maritime mortgage. Summary proceedings have been incorporated in the Maritime Navigation and Commerce Law in order to expedite foreclosure. The right to initiate foreclosure on a maritime mortgage expires on the third anniversary of the date on which the debtor fails to comply with the secured obligations.

### *(c) Communications mortgage*

The General Communications Law contemplates a floating lien mortgage over the assets of communication companies.

Unless otherwise agreed between the parties, a communications mortgage covers:

- the concession;
- the means of communication (eg, radio spectrum, telecommunications networks, satellite communication systems) and accessories;
- fixed and movable equipment used in the construction and exploitation, repair and maintenance of the means of communication;
- investment for the exploitation and administration of the means of communication;
- cash deriving from normal operations; and
- accounts receivable.

Mortgagees shall not have the right to obstruct exploitation of the corresponding means of communication, or to block any modifications or alterations to buildings, premises or means of communication. However, they are entitled to oppose the sale of the corresponding communications system if this would represent a risk to the mortgage guarantee.

Formalities to create and perfect a communications mortgage are similar to those required for an industrial mortgage, as described above.

## 2.4 Commercial pledge

A pledge is a security *in rem* created over certain rights or movable assets to guarantee payment and priority of guaranteed obligations, including machinery and equipment, accounts receivable, equity interests and negotiable instruments. The traditional pledge[5] requires actual or virtual possession of the pledged assets by the creditor, which in certain cases limits the pledgor's opportunity to use such assets. Like a mortgage, a pledge does not transfer title to the pledged assets and creates a lien which attaches to the collateral until the secured obligations are paid in full.

Only transferable assets can be pledged. Therefore, non-transferable assets and rights, and rights which require special consent in order to be transferred, cannot be

5 As opposed to the pledge without transfer of possession described below.

pledged unless the relevant consent is obtained.

The commercial pledge is regulated under the General Law of Negotiable Instruments and Credit Operations,[6] which establishes the various methods to create and perfect the pledge depending on the nature of the pledged assets. Article 334 of the law states that the commercial pledge is perfected by:

- delivery to the creditor of the goods or negotiable instruments, when issued to the bearer;
- endorsement of the negotiable instruments in favour of the creditor, in the case of nominative instruments, and by such endorsement and the corresponding notation in the relevant registry if the instruments are subject to registration;
- delivery of the instrument or the document representing the credit to the creditor, in the case of non-negotiable instruments, and recordal of the lien in the applicable register or notification of the debtor;
- deposit of the goods or bearer instruments, at the disposal of the creditor, with a third party designated by the parties;
- deposit of the goods, at the disposal of the creditor, in a place to which the creditor has keys, even if this place is owned by or located within the establishment of the debtor;
- delivery or endorsement of the instrument representing the goods, or issue or endorsement of a pledge bond in relation thereto; or
- registration of a contract for equipment or operating credit in the case of claims for working capital.

The procedure to foreclose on a pledge is regulated in Article 341 of the law, which contemplates a summary process to obtain court authorisation to sell the pledged assets. Some critics maintain that this breaches the principle of due process, arguing that the debtor is not given an opportunity to be heard in court and oppose the sale of the pledged assets. According to Articles 340, 341 and 342 of the law, a creditor is entitled to require the court to authorise the sale of the pledged assets if any of the following occurs:

- a default on the underlying obligations;
- a drop in the value of the pledged assets to an amount which is insufficient to cover the amount of the underlying obligation plus 20%: or
- the pledgor's failure to provide the creditor with the necessary funds to pay any required funds under negotiable instruments (eg, shares) on time.

Under Article 341, after the court receives a petition to sell the pledged assets, it will serve process on the debtor, which will have 15 working days in which to respond and present its defence. If the pledgor opposes the petition, the court will make its decision within 10 working days. If there is no opposition from the pledgor, the court will authorise the sale of the pledged assets.

---

6 The General Law of Negotiable Instruments and Credit Operations is a federal law and is thus applicable in all Mexican states.

The court will authorise the sale of the pledged assets even before the pledgor is notified of the petition if the situation is urgent and the court determines the corresponding liability of the creditor. The proceeds of sale will be kept in pledge by the creditor in substitution of the pledged assets. Sale of the pledged assets does not prevent the pledgor from initiating an action to determine the enforceability of the underlying obligations.

### 2.5 Civil pledge

The civil codes of the different states of Mexico regulate the civil pledge. Although this is similar to the commercial pledge in many respects, the two differ in their methods of creation and perfection. A pledge is regulated by the General Law of Negotiable Instruments and Credit Operations if the subject matter of the pledge is considered to relate to commerce in accordance with Article 75 of the Commercial Code, or if a party to the pledge agreement is a businessperson or entity engaged in commerce. All other pledges shall be considered civil pledges and shall therefore be regulated by the corresponding civil code. Civil pledges are perfected by physical delivery of the pledges asset to the creditor.

### 2.6 Pledge without transfer of possession

This type of commercial pledge is also regulated in the General Law of Negotiable Instruments and Credit Operations and is similar to a floating lien as contemplated in Article 9 of the US Uniform Commercial Code. It was recently introduced into Mexican law and has been widely used in financing projects in Mexico.

A pledge without transfer of possession allows the debtor or a third party to grant a security interest over certain specifically identified movable assets or all of its movable assets identified generically (including raw materials, inventory, cash and accounts receivable), depending on the scope of the agreement, and to continue using and exploiting such assets pursuant to certain legal and contractual rules.

Article 355 of the law provides that the following movable assets may be subject to a pledge without transfer of possession:

- assets and rights owned by the debtor at the time of granting the pledge, including trade names, trademarks and other rights;
- movable assets that the debtor acquires after the pledge has been granted;
- assets in the form of future income or products, pending or obtained, deriving from those assets mentioned above;
- assets resulting from transformation processes of the above assets; and
- assets and rights that the debtor receives or is entitled to receive as payment for transfer of the pledged assets in favour of third parties or as an indemnity in the event of damage or destruction of such assets.

The pledge must be executed by written agreement and if it exceeds a certain threshold value, the parties must ratify their signatures before a notary public. In order to be enforceable against third parties, the pledge must be recorded with the Public Registry of Commerce in the place of the pledgor's domicile.

This type of pledge allows the debtor to use the collateral and even sell the pledged assets, as long as certain rules are observed. For example, the pledge will cover any proceeds resulting from sale of the assets and the parties may agree to restrict such rights by means of covenants.

Future obligations may be secured by the pledge – in other words, the amount of the principal obligation need not be determined at the time of creating the pledge on the understanding that the pledge may be foreclosed only while the principal obligation is enforceable.

The General Law of Negotiable Instruments and Credit Operations previously imposed a limitation on this type of pledge in the form of the so-called 'Barzón clause', which provided that if the proceeds of sale of the pledged assets were insufficient to cover the full amount of the secured obligations, the debtor was discharged from its obligation to pay any outstanding amounts. This provision could not be waived. However, the law was recently amended to remove the Barzón clause, giving the creditor the right to seek payment of any outstanding amounts once the collateral has been exhausted.

## 2.7 Guarantee trust

Any kind of asset, whether movable (including intangibles) or immovable, as well as all kinds of property, real or personal, may be subject to a guarantee trust. Unlike a mortgage or a pledge, a guarantee trust is not limited to certain assets; as a result of this flexibility, guarantee trusts have become increasingly popular in recent years, particularly with respect to project and structured finance. Trust agreements may be executed only with certain institutions which are authorised under the General Law of Negotiable Instruments and Credit Operations to act as trustees. Traditionally, only banks and certain governmental institutions could act as trustees; however, in recent years this limited number of institutions which could act as trustees (particularly regarding guarantee trusts) has been extended to include insurance and bonding companies, brokerage houses, limited scope financial entities and deposit institutions, among others.

Under a guarantee trust, the settlor (generally the debtor or a guarantor) transfers title of certain moneys, rights, property and/or other assets to a trustee, which will hold title thereto until the underlying obligation is fully satisfied or until a default occurs. Likewise, the guaranty trust may cover the assets used in a business operation. Article 398 of the General Law of Negotiable Instruments and Credit Operations provides that the parties to a guaranty trust over movable assets may agree that the settlor(s) shall have the right to:

- use and combine the trust assets for the production of other assets, provided that they do not decrease in value and the produced assets become subject to the guaranty trust;
- obtain and use income and products deriving from the trust assets; and
- instruct the trustee to transfer the trust assets, provided such transfer is consistent with the ordinary course of business of the settlor, in which case the assets and rights that the trustee receives or has the right to receive as payment for the transfer of assets shall become subject to the guaranty trust.

Additionally, a trustee, as owner of the trust assets, may be authorised under the trust agreement to create certain guarantees, such as a mortgage or a pledge over its assets, providing enhanced security for the creditor.

In the event of default, provided that the procedure set forth under the trust agreement (which must conform to the guidelines determined by the General Law of Negotiable Instruments and Credit Operations) is followed, the trustee may sell such assets and the proceeds thereof will be delivered to the trust beneficiary (secured party).

The General Law of Negotiable Instruments and Credit Operations, which governs guarantee trusts, is a federal law and is thus applicable in all Mexican states and in the federal district, ensuring legal and regulatory uniformity. Notwithstanding the foregoing, and the fact that trusts have been regulated under Mexican law since 1932, provisions governing guarantee trusts have been subject to numerous amendments recently. There is thus no definitive court precedent on the matter, causing uncertainty as to how a guarantee trust or foreclosure thereunder maybe interpreted by the Mexican courts.

In order to be valid, a guarantee trust must be executed in written form; if it involves real estate, it must be executed before a notary public and registered with the Public Registry of Property in the state or municipality where the real estate is located in order to be binding against third parties.

Although there are certain exceptions,[7] as a general rule, Mexican law does not allow creditors to foreclose on guarantees without prior due process. As set forth under the General Law of Negotiable Instruments and Credit Operations, the trust beneficiary (secured party) under a guarantee trust may request that the trustee foreclose on the conveyed assets without resorting to the courts or requiring a prior court order by following the non-judicial procedure set forth under the trust agreement. This notwithstanding, the General Law of Negotiable Instruments and Credit Operations requires the inclusion and observance of certain prerequisites, such as:

- notice by the trust beneficiary to the trustee describing the default of the underlying obligation and requesting commencement of the agreed foreclosure procedure;
- notice thereof by the trustee to the settler; and
- opportunity to oppose foreclosure by:
  - paying all amounts overdue;
  - attesting fulfilment of the underlying obligations; or
  - showing the document whereby the obligations were novated or their term was extended.

Notwithstanding the existence under Mexican laws of certain non-judicial or extra-judicial foreclosure processes, such as that described for the guarantee trust, under the Mexican Constitution no one may be deprived of his property, possessions or rights without a trial conducted before established courts pursuant to due process

7 The constitutionality of these exceptions has not always been upheld by the Mexican courts in the past.

and previously enacted laws.[8] In the event that this constitutional guarantee is violated, affected individuals are entitled to launch an *amparo* proceeding.[9] As guarantee trusts have not yet been sufficiently tested before the Mexican courts, it is difficult to foresee the outcome of a foreclosure of a guarantee trust contested through an *amparo* proceeding or in any other manner. In order to mitigate the possibility of an *amparo* proceeding being filed and to establish a reasonable defence in relation thereto, it is advisable to include in the trust agreement clear rules aimed at demonstrating that the settlor (debtor) was duly notified of the commencement of the foreclosure procedure, and was given the opportunity to cure the relevant default or to prove to the trustee that the secured obligations were in fact fulfilled.

## 3. Personal guaranties

Personal guaranties do not create a lien on any specific assets, but require an individual or legal entity to comply with the obligations of a third party as if such obligations were its own. The following is a description of the personal guaranties available under Mexican laws.

### 3.1 Civil guarantee

The Federal Civil Code establishes that the civil guarantee is an agreement by means of which a third party undertakes to pay the creditor if the debtor does not meet its obligations. A civil guarantee cannot exist without a valid principal obligation.

Guarantors are granted certain benefits under Mexican law, known as the benefits of '*orden*', '*división*' and '*excusión*'. The benefit of *orden* requires the creditor to proceed against the debtor before proceeding against the guarantor. The benefit of *excusión* requires the creditor to ensure the assets of the debtor are first exhausted in payment of its obligations before any amounts are claimed from or paid by the guarantor.[10] The benefit of *división* exists when there are multiple guarantors: it allows one of the guarantors which has been called to trial to have the other guarantors appear at the same trial in order to defend themselves jointly, with each guarantor being liable for its proportionate share of the principal obligation.[11]

In order for the guarantor to waive such benefits, pursuant to the Federal Civil Code the waiver must be executed in "clear and precise terms, in a manner that there is no doubt of the right being waived".[12] This is why cross-border credit facilities generally contain an express and detailed waiver by the guarantor for all applicable articles of the local regulations establishing the guarantor's benefits.

---

8 Similar to the 14th Amendment to the US Constitution.

9 The *amparo* proceeding is a constitutional challenge directed at preserving constitutional rights, such as the guarantee of due process.

10 The benefit of *excusión* will not apply in the following cases, among others:
- The debtor is proved insolvent;
- The debtor cannot be sued in Mexico; or
- The business for which the guarantee was granted is the business of the guarantor.

11 The benefit of *división* will not apply among the guarantors in the following cases, among others:
- One or more of the guarantors are insolvent;
- One or more of the guarantors cannot be sued in Mexico; or
- The business for which the guarantee was granted is the business of the guarantor.

12 Article 7 of the Federal Civil Code.

Likewise, as there is doubt as to whether these benefits may be considered as a matter of public order, there is also doubt as to whether a Mexican court would enforce a court resolution obtained in a foreign jurisdiction that did not uphold the benefits.

Since the guarantor's obligations derive from an underlying agreement and therefore depend directly on the debtor's obligations thereunder, the guarantor is entitled to utilise and oppose the same exceptions, defences and arguments as the debtor under the underlying agreement, other than certain exceptions or defences which are personal or exclusive to the debtor (eg, a right of set-off under a different contract between the debtor and the guaranteed party).

### 3.2 Bond

Under Mexican law, a bond is a guaranty issued by an authorised entity which grants bonds on a customary basis. The bond is an agreement between a guarantor and the creditor of the original debtor under which the guarantor undertakes to pay or otherwise comply with the debtor's obligations in case the debtor defaults. The bond can be granted only if a valid underlying obligation exists. A guarantor may validly agree to pay a certain amount of money which is owed and not paid by the debtor, or if the debtor does not comply with a payment obligation.

A bonding company is a legal entity whose corporate purpose is the granting of guaranties on a customary basis. Therefore, the rules applicable to the civil guarantee are also applicable to bonds issued by bonding institutions. In addition, because of their responsibility to the public, the creation and operation of bonding institutions are also regulated by the Bonds Law, which contains additional requirements relating to the issuance and operation of bonds granted by bonding institutions.

Article 2 of the Bonds Law provides that "the bonds and the agreements related thereto issued or entered into by bonding companies shall be of a commercial nature for all parties involved, either as beneficiaries, applicants, guaranteed parties, counter-guarantors or joint and several obligors". Therefore, the provisions of the Bonds Law relating to bonds and guaranty agreements may be modified by agreement of the parties.

### 3.3 Unconditional endorsement (*aval*)

According to the General Law of Negotiable Instruments and Credit Operations, by means of an unconditional endorsement a person guarantees total or partial payment of amounts described in a negotiable instrument. The guarantor is jointly liable with the principal obligor and its obligations are valid notwithstanding that the principal obligation is null for any reason whatsoever.

Mexican courts have established that the unconditional endorsement refers only to negotiable instruments, whereas civil or commercial obligations not incorporated into a negotiable instrument are considered a guaranty. As a result, guarantors sign credit agreements as guaranties and the relevant promissory notes as unconditional endorsements or '*aval*'.

### 3.4 Joint obligations

Although not a security interest *per se*, it is common practice to have persons (whether individuals or entities) execute loan documents as joint and several obligors, entitling the creditor to claim payment directly from these joint and several obligors without first having to proceed against the principal obligor.

## 4. Conclusions

Mexican law affords a wide range of mechanisms and schemes to create security interests which do not exclude each other and can be combined to create different security packages that can be adapted to the specific characteristics of the transaction.

The schemes available may create security interests on specific assets, a 'floating lien' on a business operation and personal obligations. Some allow for non-judicial foreclosure (eg,, guaranty trust) and some require court intervention (eg, mortgage); some are available only to Mexican banking institutions (eg, industrial mortgage) and some are generally available.

Mexican law has recently been amended to provide alternatives for Mexican companies seeking more flexible ways of obtaining financing, as well to foreign banks and other lending institutions which were previously reluctant to provide financing in Mexico because of the lack of clear regulations.

An adequate security package should address the concerns of the lending entities while also being compatible with the nature of the business. The different types of security interest contemplated under Mexican law provide various options to structure security packages that can address such concerns.

# China

**Betty Tam**
**Jeremy Xiao**
Herbert Smith LLP

China's investment regime has matured significantly over the last decade. However, the same cannot be said of its regime governing the granting of security to foreign parties and the enforcement of security: those seeking security in China can be challenged by laws that give inadequate protection to various security interests and give rise to various timing difficulties.

This chapter outlines the types of security interest that are available under Chinese law and matters that grantees of such security interests should take into account to ensure the effectiveness of the security. It also identifies certain legal issues as well as some solutions for those wanting to take effective security over assets in China.

## 1. Available security

In order to be effective, security interests in China must be created in accordance with China's Security Law and, from October 1 2007, China's Property Law. The Security Law recognises five basic types of security: guarantees, mortgages, pledges, liens and deposits. The Property Law recognises mortgages, pledges and liens, but allows more possibilities in terms of the property over which mortgages and pledges may be created.

Liens and deposits may not be given as security in favour of foreign parties. Accordingly, liens and deposits are not discussed in this chapter.

### 1.1 Guarantees

Under the Security Law, a 'guarantee' is defined as an act whereby a guarantor and a creditor agree that the guarantor will perform the obligation of a debtor should the debtor fail to do so. A guarantee contract must be in writing and may take various forms, including letters of guarantee, standby letters of credit and bills of exchange.

Guarantees under Chinese law may impose either a primary or secondary obligation on the guarantor. A creditor that wants to create a 'guarantee' in the more traditional sense of the term, whereby the guarantor has a primary obligation towards the creditor, must be careful not to enter into a 'general guarantee'. If the guarantee is unclear or silent as to the secondary nature of the guarantee, the guarantor and the debtor will be deemed to have joint and several liability and a creditor may bring an action against the guarantor before exhausting options against the debtor.

## 1.2 Mortgages

A mortgage under Chinese law is a type of security whereby a debtor or a third party uses property as security for an obligation without the transfer of possession or title of such property. If possession is transferred, the security will be treated as a pledge, which is discussed further below. However, a pledge is restricted to security over movable properties and certain rights.

Mortgages over the following types of property are effective only upon the date of registration with the relevant governmental authority (noted in brackets):

- land use rights (Land Bureau);
- buildings lawfully constructed with requisite construction permissions (including partly constructed buildings), which must be mortgaged together with the corresponding land use rights (Real Property Bureau); and
- forestry resources (Forestry Administration Bureau);

Mortgages over the following types of property are effective as between the parties when the mortgage contract itself comes into effect, but will be effective against, and therefore take priority over, a good-faith third party only upon registration with the competent registration authority (noted in brackets):

- means of transportation, including aircraft, vessels and motor vehicles (Civil Aviation Administration, Maritime Safety Administration and Motor Vehicle Administration Bureau of the Public Security Administration, respectively);
- vessels and aircraft which are under construction (see below); and
- both existing and future equipment, raw materials, semi-finished and finished products (Administration of Industry and Commerce).

The possibility of creating mortgages over vessels and aircraft which are still under construction is newly recognised under the Property Law. However, the Property Law does not set out the registration authority for such mortgages. Subject to any implementing rules that may be promulgated, it is likely that the registration authority for vessels and aircraft under construction will be the Civil Aviation Administration and the Maritime Safety Administration, respectively.

Providing for mortgages over future equipment, raw materials, semi-finished and finished products is another innovation of the Property Law. This will in effect allow the creation of a floating charge, which was previously not recognised under Chinese laws and regulations. A floating charge under the Property Law will crystallise upon the occurrence of the following events:

- The debt is not repaid upon the expiry of the loan;
- The mortgagor becomes bankrupt or is dissolved;
- An event that may result in enforcement of the mortgage as agreed by the parties occurs; or
- Another event which materially affects the realisation of the creditor's rights occurs.

Except for property over which mortgages are expressly prohibited (including certain collectively owned land use rights and facilities of institutions established for the purpose of providing social welfare), mortgages may also be created over any type of property. Mortgages created over such other types of property become effective upon the date of signing the relevant contract. However, registration of these contracts remains a necessary step to protect security interests created under them against any rights that may arise in favour of third parties. For such other types of property, the relevant governmental registration authority is the notary public of the place where the mortgagor is located.

The parties to a mortgage may not agree for the mortgagee to take title to the mortgaged property directly if the secured obligation is not satisfied upon expiration of the term of a mortgage. Instead, the mortgaged property must be sold or auctioned or otherwise converted into value and the excess funds returned to the mortgagor. Unless the mortgagee can reach agreement with the mortgagor, the mortgagee must make an application to the court in order to enforce the mortgage.

### 1.3 Pledges

A pledge, under Chinese law, is categorised as either a pledge over movable property (which involves the transfer of possession of movable property as security) or a pledge over rights.

#### *(a) Pledges over movable property*

Pledges over movable property must be concluded in the form of a written contract, although the pledge becomes effective only upon transfer of the possession of the property to the pledgee. As in the case of mortgages, the parties to a pledge may not agree for the pledgee to take title to the pledged property directly if the secured obligation is not satisfied upon expiration of the term of a pledge; the pledged property must be sold or auctioned or otherwise converted into value, and the excess funds returned to the pledgor. The main difference between a mortgage and a pledge is that upon enforcement, a pledgee may dispose of the pledged property without making an application to the court, while a mortgagee is required to do so if a mutual agreement with the mortgagor is not reached.

#### *(b) Pledges over rights*

In relation to pledges over rights, the following rights may be pledged (with the time of effectiveness of the pledge noted in brackets):

- bills of exchange, cheques, promissory notes, bonds, certificates of deposits, warehouse receipts and bills of lading (effective upon delivery of title certificate or, in the absence of any title certificate, upon registration with the competent authority);
- unit trusts and equity interests (effective upon registration of the pledge with the relevant unit trusts or securities registry or, for equity interests not registered with a securities registry, effective upon registration with the local branch of the State Administration of Industry and Commerce (SAIC); see below for equity interests in foreign investment enterprises (FIEs));
- trademarks, patents and copyrights that are transferable according to law (effective upon registration of the pledge with relevant governmental authority);

- receivables (effective upon registration with the official credit agency); and
- other rights that may be pledged according to law.

Prior to the promulgation of the Property Law, the procedures for the granting and perfection of security over receivables such as earnings from power plants and highways, as well as the legal effect of such security, was uncertain. Whether such security could be registered depended on local practice. This lack of uniformity and uncertainty has now been addressed with the promulgation of the Property Law.

*(c)* ***Pledge over equity***

Equity contributions to FIEs in China may be pledged, although some restrictions apply. First, only that portion of the equity which has been paid up may be pledged. Second, the pledge must be approved by the relevant local branch of the Ministry of Commerce and registered with the relevant local branch of the SAIC before it becomes effective. These first two restrictions can create difficulties in some acquisition finance transactions where the investor needs the loan to make the capital contribution, but lenders may be reluctant to advance the loan before security is given. In such situations, lenders generally need to compromise by giving the investor a certain amount of time after drawdown to create and perfect the pledge. Failure to perfect the pledge within that the prescribed time may be stipulated as an event of default under the loan facility.

Finally, the consent of other investors in an FIE is required before equity can be pledged. Accordingly, a Chinese joint venture party can effectively veto a foreign party's financing arrangements for the payment of its capital contribution. In practical terms, however, this means that a foreign joint venture party should procure its Chinese party's consent prior to going ahead with financing arrangements involving the giving of a pledge over equity. Such consent should also waive the right of first refusal given to the other joint venture parties under the relevant joint venture laws and regulations when the equity in a Chinese foreign joint venture is transferred upon enforcement of the pledge.

## 1.4 Other types of security

Certain types of security interest commonly seen in international financing arrangements, such as security over contractual rights and security over bank accounts, are not expressly recognised under Chinese law. This notwithstanding, lenders (especially foreign lenders) generally insist upon some form of contractual security arrangement over bank accounts and contractual rights for project finance or other substantial financing arrangements. Although Article 223(7) of the Property Law provides that a pledge may be created over "other property rights that can be pledged according to laws and administrative regulations", in the absence of any express legal provision giving effect to those security interests mentioned above, it remains uncertain whether such security interests are legally effective. In particular, it is unclear how these types of security may be perfected so that they may be legally enforceable.

### *(a) Security over contractual rights*

Chinese law does not expressly permit the giving of contractual rights as security. The traditional approach adopted in project financing involves a security assignment (usually translated as 'pledge' in Chinese) by the borrower of its rights under project documents governed by Chinese law to an onshore security agent (a Chinese bank). Any relevant project document governed by foreign law is then given as a security assignment to an offshore agent and the assignment agreement is governed by foreign law. However, this type of arrangement has yet to be tested in Chinese courts.

Some have taken the view that an 'assignment' (often translated as '*zhuanrang*', meaning 'transfer') of contractual rights should be treated as a present transfer of the contractual rights, an arrangement more akin to a novation. In some major financings in China, the insurances of the borrower have been 'assigned' (in the sense of 'transfer') to the security agent, which then authorises the borrower to exercise its rights under the insurance policies (within a specified monetary limit) prior to the issuance of an enforcement notice. Insofar as insurance policies are concerned, the Supreme People's Court has ruled that security interest cannot be created over policies for property insurance. However, security over personal insurance policies is generally accepted in practice.

It also appears that it is currently possible, on a more general basis, to give legal effect to security over contractual rights by way of notarisation. In particular, the Registration of Mortgages by Notaries Public Procedures issued by the Ministry of Justice provide that where security is created over property rights such as the right to contract for business and other contractual rights, the notary public may carry out registration by reference to the procedures. According to the procedures, the security will be perfected upon the issuance of a registration certificate by the notary public. However, the authority of the Ministry of Justice (as a government department only) to issue and implement such procedures (which provide for matters not covered by the Security Law, a law passed by the Standing Committee of the National People's Congress) is not without question. Notwithstanding these concerns, the procedures do serve to give lenders a certain degree of comfort if security documents are notarised.

### *(b) Security over bank accounts*

Chinese law provides for the pledge of fixed deposits, but does not recognise the granting of a security interest over an account with a fluctuating balance. This position remains the same under the Property Law. On the basis of a Supreme People's Court interpretation of the Security Law, which recognises the creation of security over cash which is "fixed and specific", the view now taken by certain academics in China is that while security over bank accounts is possible, the security interest created attaches only to an amount 'frozen' at the time when security is granted. This renders a security over bank accounts unworkable in China because the bank account holder will then be unable to use the 'frozen' funds in the account.

One approach adopted by financial institutions lending in China is to enter into an accounts supervision agreement with the borrower, under which the borrower is obliged to open all its accounts with the lender(s) so that the lender(s) may monitor the use of funds by the borrower. A cash waterfall mechanism like those typically adopted in a charge over accounts may be included in the accounts supervision agreement. Such agreement, however, does not constitute a security interest and the lenders will not have priority over third parties to any amount standing to the credit of these accounts. A final possibility is to take an assignment of the borrower's bank accounts under a security document governed by and drafted in accordance with a foreign law. However, this arrangement requires at least one foreign party, such as an offshore security agent, to be a party to the security contract because a contract between Chinese parties must be governed by Chinese law unless a certain foreign element is present. Enforcement of such an arrangement in China also remains uncertain.

## 2. Foreign security

The giving of security to a foreign party introduces an additional layer of registrations and may also require Chinese governmental approvals.

### 2.1 Definition

'Foreign security' is defined as security given by an institution in China (the security provider) in favour of an entity outside of China (the beneficiary) to secure the obligations of a debtor (the secured party). The rights of the different parties are explained in more detail below.

### 2.2 Security provider

Institutions in China include FIEs (whether they are wholly foreign owned or Sino-foreign joint ventures). Therefore, security given by FIEs in favour of overseas lenders falls within the scope of foreign security.

### 2.3 Beneficiary

For the purpose of the foreign security regulations, the term 'beneficiary' refers to any organisation outside China and, in some instances, may also include foreign-invested financial institutions in China.

Prior to June 2004, all security given to foreign-invested financial institutions in China was considered to be foreign security. However, a circular issued by the State Administration of Foreign Exchange (SAFE) in June 2004 removed the registration requirements for security granted in favour of a foreign-invested financial institution in China if the security is granted as collateral for the debt of a Chinese entity.

### 2.4 Secured party

For the purpose of the foreign security regulations, the term 'secured party' refers to a debtor, which essentially means a borrower in a loan agreement. The party must fall within one of the following categories in order to qualify as a secured party so that its debt may be secured by foreign security:

- domestic enterprises in China;
- FIEs in China;
- entities registered outside China as wholly owned subsidiaries of entities in China; and

- enterprises in which Chinese parties have equity participation.

In essence, a secured party must either be established in China or have at least one shareholder which is a Chinese enterprise.

Secured parties that are registered outside China and meet the third or fourth categories referred to in the beginning of this section cannot be loss-making and must have ratios of net assets to gross assets of at least:

- 10% for trade-type enterprises; and
- 15% for non-trade-type enterprises.

Audited balance sheets and profit and loss statements of the secured party must be submitted to SAFE as part of the application for approval of the security.

If an entity does not fit within any of the above categories, then the loans it raises outside China may not be secured by any security granted by a Chinese entity. In particular, this means that in an acquisition finance scenario, where an offshore holding company is the borrower but the main assets are in China, the Chinese subsidiary cannot give security to foreign lenders to secure the debt of its parent company.

This problem may be resolved if the security provider is the direct sole owner of the Chinese subsidiary; some local branches of SAFE (eg, in Shenzhen) are known to be more flexible towards security given by a wholly foreign-owned enterprise (WFOE) and have registered foreign security where the secured party does not fall within any of the above four categories. However, such registration will generally be given only if the secured party is the WFOE's direct 100% equity stakeholder. Presumably, this is because the secured party in such cases is closely and directly related to the security provider whose registered capital is wholly paid up by foreign funds; hence, the issue of outflow of foreign exchange may not be a significant concern for Chinese governmental authorities.

In a group financing scenario, where the borrower may not be the direct shareholder of the Chinese subsidiary providing the security, consideration may be given to structuring the finance documents in such a way that the Chinese subsidiary is securing the debt of its immediate shareholder. For instance, the immediate shareholder in the WFOE may issue a guarantee in favour of the overseas lender in respect of the obligations of other group companies under the finance documents. In these circumstances, the principal debt for which the security is given may be said to be a guarantee provided by the immediate shareholder of the Chinese subsidiary. However, SAFE's approval in cases that do not clearly meet the regulatory guidelines should be treated as exceptional and discretionary, and should by no means be treated as binding precedents. Enquiries should be made with the local SAFE based on the facts of each specific occasion. Moreover, even where SAFE approval and registration is granted to cases that do not clearly meet the regulatory guidelines, enforcement problems may exist if the approval and registration are subsequently challenged.

An alternative solution to the restrictions on a secured party is for a foreign lender to work in conjunction with a local bank such that while the loan is advanced to an overseas borrower, the security is given by a Chinese entity to a local bank. Such security will not constitute foreign security and hence will not be subject to SAFE scrutiny. In case of default under the principal loan, the local bank may enforce the security granted by the Chinese entity. To do so, certain arrangements such as a letter of credit will need to be put in place between the foreign lender and the local bank which acts as beneficiary of the security so that the local bank may eventually remit to the foreign lender any proceeds from enforcing the security. This is not dissimilar to the structure adopted in some project financing transactions in relation to Chinese infrastructure projects, where a foreign syndicate appoints a Chinese bank (which is not itself a member of the syndicate) to act as the security agent on the basis of an intercreditor agreement entered into with the syndicate. However, this structure will work only where a Chinese bank (as opposed to a foreign-invested financial institution in China) is involved, because the June 2004 SAFE circular mentioned above applies only to situations where the borrower is a Chinese entity. In other words, SAFE approval will still be needed if an entity in China gives security to a foreign-invested financial institution in China for the debts of an overseas borrower.

### 2.5 Limits on amounts of secured indebtedness

Based on the Security Law and the relevant foreign security regulations, the amount of indebtedness that may be secured by security providers which are non-financial institutions is limited to the lowest of:

- the value of the security, for which appraisal evidence is required;
- 50% of the net asset value of the security provider (to be shown by audited financial statements); and
- the security provider's foreign exchange earnings for the previous year (which must be certified by SAFE).

This poses the question of whether such limits will remain relevant if by the time of enforcement the above figures have already changed. According to a Supreme People's Court judicial interpretation issued in 2000, the value of the security should be confirmed at the time the security is enforced. However, in the case of foreign security, the situation is complicated by the fact that when the lender has to remit the enforcement proceeds out of China, SAFE will likely take the view that the amount that may be remitted should be limited to the amount of secured indebtedness registered with SAFE. This appears to be the position taken by various local branches of SAFE. Some practitioners have suggested that lenders should therefore constantly review the financial situation of the security provider and the value of security so that application may be made to SAFE to increase the amount of secured indebtedness. Appropriate undertakings should be included in the security documents because any such application will require the cooperation of the security provider.

### 2.6 Approvals and registrations

In addition to any required registrations for domestic security (see above), foreign security must be registered with SAFE to be valid. If the security provider of mortgages or pledges to a foreign party is different from the secured party, approval by SAFE is also required. Mortgages may be registered with the relevant domestic authority only after being approved and/or registered with SAFE. SAFE approvals for other types of security must also generally take place prior to any asset-specific registrations in China.

If a WFOE is providing security, such security is not subject to SAFE approval requirements, although the WFOE must register any foreign security with SAFE after the security document is signed. This exemption from SAFE approval may be regarded as an indication that the Chinese government is willing to impose less stringent requirements on and show more flexibility towards WFOEs. However, it should be borne in mind that even though approval is not required, the giving of foreign security by WFOEs is still subject to other requirements on foreign security, such as the qualification of the secured party and the restriction on the value of security. Further, if a mortgage over a WFOE's assets is created in favour of a foreign party, such mortgage must be approved by the local branch of MOFCOM.

Guarantees given to a foreign party by a non-financial institution in China are subject to SAFE approval and registration. Certain guarantees, such as finance guarantees and foreign currency performance bonds, given by Chinese financial institutions are also subject to approval and registration.

Chinese financial institutions satisfying the following ratios, however, may issue other types of guarantee on their own authority without the need for SAFE approval and registration:

- Outstanding foreign exchange debts and security commitments may not exceed 20 times the Chinese financial institution's foreign exchange funds; and
- Foreign exchange debt and security commitments to any one of the Chinese financial institution's clients may not exceed 30% of its foreign exchange funds.

A contract creating security in favour of a foreign entity will be void if it is not duly registered or approved. Accordingly, any party taking security in China must be diligent in ensuring that the security is duly registered and, if required, approved.

Finally, in cases where SAFE approval is required, foreign security should be granted promptly following issuance of any SAFE approval. Although this will usually be the case, SAFE approvals automatically become void if the security provider does not issue the security to the foreign secured party within six months of the corresponding SAFE approval.

## 3. Timing and registrations

As noted above, foreign security requires registration with SAFE, and may also require SAFE approval, before becoming effective. In addition, and following SAFE procedures, many types of security also need registration with other particular Chinese governmental authorities in order to ensure priority over unsecured creditors and other third-party rights.

The approval and registration requirements create significant practical hurdles for many transactions. In particular, the simultaneous drawdown and giving of security is generally not possible. This affects both the initial setting up of a project and any subsequent refinancing. For the initial setting up of a project, if lenders want to take security over a foreign borrower's equity interest in the Chinese subsidiary to be established, the interest in the subsidiary will not be legally vested in the borrower until it has injected its capital into the subsidiary. This will mean that the equity pledge may not be granted and perfected until some time after the lender has advanced the funds to the borrower and the capital is duly injected. For subsequent financings, the original lender will typically want to be repaid before releasing its security. However, the new lender will typically want to have its security registered before advancing the money. These competing demands cannot generally both be accommodated within China's regulatory regime.

In practice, lenders faced with timing issues need to compromise. Usually the compromise will include an undertaking in loan documents that registration will be completed within a certain period, failing which an event of default is deemed to occur. This at least gives lenders a chance to restrict any further advances while appropriate measures are taken to rectify the situation. The threat of calling in the loan should be sufficient to ensure that registration is duly completed.

An alternative is the payment of funds into escrow. For instance, in an acquisition finance scenario, the foreign lender, instead of advancing the funds to the foreign borrower for payment into China, may transfer the funds to an escrow account opened in the name of the vendor with a bank in China. The balance of those funds may then only be drawn by the vendor upon completion of the security registration procedures.

## 4. Conclusion

As can be seen, taking security in China is not a straightforward exercise. While the Property Law, once implemented, will help resolve some of the issues that previously existed, a lot of the hurdles now facing foreign lenders which seek to take security in China (in particular those relating to foreign security) are likely to remain. Therefore, special care must be taken in both the planning and execution stages to ensure that security is valid.

# Brazil

**Silvia Rajsfeld Fiszman**
**José Ribeiro do Prado Jr**
Machado, Meyer, Sendacz e Opice Advogados

## 1. Introduction

As elsewhere in the world, investors intending to invest capital in Brazil need to evaluate the risks involved in the project, including cash flow and the liquidity of collateral. The financing structure itself must take account of:

- the length of time it will take to implement the project;
- the resources allocated to the project;
- the risks involved in the project; and
- the expected return on the investment.

The growth of the global economy in recent years, combined with increased demand worldwide for Brazilian commodities and industrial goods, has had an impact on the cost of financing projects within Brazil. As key variables such as internal inflation and country risk have fallen, there is likely to be downward pressure on interest rates in Brazil and therefore greater demand for debt financing.

Further, in January 2007 the government launched the Growth Acceleration Programme to address the shortage of infrastructure investment in Brazil and the need to remove regulatory barriers to private sector investment. The programme aims to boost Brazil's economic growth and increase investment in infrastructure.

The macroeconomic measures taken by the government under the programme – including tax reforms, incentives for infrastructure investment and enhanced legal assurance levels – amount to approximately R$503.9 billion for the period from 2007 to 2010. These funds will be used to construct and repair highways, airports and ports nationwide, boost energy development in the north of Brazil and provide housing, water and sewage systems to the underprivileged. Of this amount, according to the government, approximately $205 billion will be provided by state-owned companies such as Petrobas and the Social and Economic National Development Bank (BNDES), and the private sector, with the balance being provided directly by the government.

In order to achieve the objectives of the Growth Acceleration Programme, the government intends to introduce legal reforms which are designed to provide a clear and stable legal and regulatory framework to attract investment in Brazil. As part of this framework for investment, investors will need to consider the legal structures available to protect their investments and to ensure that these can generate the expected returns.

## 2. Safe environment for investors – legal structures

The availability of legal structures that enable investors to recoup their investments or look to some other source to service those investments on the default or insolvency of the borrower is of major importance. A prime example of such a legal structure is the security package commonly encountered in Brazilian project finance and corporate finance transactions.

This chapter provides an overview of these security packages – in particular, the different types of security interest available under Brazilian law, and the bankruptcy regime in Brazil and its application to corporate insolvencies and reorganisations. In general, as regards the use of security packages in financing transactions in Brazil, the security package will include legal protection in the form of guarantees covering:

- the construction phase of the project (if relevant);
- the operation phase of the project (if relevant); and
- the entire term or tenor of the financing.

### 2.1 Construction and operation phases

In broad terms, during the construction phase, the typical requirement is a corporate guarantee from project sponsors up to project completion. Nevertheless, some banks (eg, BNDES) require an 'insurance completion': a special type of guarantee provided by a specialised insurance company which is non-recourse to the sponsor. In addition, the shareholder must sometimes commit to provide additional equity contributions if these are necessary to reach project completion. Generally, the minimum equity/total investment requirement is 20% to 30%.

During the operation phase, an escrow account is usually required with a debt service volume of three to six months. Restrictions relating to distributions to shareholders may be established in the financing documents.

### 2.2 Entire tenor of financing

During the entire tenor of the project financing, the usual structure includes a security interest, as discussed below.

#### *(a) General*

Under Brazilian law, there are two main types of guarantee under which creditors may have their obligations secured or guaranteed: security interests and personal guarantees.

The main difference between a personal guarantee and a security interest is that the former entitles the creditor to enforce a claim against any asset of the guarantor on a *pari passu* basis with all other unsecured creditors, whereas the latter allows the creditor to enforce its rights with respect to a secured obligation by means of realising upon a specific asset of the guarantor (which may be the debtor or a third party).

#### *(b) Security interests*

A security interest takes one of the following forms:

- pledge on movable assets (including cash and shares), rights or receivables;
- mortgage on immovable assets; or
- chattel mortgage or fiduciary assignment.

Any of those forms may be used in a wide variety of deals, such as project financings, public offerings and ordinary financing transactions. The security package adopted in such deals may include more than one type of security interest. Obviously, a sophisticated security package strengthens any debt transaction.

In this sense, one interesting example worth mentioning is the security package for a debenture offering that occurred last year. A highway concessionaire made a public offering of debentures in the amount of R$510 million. The security package encompassed a pledge of receivables including toll revenues and all emerging rights of the concession, as well as a pledge of the shares of its controller (one of the biggest companies in Latin America). Through this structure, the collateral for the transaction exceeded R$2 trillion.

Security interests are ruled mainly by the Civil Code. Other laws also set forth complementary provisions, such as Law 10.391/04, which broadened the fiduciary assignment instrument.

The different forms of security interest are analysed further below.

*(i)* *Pledges*

A pledge is a security created on movable assets by means of a private or public pledge agreement. All kind of equipment, goods, fixed assets and rights may be pledged, as long as the owner may legally dispose of them.

The pledge agreement must contain a detailed description of the pledged assets and disclose other terms provided in the law (ie, the amount of the debt, the term established for repayment and the interest rate). Also, except as otherwise provided in the law, for an asset to be pledged it must be transferred to the possession (actual or deemed) of the creditor or a third party acting on its behalf. However, title thereto remains with the owner of the property.

It is common practice in Brazil to have more than one pledge on the same asset. This means that an asset can be pledged to more than one person to secure different obligations. However, such pledges have different rankings – thus, in the event of the debtor's default against a creditor under a second-ranking pledge, that creditor will not be allowed to enforce its rights until the pledge of the first-ranking creditor is extinguished.

One basic element of the pledge is that, where authorised by law or agreement, the creditor may privately sell, transfer or otherwise dispose of the assets should the debtor fail to pay the debt or interest thereon This is the so-called 'amicable sale' under the Civil Code. As a general rule, the secured creditor must sell the collateral and apply the proceeds of such sale to satisfy its claim; any proceeds remaining must be returned to the debtor.

The above notwithstanding, there are two cases in which a creditor may take title to the collateral in order to satisfy its claim:

- where the creditor and the debtor have entered into a specific agreement after the event of default by which the pledged assets are given in payment of the debt; or
- in case of foreclosure, if the public auction required by law has taken place and no bids were made for the pledged assets.

Brazilian law does not recognise a general pledge agreement, whereby assets not yet acquired by the pledgor may be pledged under a single security document. Hence, each asset given as collateral must be described in the pledge agreement, and every time the pledgor acquires a new asset an amendment to the pledge agreement must be executed and filed with the competent public registries in Brazil.

Additionally, any of the parties to the pledge agreement may register the collateral document with the competent public registries. In general terms, pledge agreements must be registered with the Registry of Titles and Deeds. There are a few exceptions under the law.

Receivables may also be pledged under Brazilian law as long as they can be individually identified. The receivables pledge agreement must be registered with the Registry of Titles and Deeds. A pledge of new receivables is perfected only upon registration of an amendment to the pledge agreement including such new receivables with the relevant registry.

A pledge of receivables usually incorporates a pledge over the rights regarding the bank accounts in which the proceeds from the receivables are deposited from time to time. In this sense, the pledge applies to the rights of the account holder against the financial institution in respect of the proceeds deposited in the bank account, and all certificates representing investments made with such proceeds. The bank holding such account must agree to be bound by the terms and conditions of the pledge agreement. The pledge is perfected by registering the security document with the Registry of Titles and Deeds in Brazil and, depending on the types of investment made with the proceeds, with other registries and clearing houses as well.

The pledge of quotas must be reflected in an amendment to the debtor's articles of association, which must be registered with the competent board of trade. The pledge agreement must be registered with the Registry of Titles and Deeds, depending on the type of security. The pledge of shares of a corporation must be recorded in the company's share register.

*(ii)* *Mortgages*

A mortgage is a security created exclusively over real estate (although ships and aircraft can also be mortgaged pursuant to specific registration and documentary rules). Title to and possession of the property remain with the debtor during the life of the secured debt. A mortgage is created by way of a public deed executed by the parties before a notary public and registered with the Real Estate Registry at the place where the mortgaged property is located. There must be one mortgage deed for each property being given as collateral and each deed must be registered with the Real Estate Registry at the place where the property is located.

Moreover, a real estate owner can create different mortgages over its property. In such case the mortgages will have different rankings; accordingly, a second-ranking creditor can enforce its rights only once the first-ranking mortgage has been extinguished.

The public deed will be registered only if the parties present certain public certificates relating to the real estate (including certificates confirming payment of taxes) to the Real Estate Registry. These formalities are also essential to ensure the validity of the security interest.

Registration with the Real Estate Registry varies from state to state in Brazil and sometimes may take 90 days or more. It is also an expensive process; the exact cost is calculated on the basis of the amount guaranteed by the respective mortgage. Once filed and registered, the mortgage will remain effective for 30 years, unless the parties agree on a shorter period of time. Once this 30-year period has expired, a new registration with the Real Estate Registry is required.

Foreclosure on the mortgaged property may be effected only through judicial proceedings.

*(iii)* *Fiduciary assignment*

Another type of security interest is a fiduciary assignment over movable assets, rights or immovable assets of the debtor. This type of security is typically used in connection with equipment and consumer credit financing. Law 4.728/65 introduced the fiduciary assignment, but only after the introduction of Law 10.391/04 did the use of this instrument increase. Law 9.514/97 also provides for the fiduciary assignment of immovable assets.

In addition, Sections 1.361 to 1.368 of the Civil Code include specific rules on fiduciary assignment.

One of the most important differences between the pledge and the fiduciary assignment is that the latter transfers title to the asset to the creditor. However, it is commonly agreed that such title is automatically transferred back to the debtor once the obligation is satisfied. In contrast, in case of default, the creditor will be entitled to foreclose on the relevant asset and to use the proceeds to satisfy its claim and pay the expenses associated with the foreclosure proceeding. Similar to the pledge, any remaining proceeds must be delivered to the debtor.

As a general rule, fiduciary assignments must be registered with the Registry of Titles and Deeds. However, the fiduciary assignment of quotas must be reflected in an amendment to the debtor's articles of association, which must be registered with the Board of Trade. The fiduciary assignment of shares of a corporation must be recorded in the company's share register or in the books of the responsible financial institution.

The fiduciary assignment of an immovable asset must be registered with the Real Estate Registry.

***(c)*** ***Bankruptcy issues***

Decree-Law 7,661 of June 21 1945 regulates the liquidation of a company and the restructuring of unsecured debt proceedings. However, it became apparent over the years that this legal framework provided inadequate protection to creditors and unsatisfactory mechanisms to preserve viable enterprises, resulting in calls for the revision and modernisation of Decree-Law 7,661.

After 10 years of discussions in Congress, a new Bankruptcy Law (Federal Law 11,101 of February 9 2005) was finally enacted.

The new law has introduced a new legal regime applicable to reorganisations (judicial reorganisation and out-of-court reorganisation) and court liquidations in

Brazil. The most significant innovation concerns reorganisations. This remedy is largely based on modern bankruptcy laws, including Chapter 11 of the US Bankruptcy Code. Among the key provisions of the new law relating to court reorganisation, the most significant are those providing for active participation of creditors.

*(i) Court reorganisation*

Court reorganisation is a judicial proceeding that aims to resolve a debtor's temporary financial distress. A debtor may become subject to court reorganisation voluntarily or involuntarily. In order to file for court reorganisation, the plaintiff must prove to the court's satisfaction that the debtor is a viable enterprise. In addition, the plaintiff must file certain documents in connection with the debtor's economic situation.

After the petition has been filed, the court will decide, on the basis of the documentation presented by the plaintiff, whether the procedure will continue. The court's decision is primarily based on its determination as to whether the plaintiff has filed the appropriate documentation.

The debtor must file a reorganisation plan within 60 days of the initial order. The reorganisation plan may propose any solutions for the debtor to recover from its financial difficulties, including:

- corporate reorganisation;
- replacement of management; and
- sale of assets.

In addition, the reorganisation plan may provide for special treatment of the debtor's obligations, including impairment and new terms and conditions. The reorganisation plan may also provide for a change in ranking or order for repayment of the company's debts, provided that the statutory priority of labour obligations is respected. Labour debt must be paid within one year of the filing of the reorganisation plan, except for a certain portion of unpaid salaries that accrued in the three months prior to the request for court reorganisation. Such unpaid salaries must be paid within 30 days and must not exceed five minimum wages per employee.

Claims arising from fiduciary trust arrangements, leases and reservation of title transactions are not affected by court reorganisation. The ownership rights and the contractual terms and conditions will prevail; however, the assets subject to such arrangements cannot be removed or sold during the period of the automatic stay[1] if they are necessary for the continuation of the debtor's business.

Another important feature of the new bankruptcy law is its introduction of an out-of court reorganisation mechanism. This allows the debtor to select and invite creditors to present a reorganisation plan. This may entail an acknowledgment of insolvency and result in the commencement of liquidation.

---

1 The judge usually declares an automatic stay on any collection proceedings against the debtor (except for labour lawsuits, tax lawsuits or lawsuits claiming an amount to be liquidated in the future). The stay lasts for 180 days after the order allowing the procedure to continue.

The out-of-court reorganisation may affect participating or non-participating creditors, and claims arising from labour and tax matters remain outside the scope of the reorganisation.

The reorganisation plan cannot provide for accelerated payment of any claim or for discriminatory treatment of creditors that are not participating in the out-of-court reorganisation.

If the reorganisation plan provides for the disposal of collateral for a certain security interest (an *in rem* guarantee), the secured creditor must approve the disposal or replacement of the collateral.

*(ii) Court liquidation*

Court liquidation is a procedure carried out in the collective interests of the creditors of an insolvent debtor. The main purpose of court liquidation is to wind up and sell the assets of the debtor in order to satisfy its obligations.

Any creditor may file for court liquidation under the following conditions:

- Creditors domiciled in Brazil must prove that they are duly registered with the Board of Commerce;
- Secured creditors must waive their security interest; and
- Creditors domiciled outside Brazil must make an escrow deposit in Brazil to secure payment of court costs and attorneys' fees (payable if the creditor's petition for court liquidation is dismissed).

The debtor and/or its shareholders (among others) may also petition for court liquidation.

The court liquidation procedure is divided into the following stages:

- Stage 1 – the period from filing of a petition for court liquidation until a court decision is issued admitting or refusing such petition;
- Stage 2 – the period from the court liquidation order until final payment of the creditors' claims from the proceeds of sale of the debtor's assets; and
- Stage 3 – the period from such payment until the debtor is finally released from any criminal or civil liability.

In Stage 1, after service of process is completed (if the court liquidation is requested by the debtor, there is no need for service of process), the debtor may present its defence. In order to defend itself, the debtor may deposit the disputed amount in escrow, in which case the petition for court liquidation will be converted into a regular collection procedure (ie, the court liquidation claim will be extinguished). If the debtor does not make such a deposit and challenges the application for court liquidation, the judge may admit and determine the commencement of the procedure if the debtor's defence is not accepted.

Stage 2 is divided into the filing stage and the liquidation stage.

At the filing stage, all creditors, other than tax and labour creditors, must file their claims, along with any supporting documentation (proofs of claim). Foreign documents must be filed alongside a sworn translation. The trustee must prepare a list of claims covered by the court liquidation. The court and the Public Attorney's

Office have a say over this list and any third party (including a creditor) has a right to challenge it. The order of payments (ranking of claims) is as follows:

- labour claims, up to a maximum of 150 minimum wages per employee, and occupational accident-related claims;
- claims with *in rem* guarantees up to the value of the encumbered property, which will be the proceeds of sale or, in the case of a block disposal, the appraised value of the individual assets;
- tax claims, irrespective of their nature and date of creation, except tax penalties;
- claims with special privileges as provided in Article 964 of the Civil Code, as well as claims thus defined under other civil and commercial laws (except as otherwise provided in the Bankruptcy Law), and claims whose holders have retention rights over the property given as guarantee;
- claims with general privileges as provided in Article 965 of the Civil Code; claims resulting from obligations undertaken by debtor during the judicial recovery process will not be included in a composition with creditors, where applicable;
- unsecured claims, including the balance of secured claims outstanding after the proceeds of sale of the collateral have been applied to satisfy such claims, and the balance of claims deriving from labour law and exceeding the thresholds established in the first bullet point above;
- contractual fines and monetary penalties for violations of criminal or administrative law, including tax fines; and
- subordinated claims – that is, those provided under law or contract, claims of partners and officers with no employment relationship to the debtor.

At the liquidation stage, the trustee has discretionary powers to dispose of the debtor's assets in the following order of preference:

- sale of the undertaking as a going concern;
- sale of branches or divisions;
- sale of assets of each division; and
- sale of assets (piecemeal).

In the case of *in rem* guarantees (ie, pledges), the creditor's claim is secured up to the value of the encumbered asset.

In addition, creditors with *in rem rights* are subject to the prior payment of claims that cannot be included in a composition with creditors, such as:

- fees owing to the court-appointed trustee;
- labour claims and claims deriving from occupational accidents relating to services rendered after the bankruptcy is adjudicated;
- sums invested by creditors in the bankruptcy estate;
- expenses incurred through the realisation of bankruptcy assets and the bankruptcy proceedings;
- court fees awarded against the bankruptcy estate; and
- obligations resulting from legal acts performed during the judicial recovery

or after the adjudication of bankruptcy, and taxes due after the adjudication of bankruptcy.

In contrast, according to Section 85 of the Bankruptcy Law, "the owner of an asset scheduled in the bankruptcy proceeding or that is in the debtor's possession on the date of decree of bankruptcy may request its restitution". In other words, creditors under a fiduciary assignment may file a restitution lawsuit in order to recover the assigned asset. The debtor is said to have direct possession of the assigned asset, while the creditor has indirect possession. Therefore, the creditor has the right to recover the asset without being included within the group of creditors which are subject to Section 83 of the Bankruptcy Law.

## 3. Conclusion

A key element of the success of a financing transaction is the identification and mitigation of the risks involved in the project. The Brazilian legal framework now contains the necessary legal protections to achieve this objective and thus protect the interests of both domestic and foreign investors. The existing legal framework facilitates the tailoring of efficient security packages to enable large-scale secured financing which is necessary for the development of Brazilian infrastructure and which is one of the chief goals of the Growth Acceleration Programme.

The programme represents an important step towards a sweeping and enduring economic, social, political and cultural transformation. In line with the goals of the programme, a legal framework already exists which should give private investors the necessary confidence to invest in infrastructure and other projects in Brazil.

# Credit derivatives

**Paul U Ali**
University of Melbourne

## 1. Introduction

Security interests are a hedge against the credit risk of borrowers. A lender, by taking a security interest over designated property of the borrower, obtains preferential rights to that property, entitling the lender, upon the default or insolvency of the borrower, to realise the property and apply the cash proceeds of realisation in satisfaction of the lender's claim against the borrower, in priority to the claims of the borrower's other creditors. An appropriately structured security interest can be used to shield a lender from the actual losses that would otherwise be incurred due to a borrower defaulting in the performance of its obligations to the lender or the borrower's insolvency, as well as more broadly against any material deterioration in the credit quality of the borrower.[1] The latter exposes the lender to a greater risk of loss on the borrower's obligations, despite the borrower having met its current obligations to the lender, as a rise in the borrower's cost of funds, or a fall in its ability to raise funds or the value of its assets, may impede the borrower's capacity to service or refinance those obligations. Equally, a fall in the value of the borrower's assets may erode the utility of the lender's security interest if there is no replenishment of those assets.

This chapter is concerned with a major financial markets innovation in the management of credit risk: the credit default swap. Credit default swaps – and the synthetic securitisations that make use of them to repackage credit risk into securities that can be traded by investors in the capital markets – have dramatically transformed the way in which lenders now deal with credit risk. The flexibility afforded by these instruments, in terms of allowing lenders the freedom to decide how much credit risk should be laid off or retained in relation to particular borrowers, industry sectors or geographic markets, has greatly enhanced the ability of lenders to diversify their credit portfolios, as well as providing lenders with an efficient means of releasing the risk capital held by them to cover losses on the credit portfolios. Equally, a lender can use these instruments to assume credit risk as an alternative to obtaining that exposure through making loans, and this again greatly facilitates portfolio diversification. It is therefore not surprising that the market for credit derivatives has grown rapidly over the last decade. The International Swaps and Derivatives Association (ISDA) has estimated that credit default swaps with an

1 As to the distinction between credit default risk and credit deterioration risk, see G Meissner, *Credit Derivatives* (Blackwell, Oxford, 2005), pp 1 and 21.

estimated aggregate notional value of $34.4 trillion were outstanding as at the end of 2006, up from $17.1 trillion as at the end of 2005.[2]

Before turning to a more detailed consideration of credit default swaps and synthetic securitisations, it is useful to refer to two other financial markets instruments that are relevant to the management of credit risk. The first of these, the 'repo', comprises back-to-back sales of securities, under which one party sells securities to another for cash with the former agreeing to buy back the same or equivalent securities for a specified price at a future date. This combination of sale and repurchase replicates the economic incidents of a secured finance transaction: the first party has effectively borrowed cash from the second party and has provided the securities as collateral for that loan, while the second party can be characterised as having borrowed the securities from the first party with cash constituting the collateral for that loan of securities.[3]

The second instrument, the 'total rate of return swap', can be characterised both as a synthetic loan (or a secured synthetic loan, since the obligations of the total return receiver under the swap may be supported by collateral) and as a mechanism for hedging credit risk (on the part of the total return payer).[4] In a total rate of return swap, one party (the total return receiver) agrees to pay a floating interest rate to a second party (the total return payer) in exchange for receiving amounts representing all of the cash flows (interest payments and also any fees, such as loan commitment fees) generated by an underlying asset. The total return receiver thus assumes all of the risks, including credit risk, associated with this reference asset (it is obligated to pay the total return payer any fall in the value of the reference asset, but is entitled to receive the benefit of any increase in the value of the reference asset). This swap can be characterised as a synthetic loan for the acquisition of the reference asset: the interest payments made by the total return receiver are akin to the cost of funds that that party must pay for the acquisition of the reference asset, with the notional principal amount of the swap on which those interest payments are calculated representing a notional or synthetic loan of that amount from the total return payer. From the perspective of the total return payer, it has been able to hedge its exposure to the credit risk and other risks associated with the reference asset.

## 2. Credit default swaps

A credit default swap is, in common with other over-the-counter (OTC) derivatives,

---

2 See ISDA, Year-End Surveys for 2005 and 2006. A summary of these and earlier surveys is available at www.isda.org. This notional value is the aggregate principal amount or face value of the debt obligations in respect of which credit risk has been transferred using credit default swaps.

3 As regards the (arguably minimal) risk that a court will characterise a repo as giving rise to a registrable charge over the securities in favour of the 'buyer' of those securities, see M Choudhry, *The Repo Handbook* (Butterworth-Heinemann, Oxford, 2002), pp 94-95 and 293-294; JL Schroeder, "Repo Madness: The Characterization of Repurchase Agreements under the Bankruptcy Code and the UCC" (1996) 46 *Syracuse Law Review* 999. A repo can also be characterised as enabling the 'seller' of the securities (the borrower of the cash) to hedge credit risk in respect of the issuer of the securities for the term of the repo: see G Chaplin, *Credit Derivatives: Risk Management, Trading and Investment* (John Wiley & Sons, Chichester, 2005), pp. 5-6.

4 See AN Bomfim, *Understanding Credit Derivatives and Related Instruments* (Elsevier Academic Press, San Diego, 2005), pp 85-87; S Das, *Credit Derivatives: CDOs and Structured Credit Products* (John Wiley & Sons, Singapore, 3rd ed, 2005), pp 8-18; Meissner, above n 1, pp 25-27.

a privately negotiated contract.[5] Basically, one party (the protection seller) agrees, in exchange for the payment to it of a periodic fee by the other contracting party (the protection buyer), to sell credit risk protection to the other contracting party (the protection buyer) on – or, in other words, assume the credit risk of a third party (the reference entity) in relation to – certain debt obligations (the reference obligations).[6] If a stipulated 'credit event' occurs, the swap will normally terminate and the protection seller will be obligated to pay a settlement amount to the protection buyer.[7] The credit events normally covered by credit default swaps include the insolvency of the reference entity and the failure of the reference entity to make payments when due in respect of the reference obligations.[8]

Credit default swaps can be structured to transfer the credit risk relating to individual reference entities (known as single name credit default swaps), multiple reference entities (known as multi-name or portfolio credit default swaps) or even the credit risk of an entire industrial sector or geographic market (via a credit index transaction).[9] It is also possible for the swap to be structured so that it does not terminate and the protection seller is not obligated to pay the settlement amount until a designated number of credit events have occurred in relation to the reference entity (in the case of a single name credit default swap) or to the reference entities

---

5 Credit default swaps and other OTC derivatives are documented using the industry standard templates published by ISDA. In the case of credit default swaps, the key legal terms distinguishing them from other derivatives are contained in the 2003 ISDA Credit Derivatives Definitions and the confirmation for the swap.

6 These are most often corporate debt securities or corporate loans, although standalone credit default swaps typically reference the former (while synthetic securitisations implemented to release risk capital typically reference the latter): see PC Harding, *A Practical Guide to the 2003 ISDA Credit Derivatives Definitions* (Euromoney, London, 2004), pp 49-50; JJ de Vries Robbe and PU Ali, *Opportunities in: Credit Derivatives and Synthetic Securitisation* (Thomson Financial, London, 2005), p 20. ISDA and the Loan Syndications and Trading Association have recently released templates for loan-only credit default swaps in a move designed to boost the use of standalone credit default swaps referencing secured syndicated loans: see Fitch Ratings, "Loan-Only Credit Default Swaps" (May 31 2006). In addition, following the publication by ISDA of templates for credit default swaps of asset-backed securities, an increasing number of credit default swaps and synthetic securitisations have been implemented where the reference obligations are residential and commercial mortgage-backed securities as well as securities issued in synthetic securitisations: see de Vries Robbe and Ali, *ibid*, pp 26-27; JJ de Vries Robbe, "CDS of ABS: Structured Credit and Securitisation at the Cutting Edge" in JJ de Vries Robbe and PU Ali (eds), *Innovations in Securitisation* (Kluwer Law International, The Hague, 2006); Fitch Ratings, "Synthetic Structured Finance CDOs" (February 17 2004); Nomura Securities, "Synthetic ABS 101: PAUG and ABX.HE" (March 7 2005); Nomura Securities, "Synthetic CMBS Primer" (September 5 2006); Fitch Ratings, "Synthetic Overview for CMBS Investors" (June 6 2007).

7 See Das, above n 4, pp 28-31; Meissner, above n 1, pp 15-19. Apart from their credit risk management function, the key motivations for the use of credit default swaps are:

- the opportunities for arbitrage provided by differences in the spreads in the market for such swaps and the underlying cash market;
- the ability of lenders, through the purchase of credit protection, to release risk capital in relation to the reference obligations held by them; and
- the opportunities provided by synthetic securitisation to repackage credit default swaps.

See Bomfim, above n 4, pp 29-39; de Vries Robbe and Ali, *ibid*, pp 10-11; Meissner, ibid, pp 62, 70, 75, 78 and 85-86; R Bruyere, Credit Derivatives and Structured Credit (John Wiley & Sons, Chichester, 2006), pp 119-120, 124 and 128; PU Ali, "Credit Derivatives and Synthetic Securitizations: Innovation and Fragility" (2005) 20 *Banking & Finance Law Review* 293, at 295-296.

8 Another credit event commonly encountered in relation to corporate reference entities is 'restructuring'. The credit events employed in credit default swaps are discussed in more detail in Harding, above n 6, pp 106-114; de Vries Robbe and Ali, *ibid*, pp 17-20.

9 See de Vries Robbe and Ali, *ibid*, pp 32-34. A credit index transaction is not a single credit default swap but comprises, instead, a series of separate and independent credit default swaps each referencing one of the reference entities that make up a credit index: *ibid*, p 29.

collectively (in the case of a portfolio credit default swap or credit index transaction). This notwithstanding, the majority of credit default swaps are first-to-default swaps where the swap will terminate upon the first occurrence of a credit event.[10]

However, regardless of the number of reference entities to which a credit default swap relates or the number of credit events that must occur before a swap will be terminated, all credit default swaps encompass two mutually exclusive scenarios. Either no credit event (or an insufficient number of credit events) occurs during the term of the swap, in which case it continues in force until maturity, or a credit event occurs that triggers the termination of the swap. In the first scenario, the protection buyer will continue to pay a periodic fee to the protection seller for the full term of the swap. In the second scenario, however, the termination of swap will also bring to an end the obligation of the protection buyer to pay a fee to the protection seller. The protection seller will be obligated to pay to the protection buyer a settlement amount that:

- for cash-settled swaps, has been calculated by reference to the fall in value of the reference obligations or is simply a fixed percentage of the face value of the reference obligations (in the case of the sub-set of cash-settled swaps known as digital or fixed recovery credit default swaps);[11] or
- for physically settled swaps, comprises the full face value of the reference obligations or other 'deliverable obligations' and represents the purchase price for those obligations with the protection buyer tendering, at its election, delivery of either the reference obligations or deliverable obligations against the payment of the settlement amount.[12]

Credit default swaps are normally physically settled, except where a credit default swap is used in a synthetic securitisation, in which case cash settlement is the norm.[13]

As described above, a credit default swap enables a lender to reduce the credit risk assumed by it on a loan made to, or other financial obligations incurred to it by, a borrower, by transferring that credit risk to a third party (the protection seller). On this basis, a credit default swap would appear to be no different from more conventional and longer-established mechanisms for hedging credit risk, including guarantees, credit insurance, syndications and cash securitisations.

There are, however, three key factors that distinguish credit default swaps (and other credit derivatives) from these other mechanisms for managing credit risk. First of all, a credit default swap enables credit risk to be disaggregated from the 'physical' loan or other reference obligations to which that risk relates and also the entire bundle of credit, liquidity, market and other risks associated with the reference obligations. A lender that is exposed to the credit risk of a borrower can, by purchasing credit protection under a credit default swap, transfer that risk independently of the underlying reference obligations. There is no need for the lender to transfer all or part of the reference obligations – as is the case with

10 *Ibid*, pp 32-33.
11 See Chaplin, above n 3, p. 153; de Vries Robbe and Ali, *ibid*, pp 24 and 53-55.
12 See Harding, above n 6, pp. 58-60; de Vries Robbe and Ali, *ibid*, pp 22-23 and 55-56; Bruyere, above n 7, p 41.
13 See de Vries Robbe and Ali, *ibid*, pp 21 and 53.

syndications and cash securitisations, for example – in order to divest itself of a corresponding proportion of the credit risk represented by the reference obligations. Credit default swaps thus permit lenders to hedge credit risk on a loan while retaining the economic benefit of the loan as well as control over the enforcement (or waiver) of loan covenants.

Second, a credit default swap creates a principal obligation – not a secondary obligation, as is the case with guarantees – on the part of the protection seller to pay the settlement amount to the protection buyer on the occurrence of a credit event. Moreover, while the protection seller's obligation to pay the settlement amount may be triggered by a failure on the part of the reference entity to make payments when due on the reference obligations, the credit default swap may equally provide for that obligation to be triggered (again, in contrast to guarantees) in circumstances where the reference entity has made and is continuing to make payments in relation to the reference obligations as they fall due, but there has nonetheless been a deterioration in the credit quality of the reference entity.[14] Also, unlike credit insurance, the protection seller's obligation to pay the settlement amount is not contingent upon the lender having actually suffered a loss that is attributable to the reference entity's default on the reference obligations or its insolvency or some other credit event. The fact that the payment of the settlement amount may have the effect of making the lender whole in respect of any losses incurred by it is merely coincidental, as the contingency whose occurrence triggers the obligation to pay the settlement amount is the credit event, not the actual losses occasioned by that event.[15]

Third, there is no requirement under a credit default swap for the protection buyer actually to hold the reference obligations or otherwise be exposed to the credit risk of the reference entity in respect of those obligations. There is on this basis nothing to guarantee or insure. Credit default swaps can be used, like any other derivative, to synthesise long and short positions in relation to financial assets. A long position in the reference obligations can be synthesised by selling credit protection on those obligations, while likewise a short position can be synthesised through the purchase of credit protection.[16] The ability to replicate exposure to the reference obligations without having to acquire those obligations has greatly facilitated the leveraged trading of credit risk and has contributed to the emergence of hedge funds as major participants in the global market for credit derivatives.[17]

## 3. Synthetic securitisations

In general, securitisation involves the repackaging of relatively illiquid financial assets into debt securities that can be traded in the capital markets. In conventional or cash securitisations, the assets repackaged are receivables, including residential and

---

14 Nor, in contrast to guarantees and credit insurance, does the payment of the settlement amount by the protection seller to the lender entitle the former to be subrogated to the latter's rights against the reference entity: see de Vries Robbe and Ali, *ibid*, p 117.

15 Credit default swaps are deliberately structured in this manner to minimise the risk of their characterisation by a court or regulator as contracts of insurance: see de Vries Robbe and Ali, *ibid*, pp 114-117; Ali, above n 7, at 308-313.

16 See Bomfim, above n 4, pp 36-38.

17 See Fitch Ratings, "Hedge Funds: The Credit Market's New Paradigm" (June 5 2007).

commercial mortgage loans, credit card debts, car loans, corporate loans and student loans. The proceeds from the issue of securities by a securitisation vehicle (normally, an orphan entity or special purpose vehicle (SPV) whose assets and liabilities will not be consolidated with the originator of the financial assets or a third-party transferor) are used by the SPV to finance the acquisition of receivables. In addition, the cash flows generated from the collection or amortisation of the receivables are used by the SPV to service principal and interest payments on the securities.

In the case of synthetic securitisations, the financial assets securitised are credit derivatives, most often credit default swaps.[18]

Synthetic securitisations enjoy a number of critical advantages over cash securitisations, which may be summarised as follows:[19]

- They enable credit risk to be hedged by lenders in relation to a substantially broader range of financial assets as, in contrast to a cash securitisation, there is no need for the SPV to hold the assets in respect of which credit risk is being hedged.
- As the securities issued by the SPV are serviced out of the cash flows from the collateral that supports the SPV's obligations under the credit default swap to the protection buyer, not out of the cash flows generated by the financial assets being securitised, synthetic securitisations facilitate the hedging of credit risk in relation to reference obligations whose cash flows are not predictable (eg, emerging market debt obligations and payment obligations under derivatives).
- The tranches of securities issued as part of the synthetic securitisation are more readily capable of being customised to meet the risk appetite of individual investors than is the case with cash securitisations that transfer to the investors the entirety of risks associated with the assets being securitised.
- Synthetic securitisations are cheaper and faster to implement than cash securitisations (eg, in contrast to cash securitisations, a perfected assignment of the financial assets being securitised is not necessary; nor does the presence of anti-assignment clauses in the underlying documentation inhibit the lender's ability to hedge the credit risk in respect of the reference obligations).
- Synthetic securitisations permit the proactive hedging of credit risk (as there is no need to wait until the protection buyer actually holds the reference obligations whose credit risk it is seeking to hedge).

---

18 See de Vries Robbe and Ali, above n 6, p 49. Total rate of return swaps have been used in a small number of synthetic securitisations: *ibid*, p 110. See also Fitch Ratings, "Synthetic CLOs using Total Return Swaps: A Primer" (May 19 2006). Increasingly, 'hybrid' cash and synthetic securitisations are being brought to market that comprise mixed portfolios of asset-backed securities and credit default swaps referencing asset-backed securities: see Fitch Ratings, "Fusion of Synthetic and Cash CDOs" (March 13 2006).

19 See M Choudhry, *Structured Credit Products: Credit Derivatives and Synthetic Securitisation* (John Wiley & Sons, Singapore, 2004), pp 264-265; CL Culp, *Structured Finance and Insurance: The ART of Managing Capital and Risk* (John Wiley & Sons, Hoboken, NJ, 2006), pp 403-405; Ali, above n 7, at 297-300; JJ de Vries Robbe and PU Ali, "Synthetic CDOs: The State of Play" (2006) 21 *Journal of International Banking Law and Regulation* 12, at 12-13. As is the case with credit default swaps, the main motivations of lenders (and other protection buyers) in resorting to synthetic securitisations are credit risk management, the potential for arbitrage profits, releasing risk capital and the potential for profits from repackaging credit default swaps as well as the securities issued in other synthetic securitisations: see above n 7 and also Bomfim, above n 4, pp 125 and 139-140; Meissner, above n 1, p 48.

- Synthetic securitisations enable leveraged positions to be taken in relation to the reference obligations, as the level of credit risk that can be hedged by the protection buyer or assumed by the investors is not limited to reference obligations with an aggregate face value matching the proceeds that can be raised by the SPV through the issue of securities (unlike cash securitisations where the SPV must issue sufficient securities to finance the acquisition of the financial assets being securitised).

The SPV normally acts as the protection seller, under one or more credit default swaps, in relation to a portfolio of reference obligations, and the proceeds from its issue of the securities are used not to finance the acquisition of the reference obligations, but to acquire collateral to support the SPV's assumption of credit risk under the credit default swap.[20] The securities are serviced out of the fees received from the protection buyer and the cash flows generated from the collateral acquired by the SPV. This collateral, which will typically comprise highly liquid, highly rated debt securities, thus supports both the SPV's obligations to the protection buyer and the SPV's obligations in respect of the securities issued by it.

The SPV, in a synthetic securitisation, acts as a conduit for the transfer of credit risk from a lender or other protection buyer to the investors in the securities issued by the SPV.[21] The protection buyer is usually a lender seeking to hedge the credit risk of a portfolio of reference obligations and to release the risk capital held by it in relation to those reference obligations.

The following figure depicts a generic fully funded synthetic securitisation.

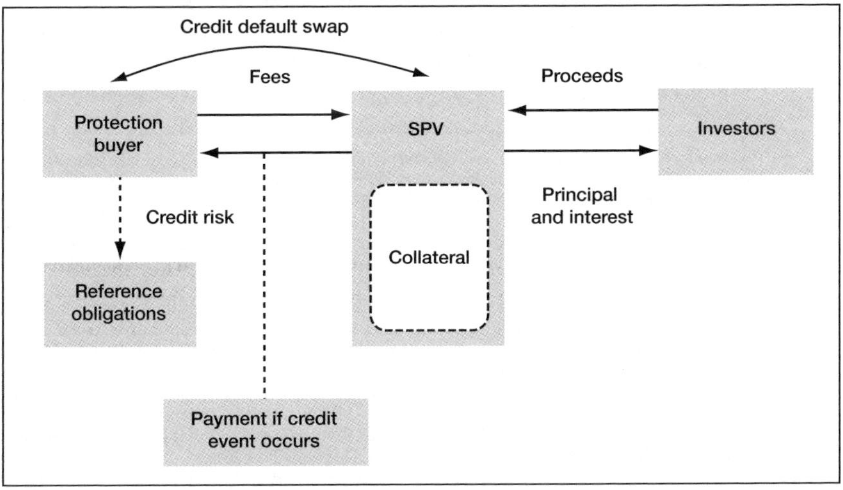


20 See Bomfim, *ibid*, pp 137-139; Ali, *ibid*, at 300-303; de Vries Robbe and Ali, *ibid*, at 13-14.

21 Synthetic securitisations can readily be customised to meet the requirements of individual investors as, for instance, where the investor in the securities issued by the SPV is also the reference entity (meaning that the investor, by selling credit protection on itself, has effectively synthesised an investment in itself): see further PU Ali, "The Conundrum of Self-Referenced Credit-Linked Notes" (2004) 19 *Journal of International Banking Law and Regulation* 326; S Firth, "Self-Referenced Credit Derivatives – Are They Enforceable under English Law?" (2006) 1 *Capital Markets Law Journal* 21.

The transfer of credit risk from the protection buyer to the investors is achieved by making the SPV's obligation to pay principal and interest on the securities conditional upon the SPV not being required to pay a settlement amount under the credit default swap entered into by it – that is, upon the non-occurrence of a credit event,[22] during the term of the securities. If no such credit event occurs, the investors will receive interest on the scheduled payment dates and the securities will be redeemed for their face value on the scheduled maturity date. The occurrence of a credit event that triggers payment of a settlement amount[23] by the SPV to a protection buyer will usually lead to the early redemption of the securities for any positive balance following the deduction of the settlement amount from the face value of the securities.[24]

This deduction is effected out of the collateral held by the SPV in reverse order to the seniority of the securities, with the settlement amount being met first out of the principal amount attributable to the junior tranche of securities, followed by the mezzanine and then the senior tranche (with any residue being applied to redeem the securities in order of seniority). The more senior tranches have the benefit of the subordination of the more junior tranches as the latter protect the former against loss.[25]

The SPV's payment of the settlement amount necessarily depletes the collateral available to meet the claims of the investors and, through this application of the investors' claims for the payment of principal in satisfaction of the settlement amount, the securities are exposed to the credit risk of the reference obligations.

The interest payment on the securities is designed to compensate the investors for uncertainty as to the likelihood of a credit event occurring and the severity of losses flowing to the investors from such an event.[26] A synthetic securitisation can thus be viewed as involving the purchase by investors of exposure to credit risk for a fee that is paid to them in the form of periodic interest payments on their securities. These interest payments are, as noted above, financed by a combination of the fees paid to the SPV by the protection buyer and the cash flows generated by the collateral held by the SPV.

---

22 The credit events provided for in credit default swaps which are used in synthetic securitisations may be markedly different from those encountered in standalone credit default swaps. The credit events, in the case of the former, will be limited to those (usually, bankruptcy and failure to pay) that meet the requirements of the prudential regulator for the protection buyer to be able to release the risk capital held by it against the reference obligations: see de Vries Robbe and Ali, above n 6, pp 51-52.

23 As stated above, the credit default swaps and other credit derivatives used in synthetic securitisations are usually cash settled: see above n 13.

24 See de Vries Robbe and Ali, above n 6, pp 58-59. Alternatively (*ibid*, pp 57 and 59), the write-down of the principal amount of the securities may take place on the scheduled maturity date for the securities, with the investors continuing to receive interest on the full face value of the securities for the term of the securities. In the case of principal-protected structures (or tranches), the settlement amount is financed by writing down the securitisation vehicle's obligations to pay interest on the securities; the investors will receive the full face value of the securities on the scheduled maturity date but may receive reduced or no interest on the securities for the remainder of their term following the occurrence of a credit event.

25 See de Vries Robbe and Ali, *ibid*, pp 57-58; G Fuller, *Corporate Borrowing: Law and Practice* (Jordans, Bristol, 3rd ed, 2006), pp 116-118; Nomura Securities, "Tranching Credit Risk" (October 8 2004). The obligation of the SPV to pay the settlement amount may depend upon a stipulated loss threshold having been reached, as regards the severity of the credit event, in which case the junior tranche can be said to be protected, itself, by the subordination offered by that loss threshold (as losses below that amount would be borne by the protection buyer).

26 The interest rate payable to the investors will depend upon the credit quality of the underlying reference, the level of correlation between the reference obligations and the level of subordination protection. The junior tranche of securities bears the highest risk of loss and will, accordingly, carry the highest interest rate: see Bomfim, above n 4, p 140; Meissner, above n 1, p 45. In addition to credit risk on the reference obligations, the investors are also exposed to the credit risk of the SPV: see Chaplin, above n 3, p 147.

## 4. Partly funded structures

The transfer of credit risk in the synthetic securitisation depicted in the previous section of this chapter is 'fully funded', as the aggregate face value of the securities issued by the SPV matches the aggregate notional value of the reference obligations in respect of which credit risk has been assumed by the SPV under the credit default swap. Fully funded structures are relatively costly to implement, due to the fee that must effectively be paid by the protection buyer to the investors to compensate them for assuming the entirety of the credit risk on the reference obligations, the transaction costs and the practical difficulties involved in the SPV having to place securities of an aggregate value matching that of the reference obligations.[27] There are also transaction costs and practical issues involved in the SPV having to acquire sufficient collateral with the proceeds from the issue of the securities to cover fully the SPV's obligation to pay the settlement amount to the protection buyer.

For these reasons, fully funded structures have been largely superseded by a more cost-effective structure, the 'partly funded' structure.[28] In a partly funded structure, the transfer of a level of credit risk, equivalent to that which could have been transferred to the investors using a fully funded structure relating to the same reference obligations, can be effected without either:

- the protection buyer having to enter into a credit default swap with the SPV to transfer the entirety of the credit risk on the reference obligations; or
- the SPV having to issue securities of an aggregate value matching that of the reference obligations.

This result is achieved by super-imposing an unfunded component – namely, a second credit default swap – over the credit default swap between the protection buyer and the SPV.[29] A substantial portion of the credit risk on the reference obligations is transferred to the protection seller under this second credit default swap, leaving only a minority of the credit risk on the reference obligations to be transferred to the SPV (and thus the investors). In addition to the different levels of credit risk borne by the SPV and the other protection seller, the two parties do not rank equally in terms of their obligations to pay the settlement amount to the protection buyer in respect of the credit risk they assume.[30] The credit default swap between the protection buyer and the SPV is subordinated to the second credit default swap: on the occurrence of a credit event, the collateral held by the SPV will first be applied towards payment of the settlement amount and the other protection seller will be liable to pay the settlement amount under its credit default swap with the protection buyer only if a portion remains outstanding after the SPV's collateral

27 See de Vries Robbe and Ali, above n 6, pp 44-45 and 60; Ali, above n 7, at 303.

28 See M Choudhry, *Corporate Bonds and Structured Financial Products* (Butterworth-Heinemann, Oxford, 2004), p 394.

29 See Bomfim, above n 4, pp 140-141; de Vries Robbe and Ali, above n 6, pp 60-62; Ali, above n 7, at 303-306; de Vries Robbe and Ali, above n 19, at 14-15. The credit risk under this swap may be transferred to a third-party protection seller or retained by the protection buyer: see Das, above n 4, p 441; de Vries Robbe and Ali, above n 6 , p 60.

30 Both swaps are usually cash settled. However, where the swap between the protection buyer and the SPV is physically settled, it is not necessarily the case that the super-senior swap will also be cash settled: see de Vries Robbe and Ali, *ibid*, p. 61.

has been exhausted. Accordingly, the protection seller under the second credit default swap ranks ahead of the senior-most tranche of securities issued by the SPV (leading to such swaps being known as super-senior swaps), and is exposed to loss only where the occurrence of a credit event has led to the SPV's collateral being exhausted and thus the investors in the securities issued by the SPV suffering a depletion of the entire principal amount of their securities.

The following figure depicts the key features of a partly funded synthetic securitisation.

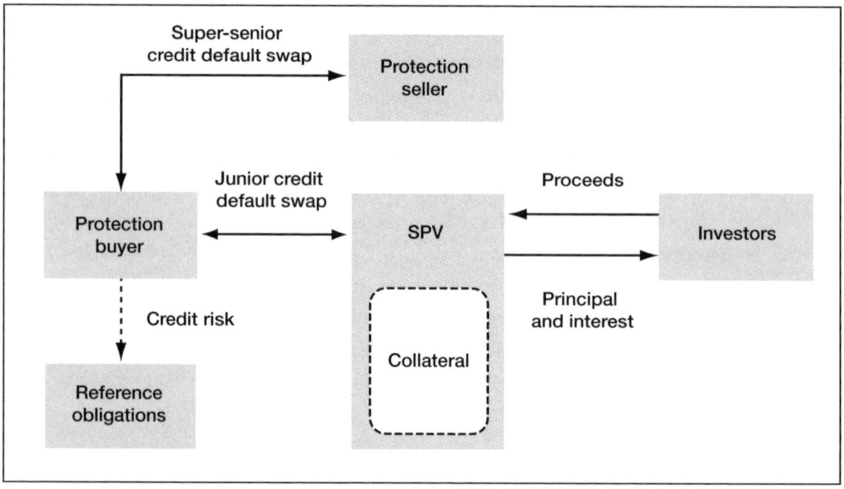


The super-senior position of the protection seller under the second credit default swap means that it is relatively cheap for the protection buyer to transfer to that party the bulk of the credit risk on the reference obligations.[31] Moreover, as only a minority of the credit risk on the reference obligations is assumed by the investors, the aggregate value of the securities that must be placed by the SPV with the investors is much lower than would have been the case had an equivalent level of credit risk (to that transferred under the super-senior swap and to the investors) been transferred via a fully funded structure.

## 5. Single-tranche structures

The capacity of credit default swaps to provide customised exposure to credit risk has led to the development of single-tranche structures.[32] These structures can be viewed as a 'cut-down' version of a fully funded structure (or the funded component of a partly funded structure), with the key difference being that in the case of a single-tranche structure, only a specific portion of the credit risk on the reference obligations is passed via the SPV to a single investor. Accordingly, the exposure to the

31 *Ibid*, p 44.

32 See Choudhry, above n 19, pp 280-281; de Vries Robbe and Ali, *ibid*, pp 30-32; J J de Vries Robbe and P U Ali, "The Continuing Evolution of the Structured Credit Market" (2005) 20 *Journal of International Banking Law and Regulation* 628, at 631-632.

credit risk on the reference obligations that is incorporated in the securities issued by the SPV can be customised to meet explicitly the risk appetites of individual investors, ranging from those that wish to acquire only senior tranches of securities in synthetic securitisations to those that are comfortable with junior tranches.

This customisation is accomplished through the protection buyer transferring a portion of credit risk on the reference obligations bounded by 'attachment' and 'detachment' points.[33] The former represents the point at which, following the occurrence of a credit event, the collateral held by the SPV must be applied towards the payment of the settlement amount under the credit default swap, while the latter represents the maximum liability of the SPV under that swap. Accordingly, one or more credit events must occur which alone or together are of sufficient severity to cause the attachment point to be breached and thus the SPV's obligation to pay the settlement amount to be triggered before the investor will bear a loss on the securities.

These two points therefore determine the extent to which the principal amount of the investor's securities is exposed to credit risk on the reference obligations (with the balance of the exposure retained by the protection buyer or hedged, using (unfunded) credit default swaps). The securities held by the SPV can be said to constitute a synthetic mezzanine or senior tranche, as the securities can be viewed as ranking ahead of that portion of the credit risk on the reference obligations below the attachment point which provides the investor with the benefit of subordination. The degree of protection provided by this subordination will be determined by the investor's particular appetite for exposure to credit risk on the reference obligations.

The following figure depicts the key features of a single-tranche synthetic securitisation.

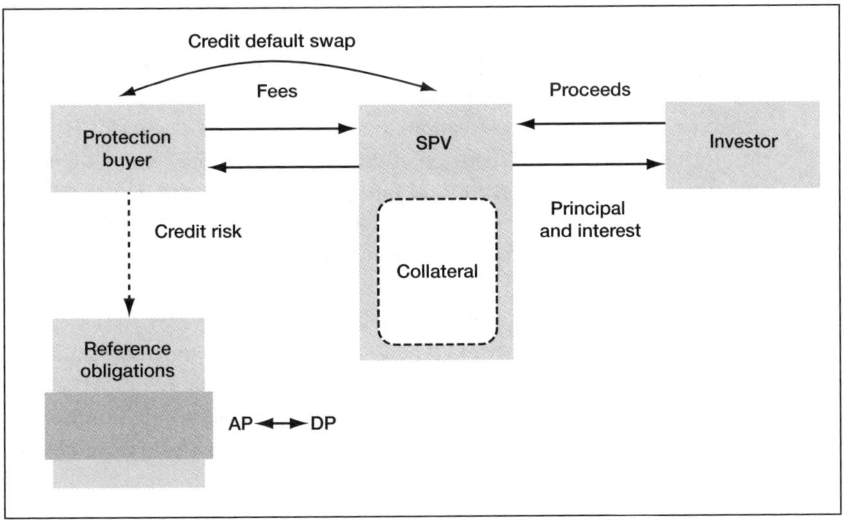


33 See Choudhry, *ibid*, p 285; de Vries Robbe and Ali, above n 6, p 31. See also Fitch Ratings, "Single-Tranche Synthetic CDOs" (June 13 2003); Nomura Securities, "'The Bespoke [*bispóuk*]' – A Guide to Single-Tranche Synthetic CDOs" (November 17 2004).

Unlike the fully funded and partly funded structures, the design of a single-tranche structure need not take into account the interests of multiple investors or, where the SPV has issued different tranches of securities, those of multiple classes of investor. The tranching of securities in fully funded and partly funded structures reflects the compromise between the competing interests of investors in the different tranches necessary for the SPV to be able to place the securities. Having to address the interests of only an individual investor – coupled with a concomitant reduction in the complexity of the transaction documentation – and being able to satisfy fully the requirements of that investor in relation to the level of credit risk it wishes to assume has led to single-tranche structures becoming the most common form of synthetic securitisation.[34]

## 6. Managed structures

### 6.1 Lightly managed structures

It is now common for synthetic securitisations to be lightly managed, at the very least, in order to overcome the problems posed by a purely static portfolio of reference obligations. If – as is the case with a purely static portfolio – the credit default swap entered into by the protection seller and the SPV remains in place for the entire term of the securities, with no ability for the SPV to alter the underlying reference obligations, the investors may find themselves locked into reference obligations of deteriorating creditworthiness and the SPV will be unable to take steps to mitigate or prevent the depletion of its collateral (and thus losses being suffered by the investors).

The adoption of a lightly managed structure enables the SPV to replenish its portfolio of reference obligations (where reference obligations have been depleted due to amortisation, pre-payments or the occurrence of a credit event) by introducing new reference obligations to the portfolio and also to substitute new reference obligations for obligations that no longer comply with the requirements for inclusion in the reference portfolio.[35] The SPV may, in a lightly managed structure, also be empowered to add further reference obligations (whether or not the existing reference obligations need to be replenished) and increase the notional amount of existing or substitute reference obligations.

### 6.2 Actively managed structures

The actively managed structures (known as collateralised swap obligations) which are now increasingly being brought to market represent a natural progression from the lightly managed structures discussed above.[36] However, in contrast to lightly managed structures, which are essentially reactive in nature (as the replenishment or

34 See Choudhry, *ibid*, pp 285-286; Das, above n 4, p 406; de Vries Robbe and Ali, *ibid*, p 30.

35 See de Vries Robbe and Ali, *ibid*, p 70.

36 See Choudhry, above n 28, pp 396-398; de Vries Robbe and Ali, *ibid*, pp 71-72; Fitch Ratings, "Managed Synthetic CDOs" (April 3 2006) This is also indicative of the increasing convergence between the securitisation and investment fund sectors, a trend that is even better illustrated by developments in relation to collateralised bond obligations: see J Benjamin, *Interests in Securities: A Proprietary Law Analysis of the International Securities Markets* (Oxford University Press, Oxford, 2000), pp 298-299.

substitution of reference obligations is a response to a deterioration in their credit quality), actively managed structures permit proactive changes to the SPV's portfolio of reference obligations.

The SPV, in an actively managed structure, is thus able to trade reference obligations in and out of its portfolio, even if there has been no deterioration in the credit quality of those obligations. In addition, the SPV can both buy and sell credit protection on reference obligations (although it will normally be precluded from purchasing credit protection other than for the purposes of closing-out or unwinding a sale of credit protection).[37] Nor is the SPV restricted in its dealings to a single protection buyer (although the SPV will normally be confined to dealing with an approved panel of protection buyers and sellers).

The securities issued by the SPV are serviced out of the SPV's trading gains (and the investors bear risk of the SPV's trading losses) rather than – as is the case with the structures discussed above – out of the passive receipt of fees from the sale of credit protection to a single protection buyer coupled with cash flows generated from the collateral held by the SPV to support its obligations to that protection buyer. The SPV's investment strategy in pursuit of these trading profits basically involves the SPV selling credit protection and crystallising gains from such sales through the early unwinding of the credit default swaps under which it has assumed credit risk, or through the SPV entering into offsetting credit default swaps (ie, buying credit protection).[38]

These actively managed synthetic structures are essentially no different from the hedge funds that actively buy and sell credit risk in the global market for credit derivatives. The issue of securities by the SPV is designed to finance its trading activities in the same way that a hedge fund might issue debt securities to finance its own trading activities.[39]

## 7. Synthetic squares

The similarities between synthetic securitisation and investment funds are equally pronounced in the case of one of the latest innovations in the global market for credit derivatives: synthetic squares, which can be likened to a fund of funds.

The outer layer of a synthetic square is no different from that encountered in the fully funded, partly funded and single-tranche structures discussed above.[40] The SPV, as is the case in these other structures, enters into one or more credit default swaps under which the credit risk on certain reference obligations is transferred to it with

---

37 See Choudhry, *ibid*, pp 403-407. The credit default swaps entered into by the SPV can be either cash settled or physically settled, although the latter are more common: *ibid*, p 398.

38 See de Vries Robbe and Ali, above n 6, pp 88-89 and 92-93; de Vries Robbe and Ali, above n 19, at 15.

39 See Ali, above n 7, at 306-307; de Vries Robbe and Ali, above n 19, at 15. This is in contrast to the motivations for other synthetic securitisations: see above n 7.

40 See JJ de Vries Robbe, "Synthetic Squares, or the Securitisation of Russian Dolls" in JJ de Vries Robbe and PU Ali (eds), *Securitisation of Derivatives and Alternative Asset Classes* (Kluwer Law International, The Hague, 2005), pp 7-8 and 10; Moody's Investors Service, "Moody's Approach to Rating Synthetic Resecuritizations" (October 29 2003); Standard & Poor's, "Drill-Down Approach for Synthetic CDO Squared Transactions" (December 10 2003); Fitch Ratings, "Synthetic Structured Finance CDOs" (February 17 2004); Fitch Ratings, "Analysis of Synthetic CDOs of CDOs" (September 13 2004); Nomura Securities, "CDOs-Squared Demystified" (February 4 2005).

that risk, in turn, being passed on to the investors in the securities issued by the SPV. Where, however, a synthetic square differs from these other structures is in terms of its inner layer, namely the reference obligations to which these swaps relate. The reference obligations are not corporate debt securities or corporate loans but, instead, comprise securities issued in other synthetic securitisations (which themselves, through the mechanism of credit default swaps, bear the credit risk on other reference obligations) or a combination of such securities and securities issued in cash securitisations.[41] Moreover, the synthetic securitisations whose securities are referenced in a synthetic square are usually implemented solely for that purpose.

Like a fund of funds, a synthetic square offers investors a higher degree of diversification than that which would ordinarily be available to them from investing directly in a single synthetic securitisation. A synthetic square typically references between five and 15 underlying synthetic securitisations, each of which may involve the transfer of credit risk on the reference obligations of 100 to 200 reference entities.[42] Even though there will usually be a high level of overlap as regards the reference entities covered by the underlying synthetic securitisations, a synthetic square can potentially offer investors exposure to substantially all, or a significant portion of, the highly liquid reference entities traded in the global market for credit derivatives.[43] Also, a synthetic square, by effectively creating a secondary market in the securities in which the SPV invests (and thus also in the reference entities that underlie those securities), enables investors to obtain exposure to securities that might otherwise be illiquid or in short supply (and reference entities that are only thinly traded in the global market for credit derivatives).

On the other hand, investors should be aware that – like a fund of funds – the synthetic square offers a "popular means by which the bits and pieces of other [synthetic securitisations] can be sold" and, accordingly, a synthetic square "provides a good opportunity for the cash flows on those otherwise-undesirable tranches to be repackaged and sold through a resecuritization".[44]

A further distinguishing feature of synthetic squares – and one that is related to the identity of the reference obligations – is the benefit offered to investors of a double layer of tranching or subordination compared to the single layer that characterises other synthetic securitisations.[45] In the latter case, the investors in the more senior tranches, where the SPV has issued multiple tranches of securities, have only the protection offered to them by the subordinated position of the more junior tranches (the junior-most tranche is not protected by subordination[46]). Likewise, where a single-tranche structure has been employed, the investors will have the benefit of the subordination represented by the attachment point. The occurrence of a credit event may lead to the erosion of this single layer of subordination, leaving

41 See above n 6. See also K Gilkes, "Modelling Credit Risk in Synthetic CDO Squared Transactions" in de Vries Robbe and Ali, *ibid*, p. 24; Nomura Securities, *ibid*.

42 See Gilkes, *ibid*, p. 24.

43 See Fitch Ratings, above n 40 (13 September 2004).

44 See Culp, above n 19, p. 407.

45 See de Vries Robbe and Ali, above n 6, p. 108; Meissner, above n 1, p. 51; Bruyere, above n 7, p. 143; Fitch Ratings, above n 40 (13 September 2004); Nomura Securities, above n 40.

46 See above n 25.

the investors exposed to loss.

The securities issued by the SPV in a synthetic square may comprise senior and junior tranches or a single tranche. However, in addition to the protection provided in this outer layer of the synthetic square (to the more senior tranches by the subordination of the more junior tranches, or to the single tranche by the attachment point), the investors will have the protection of subordination, in the inner layer of the synthetic square, in respect of the securities issued in synthetic securitisations that comprise the reference obligations. These underlying synthetic securitisations are typically single-tranche tranches due, as stated above, to their having been customised for the purpose of utilisation in the synthetic square.[47]

Accordingly, for the investors in the securities issued by the SPV to suffer a loss, the subordination in each of the inner and outer layers of the synthetic square must be overcome.[48]

This requires, first, a credit event (or successive credit events) to have occurred in relation to one of the tranches of securities that make up the reference obligations, which alone or together are of sufficient severity to cause the attachment point applicable to that tranche to be breached, resulting in a loss on the securities.[49] Second, that loss (taking into account the fact that this will be capped by the detachment point referable to the securities and also the aggregate principal amount of the securities) must be sufficiently great[50] so as to constitute or lead to the

---

47 The securities referenced by a synthetic square may represent an unsold tranche from a conventional tranched structure, the super-senior position in a partly funded structure or one of the layers of credit risk that would otherwise be retained by the protection buyer in a single-tranche structure: see above n 44.

48 Where the SPV has issued multiple tranches of securities, the junior tranche may – but will not always – be protected by the obligation of the SPV to pay the settlement amount being contingent upon a loss threshold having been reached (as is the case with the junior-most tranches in fully funded and partly funded structures). Equally, it is possible that the particular single tranche to which the credit event relates is not protected by an attachment point (although the losses are capped by a detachment point) and thus occupies a position no different from that of the junior-most tranche in a conventional tranched structure.

49 Depending on the degree of overlap between the underlying tranches of securities, a deterioration in the credit quality of a single reference entity may trigger credit events under more than one of the underlying tranches, eroding the diversification benefits offered by the synthetic square: see de Vries Robbe and Ali, above n 6, pp 103-104; Nomura Securities, above n 40. The inclusion of securities issued in cash securitisations as reference obligations may reduce this degree of overlap, but may in turn introduce significant systematic risk due to the correlation between such securities: see Gilkes, above n 41, pp 25-26.

50 Where cross-subordination is used, the loss or cumulative losses flowing from one or more successive credit events in relation to any of the tranches of securities in the inner layer must be sufficiently great so as to erode completely the subordination that protects all of those tranches, before that loss can be passed on to the SPV: see de Vries Robbe and Ali, *ibid*, p 108; Fitch Ratings, above n 40 (September 13 2004).

51 The credit events in the credit default swap in the outer layer of a synthetic square are typically broader than those encountered in synthetic securitisations that have implemented to release risk capital: see above n 22. These events may include bankruptcy, failure to pay, restructuring, loss event, write-down, principal or interest shortfall, and ratings downgrade: see de Vries Robbe, above n 6, pp 163-165, 169-172 and 173-164. Where a protection buyer holds securities (issued in a synthetic securitisation or otherwise) referenced by the credit default swap between it and the SPV in the outer layer of a synthetic square and that swap contains credit events including, for example, restructuring, loss event, writing down or downgrade, there is a risk that the payment of the settlement amount under the swap may be seen by a court or regulator as compensation for the loss actually incurred by the protection buyer on the securities, leading to the swap being treated as in-substance insurance: see Culp, above n 19, pp 409-410; P Forrester, "Why Uncertainty could Stall Synthetic CDOs", *International Financial Law Review* (December 2003) 24, at 25.

occurrence of a credit event[51] in relation to the securities held by the investors and also cause the erosion of any subordination that protects the investors.[52]

The following figure depicts the key features of a synthetic square.

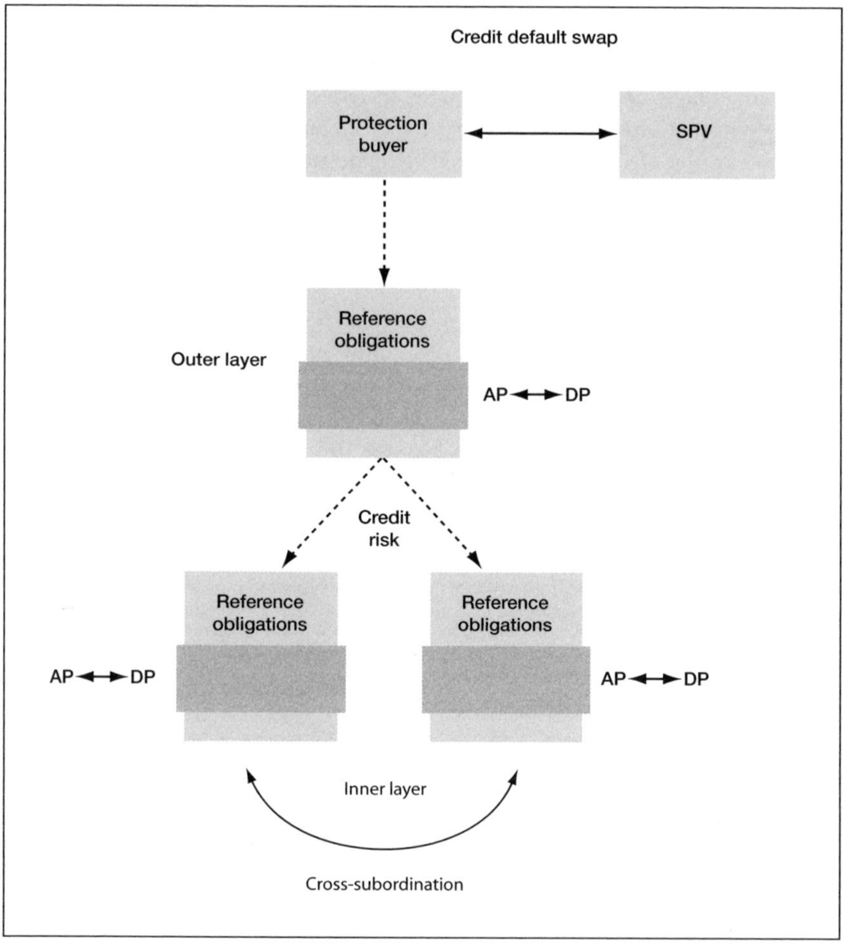


Finally, there is, in principle, no bar to the securities issued by the SPV themselves forming the reference obligations in another synthetic securitisation – and such synthetic cubes have already been brought to market.[53]

## 8. Synthetic securitisation and proxies for credit risk

Although credit default swaps and the synthetic securitisations that make use of them are now important tools for managing credit risk, they are not without some

52 See also above n 48.

53 See M Choudhry, Foreword to C Evans (ed), *The Euromoney Structured Credit Products Handbook 2005/06* (Euromoney, Colchester, 2006).

significant drawbacks. In particular, the number of highly liquid reference entities whose credit risk is traded in the global market for credit derivatives is relatively small compared to the number of entities to which credit risk lenders are exposed and even to the number of entities whose shares are traded in any of the major stock markets. In addition, determining when a credit event has occurred in respect of a reference entity, calculating the amount of the settlement payment (for cash-settled credit default swaps) or sourcing deliverable obligations (for physically settled credit default swaps) can pose practical difficulties for the parties involved.

These factors have provided a major impetus for the development of synthetic securitisations that use some other form of risk as a proxy for credit risk.[54] In this way, lenders have, for instance, been able to manage their exposure to the credit risk of a far wider range of borrowers, as well as overcoming issues as to the transparency of credit events and the practical difficulties posed by the settlement requirements for credit default swaps. This has significantly enhanced the ability of lenders to diversify their portfolios.

So far, synthetic securitisations have been brought to market in which the price risk of the shares in corporations, the price risk of major commodities and the price risk of currency have been employed as proxies for credit risk. For example, a significant or sudden fall in the price of the shares of a listed borrower may represent a situation equivalent to that captured by a credit event – namely, a material decline in the creditworthiness of the borrower. Equally, an adverse movement in commodity prices or exchange rates may herald a material decline in revenues or increase in costs and thus a material diminution of a borrower's ability to service or refinance its obligations to a lender – again a situation against whose consequences the hedging of credit risk is designed to protect a lender. Moreover, on a broader scale, adverse movements in a major equity index, commodity prices or exchange rates may be indicative of the diminished creditworthiness of the borrowers in a particular industrial sector or geographic market (in equivalent fashion to an adverse movement in a credit index).

The information content of a borrower's share price and the exposure of a borrower to commodity price risk and exchange rate risk have enabled lenders to use instruments to manage that particular risk as a substitute for credit default swaps as regards the hedging of the credit risk of that borrower. Just as credit default swaps lie at the heart of the synthetic securitisations discussed in the previous sections of this chapter, so too are these new forms of synthetic securitisation structured around these new instruments which reference shares, commodities and foreign exchange.

The following figure depicts the use of these price risks as proxies for credit risk.

---

54 See de Vries and Robbe, above n 6, p 109; Bruyere, above n 7, pp 54-55; MJ Logie and JP Castagnino, "Equity Default Swaps and the Securitisation of Risk" in de Vries Robbe and Ali, above n 6, pp 51-53.

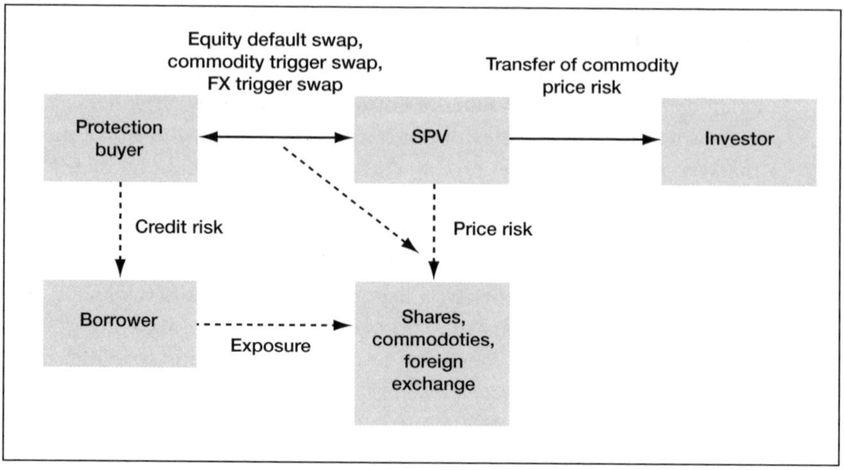


As indicated by the above figure, the synthetic securitisations that effect a transfer of these price risks to investors in the capital markets are structurally similar to the fully funded, partly funded and single-tranche structures encountered previously in this chapter.[55] The lender expects to receive the settlement amount from the SPV on the occurrence of a default event while the investors expect to receive principal and interest on their securities on the scheduled payment dates if no default event occurs during the term of the securities. The occurrence of a default event will lead to the investors' claims for payment of the principal amount of the securities being applied, in reverse order of seniority, to satisfy the settlement amount.

Equity price risk is transferred from the protection buyer to the SPV, as the protection seller, in the same way that credit risk is transferred under a credit default swap.[56] The SPV, in exchange for the payment to it of a periodic fee by the protection buyer, agrees that if the price of a certain share, basket of shares or share index falls below a stipulated threshold, it will pay a settlement amount to the protection buyer. The threshold is set at a level designed to simulate the occurrence of a credit event.[57] Equity default swaps are cash settled, typically according to a fixed recovery rate, with the settlement amount representing a fixed percentage of the notional amount of the shares referenced by the swap. As with synthetic securitisations involving credit default swaps, the SPV will satisfy its payment obligation out of the collateral held by it which has been purchased using the proceeds from its issue of securities.

Commodity trigger swaps[58] and foreign exchange trigger swaps transfer commodity price risk and exchange rate risk in the same way.[59]

A key feature of all of these swaps – compared to credit default swaps – is the ease

55 See Logie and Castagnino, *ibid*, pp 56-58; Standard & Poor's, "Global Methodology for CDOs of Equity and Credit Default Swaps" (February 17 2004).

56 See Logie and Castagnino, *ibid*, p 49.

57 See de Vries Robbe and Ali, above n 6, p 109.

58 See JJ de Vries Robbe, "That's One Small Step for Man ... Securitising Commodity Risk through Apollo" in de Vries Robbe and Ali, above n 6, pp 75-77; Fitch Ratings, "Considerations for Rating Commodities-Linked Credit Obligations ('CCOs')" (November 14 2006).

59 See Fitch Ratings, "Considerations for Rating Foreign Exchange-Linked Credit Obligations ('CFXOs')" (April 23 2007).

with which the occurrence of a default event triggering the payment of the settlement amount can be determined – namely, by reference to share prices, or spot or futures contract prices for commodities and currencies.

## 9. Conclusion

The ease with which credit risk can be separated from loans using credit default swaps and synthetic securitisation has resulted in those instruments now being used on a regular basis by lenders worldwide to hedge the credit risk of borrowers. They have proved to be an invaluable addition to the more conventional tools – including security interests – available to lenders for mitigating the credit risk assumed when making loans to borrowers. Moreover, in situations where taking a security interest over a borrower's property is not a feasible option – due, for instance, to the greater bargaining power of the borrower relative to the lender, or the barrier posed by a negative pledge or a restrictive covenant that accompanies an earlier created security interest – a credit default swap or synthetic securitisation, neither of which requires the consent of the borrower or the borrowers' other lenders, can be substituted for a security interest.

Further, the efficacy of credit default swaps and synthetic securitisations in managing credit risk continues to be enhanced by the ongoing – and rapid – evolution of the global market for credit derivatives. The extension of single-tranche structures to novel financial assets, the use of proxies for credit risk in synthetic securitisations and the heavy issuance of synthetic squares have all contributed to an increased capacity, on the part of lenders, to 'fine-tune' their exposure to credit risk.

# About the authors

**Paul U Ali**
Associate Professor, University of Melbourne
p.ali@unimelb.edu.au

Paul U Ali is an associate professor in the Faculty of Law, University of Melbourne and a member of the faculty's Centre for Corporate Law and Securities Regulation. Prior to becoming an academic, Dr Ali was, for several years, a lawyer in Sydney. Dr Ali has published widely on banking and finance law, securitisation and structured finance, including two books on secured finance, *Marshalling of Securities* (Clarendon Press, Oxford, 1999) and *The Law of Secured Finance* (Oxford University Press, Oxford, 2002). In 2006, Dr Ali was appointed by the Australian federal attorney general as a member of the Personal Property Securities Review Consultative Group.

**Spiros V Bazinas**
Senior Legal Officer, United Nations Office of Legal Affairs
spiros.bazinas@uncitral.org

Spiros V Bazinas is a senior legal officer in the International Trade Law Division of the United Nations Office of Legal Affairs, the Secretariat of the United Nations Commission on International Trade Law (UNCITRAL). He is currently the secretary of Working Group VI (Security Interests), which is preparing a Legislative Guide on Secured Transactions. He served as secretary of the UNCITRAL Working Group on International Contract Practices, which prepared the draft Convention on the Assignment of Receivables in International Trade. He has also been involved in UNCITRAL's work on e-commerce, cross-border insolvency, procurement and bank guarantees. He has co-authored/edited four books and has published several articles and lectured all over the world on various international trade law topics and, in particular, on receivables financing and secured financing law.

**Carlos de Maria y Campos Segura**
Partner, Galicia y Robles, SC
cdemaria@gr.com.mx

Carlos de Maria y Campos Segura became a partner of Galicia, y Robles, SC in 1995. His practice areas include banking, financial and securities law, international joint ventures, mergers and acquisitions, project financing, energy, gas and petrochemical projects, corporate and debt restructuring and general corporate matters.

During the negotiations on the North American Free Trade Agreement (NAFTA), Mr de Maria acted as legal adviser to the *Coordinadora de Organizaciones Empresariales de Comerico Exterior* - a private sector organisation established to act as a point of liaison between the private sector and the Mexican government in relation to the negotiation and implementation of NAFTA.

Mr de Maria studied law at *Universidad La Salle*, AC in Mexico City, graduating in 1988, and received a master of laws from Southern Methodist University.

Mr de Maria served as a foreign associate in the Washington offices of Cleary, Gottlieb, Steen & Hamilton in 1991.

**Grzegorz Dyczkowski**
Partner, Norton Rose Piotr Strawa and Partners, LP
grzegorz.dyczkowski@nortonrose.com

Grzegorz Dyczkowski is a Norton Rose banking partner based in Warsaw and a Polish legal adviser.

Mr Dyczkowski has advised international and domestic financial institutions and major multinational and domestic corporations on a variety of financial transactions, including secured and unsecured lending and borrowing, debt instruments, asset finance, securitisations, derivative transactions and banking and finance regulatory matters.

*Chambers Europe 2007* comments that "clients

are impressed by his diligence in regulatory work and his negotiation skills". He is said "not only [to[ advise, [to] but mediate".

**Jeremy Edwards**
Partner, Norton Rose LLP
jeremy.edwards@nortonrose.com

Jeremy Edwards is a partner in the banking department at Norton Rose, a leading international law firm with 21 offices in 16 countries and over 2,000 employees. Mr Edwards started working at Norton Rose as a trainee in 1987, qualifying into the asset finance team in 1989, where he specialised in aviation-related matters. He spent three years in the firm's Paris office between 1992 and 1995 and became a partner in 1997 following his return to London. He is recognised as a top-tier leading individual in *Chambers Global 2007* and is currently head of the firm's global aviation practice group.

**Silvia Rajsfeld Fiszman**
Senior Associate, Machado, Meyer, Sendacz e Opice Advogados
silvia@mmso.com.br

Silvia Rajsfeld Fiszman is a senior associate in the banking and finance departments of Machado, Meyer, Sendacz e Opice Advogados. She is a specialist in project finance and cross-border financial transactions, and has been involved in some of the largest project financings in the Brazilian energy sector. She has also represented commercial and investment banks in debt restructurings, and multilateral agencies, financial institutions and corporations in syndicated loans. Ms Fiszman was admitted to practise law in São Paulo in 1995. She received her LLB from the *Universidade de São Paulo* in 1994 and a master's in civil procedure law in 2002. She also holds an LLM from New York University School of Law, United States (2003). She is a member of the Brazilian Bar Association.

**John Forrester**
Partner, Holman Fenwick & Willan
john.forrester@hfw.co.uk

John Forrester is a partner in the London office of Holman Fenwick & Willan, an international firm which is widely regarded as one of the world's leading shipping law firms. He specialises in international ship finance and has worked in this field since his qualification as a solicitor in 1989. During this time he has acted for a wide range of banks and export credit agencies on their shipping and offshore loans, including many of the shipping industry's leading banks, and has also represented shipbuilders, shipowners, operators and investors on various shipping and offshore-related transactions. He is recognised as a leading ship finance practitioner by independent legal directories such as *Chambers* and *Legal Business*, and is currently head of Holman Fenwick & Willan's international ship finance group.

**Tomas Gärdfors**
Partner, Norton Rose LLP
tomas.gardfors@nortonrose.com

Tomas Gärdfors is a Norton Rose banking partner based in Frankfurt. He is qualified both as an *advokat* in Sweden and as a solicitor in England and Wales.

Before joining the Frankfurt office, Mr Gärdfors worked in Sweden and in London, specialising in structured cross-border deals. He has advised financial institutions, banks and borrowers in relation to debt financing facilities for leveraged acquisitions, project finance and other structured finance transactions, including syndicated and bilateral credit facilities.

Mr Gärdfors was cited in *The Legal 500 Europe, Middle East and Africa 2006* as "widely praised for understanding the commercial fundamentals and economics of transactions". He was ranked in Band 1 in *Chambers Global, Germany 2006/07* for project finance and was cited as "refreshingly down-to-earth", impressing clients with his "efficiency and amiable nature".

Mr Gärdfors is a regular speaker at conferences and seminars.

**Dmitry Gravin**
Partner, Norton Rose (Central Europe) LLP
dmitry.gravin@nortonrose.com

Dmitry Gravin is a Norton Rose banking partner based in Moscow.

Mr Gravin has advised on a wide range of Russian financings, including guarantees and moratorium requests, security for loans and legal opinions for loans covered by political risk insurance. He has also been responsible for preparing the documentation for the financing of several substantial and complex projects in Russia.

Mr Gravin's clients include international institutions, foreign and Russian banks, and other providers and arrangers of finance.

The 2005 edition of *European Legal 500* comments: "Dmitry Gravin has established himself a strong reputation in transport, particularly on the aviation side."

Mr Gravin studied law at the Moscow State University from 1980 to 1985. He became a partner in May 1997.

**Christian Johnson**
Professor of Law, Loyola University Chicago
cjohns6@luc.edu

Christian Johnson is a law professor at Loyola University Chicago School of Law and a frequent consultant on derivatives for large derivative dealers and corporations. At Loyola, Professor Johnson teaches a law school course on derivatives and corporate finance. Professor Johnson has published several books and over two dozen articles on derivatives. He is a frequent presenter on derivative documentation and banking issues, having made presentations to the International Money Fund, the Federal Reserve Bank of Chicago, the American Bar Association and the Futures Industry Association, among others. Professor Johnson is a graduate of Columbia Law School, where he was executive editor of the *Columbia Law Review*. He is also a certified public accountant.

**Pavel Kvícala**
Partner, Norton Rose vos
pavel.kvicala@nortonrose.com

Pavel Kvícala is a Norton Rose partner based in Prague. He joined the Prague practice in 1998 and became a partner in 2006.

Mr Kvícala specialises in corporate finance and banking. His previous experience includes advising major Czech and international banks and corporates on a number of high-profile privatisations and restructurings and foreign investments. His regulatory expertise includes advising a major Czech telecommunications company on corporate governance and shareholder relations issues and advising a US multinational on acquisition-related competition and regulatory issues.

Mr Kvícala graduated from the Law Faculty of Charles University in 1997. A native Czech speaker, he speaks fluent English. He is a member of the Czech Bar and is also registered as a foreign lawyer with the Law Society of England and Wales.

**Christopher Lawrence**
Partner, Macfarlanes
christopher.lawrence@macfarlanes.com

Christopher Lawrence qualified as a solicitor in 1998 and is a partner in the debt finance group at Macfarlanes, having previously worked at another major City law firm. His practice encompasses a broad range of debt finance transactions, advising on both the lender and the borrower sides. Mr Lawrence specialises in acting for borrowers and private equity sponsors on acquisition finance transactions, advising on the structure and terms of debt finance packages for private acquisitions in the United Kingdom and internationally, and public-to-private acquisitions of UK listed companies.

Outside the leveraged finance area, Mr Lawrence advises on general debt finance matters, including investment-grade syndicated and bilateral facilities, International Swaps and Derivatives Association documentation, workouts and restructurings, guarantee and security issues, second lien debt, mezzanine debt and inter-creditor issues.

**Gerard McCormack**
Professor of Law, University of Leeds
g.c.mccormack@leeds.ac.uk

Gerard McCormack is a professor of law in the University of Leeds, specialising in secured credit and corporate insolvency law. He has taught in a number of different universities, including the National University of Singapore. He has consulted widely and has had experience of the secured transactions law reform process in many jurisdictions, including Hong Kong and Singapore. He is the author of *Secured Credit under English and American Law* (2004), among other things.

**Robin Parsons**
Partner, Sidley Austin LLP
RParsons@Sidley.com

Robin Parsons is a partner of Sidley Austin in London. His practice ranges from structured finance and securitisations to consumer finance, but with particular emphasis on restructurings, workouts and insolvency. He handled many of the high-profile workouts of the 1980s involving cross-border restructurings, debt/equity swaps, success fees and other incentives. He chaired a Law Society working group on the EU Financial Collateral Arrangements Directive, as well as a

Financial Law Panel working group on security over book debts and the future of the London Approach. High-profile restructurings have included acting for the lead bank on Goodman International and numerous other bank-led rescues; acting for Federal Mogul Corporation in connection with the dual Chapter 11 and administration proceedings of its UK subsidiaries; and acting for bondholders and banks in distressed situations in the energy sector. Acquisition finance experience has included buybacks through schemes of arrangement and bid finance. He has been nominated by Euromoney in its *Guide to the World's Leading Banking Lawyers*, included in Law Business Research International's *Who's Who of Banking Lawyers* and "recommended" in the banking section of *Legal Business*.

**José Ribeiro do Prado Jr**
Partner, Machado, Meyer,
Sendacz e Opice Advogados
jprado@mmso.com.br

José Ribeiro do Prado Jr is a partner in the infrastructure and banking and finance departments of Machado, Meyer, Sendacz e Opice Advogados. He has extensive experience in project finance, cross-border financial transactions, public-private partnerships, administrative law and regulatory matters. Mr Prado was admitted to practise law in São Paulo in 1994. He received his LLB from the *Universidade de São Paulo* in 1994 and his LLM from King's College, London in 1997. He was an associate with Cameron McKenna, London, from 1998 to 1999. He is a member of the Brazilian Bar Association and the São Paulo Lawyers Association.

**Betty Tam**
Senior Associate, Herbert Smith LLP
betty.tam@herbertsmith.com

Betty Tam is experienced in cross-border M&A transactions with a focus on China-related projects. Ms Tam has considerable experience in infrastructure projects in China, including telecommunications, water and waste-water treatment and power plants. She has also acted on various project finance and acquisition finance transactions in China.

Ms Tam is fluent in Cantonese, Putonghua, English and French.

**Jeremy Xiao**
Partner, Herbert Smith LLP
jeremy.xiao@herbertsmith.com

Jeremy Xiao is the managing partner of Herbert Smith's Beijing office and specialises in corporate and corporate finance work in Hong Kong and China. He has acted on a number of groundbreaking transactions, including the first Chinese B-share international offering which was listed on the Shanghai Securities Exchange in 1992 and the first Chinese H-share international public offering (IPO) and listing in Hong Kong in 1993.

Mr Xiao was the founding member of the Law Society of England and Wales and the Bar Council's joint working group on China.

Mr Xiao is fluent in both English and Putonghua.